ROGUE JUSTICE

ROGUE JUSTICE

THE MAKING OF THE SECURITY STATE

KAREN J. GREENBERG

CROWN PUBLISHERS
NEW YORK

Published in the United States by Crown, an imprint of the Crown Publishing Group, a division of Penguin Random House LLC, New York.
crownpublishing.com

CROWN is a registered trademark and the Crown colophon is a trademark of Penguin Random House LLC.

Library of Congress Cataloging-in-Publication Data
Names: Greenberg, Karen J., author.
Title: Rogue justice : the making of the security state / Karen J. Greenberg.
Description: First edition. | New York : Crown Publishers, 2016. | Includes
    bibliographical references and index. | Description based on print version
    record and CIP data provided by publisher; resource not viewed.
Identifiers: LCCN 2016001224 (print) | LCCN 2015041144 (ebook) |
    ISBN 9780804138222 (ebook) | ISBN 9780804138215 (hardback)
Subjects: LCSH: Criminal justice, Administration of—Political aspects—
    United States. | National security—Law and legislation—United States. |
    Civil rights—United States. | Political questions and judicial power—United
    States. | War on Terrorism, 2001–2009—Political aspects—United States. |
    Human rights—Government policy—United States. | Detention of persons—
    United States. | Internal security—United States. | United States—Politics and
    government—2001–2009. | United States—Politics and government—2009– |
    BISAC: POLITICAL SCIENCE / Political Freedom & Security / Intelligence. |
    POLITICAL SCIENCE / Government / Executive Branch. | POLITICAL
    SCIENCE / Political Freedom & Security / Terrorism.
Classification: LCC KF9223 (print) | LCC KF9223 .G74 2016 (ebook) |
    DDC 364.973—dc23
LC record available at http://lccn.loc.gov/2016001224

ISBN 978-0-8041-3821-5
eBook ISBN 978-0-8041-3822-2

PRINTED IN THE UNITED STATES OF AMERICA

Book design by Anna Thompson
Jacket design by Tal Goretsky
Jacket illustration by Tim O'Brien

10 9 8 7 6 5 4 3 2 1

First Edition

For Gary

CONTENTS

PART III
THE LONG GAME

INTRODUCTION

For a man who had just suffered one of the biggest losses of his professional life, Attorney General Eric Holder seemed anything but chastened. He might not have had his boss's gift for soaring rhetoric, but as he stood at the Department of Justice podium on April 4, 2011, his anger was palpable and his meaning clear: the decision he was announcing—to turn over prosecution of Khalid Shaikh Mohammed and four other conspirators in the September 11 attacks to the Department of Defense—was not one he had made willingly.

Just a year and a half earlier, from the same podium, he had told the country that the men would be tried in federal court in Manhattan, less than a mile from ground zero. The venue, Holder argued at the time, would be a testament to America's pride and trust in the rule of law and the American courts. "I am confident," he said, "that our justice system would have performed with the same distinction that has been its hallmark for over two hundred years." But members of Congress, determined to show their constituents just

how tough on terrorism they were, had thwarted Holder by passing a law prohibiting the Department of Justice from bringing any
Guantánamo detainees onto American soil for prosecution or imprisonment. Since the law required their presence, trials could not
go forward; military commissions, cobbled-together boards that operated offshore and under looser rules and regulations than those required in the civilian federal courts, were the only remaining option.
Years of labor by his prosecutors—"some of the most dedicated and
patriotic Americans I have ever encountered," Holder said—had
gone up in the smoke of political posturing.

The prohibition was unwise on its face. After all, Holder said,
"members of Congress simply do not have access to the evidence . . .
necessary to make prosecution judgments." Federal prosecutors had
convicted and imprisoned "hundreds of terrorists since September 11"—cases that aided in intelligence collection even as they in-
capacitated the convicted. In passing the law, Congress had "taken
one of the nation's most tested counterterrorism tools off the table."
But there were bigger issues at stake. Under the Constitution, Holder
pointed out, "decisions about who, where, and how to prosecute have
always been—and must remain—the responsibility of the executive
branch." And perhaps worst of all, by calling into question the ability of lawyers and courts to bring the terrorists to justice, Congress
had tarnished the shining jewel of American democracy, "a court
system that has distinguished this nation throughout its history."

Holder's decision to abandon the federal prosecution was a ca-
pitulation to forces that had been gathering in Washington, DC,
even before the capture of the 9/11 terrorism defendants. The threat
was so dire, the situation so precarious, and the stakes so high that
transparency and due process and the other staples of American democracy would have to take a backseat to the war on terror. Politicians, lawyers, and bureaucrats had been working hard to counter
the terrorist threat by going right to the edge of the law and, when
the law proved too restrictive, by massaging its boundaries to include the measures they wanted to take. The rationale for subverting

the rule of law had been established almost immediately by Vice President Dick Cheney, who just five days after the attacks told *Meet the Press* host Tim Russert that counterterrorism efforts would require the use of "any means at our disposal." The country would "have to work the dark side," he said.

By the time of Holder's about-face, many of the results of the Cheney doctrine were well known. Torture had been sanctioned at the highest levels of government. Indefinite detention, even for Americans, had been embraced as essential to the nation's security. An offshore prison had been created to bypass the protections of the rule of law. Mass warrantless surveillance had been used against Americans who were not suspected of criminal behavior. And overseas assassinations of terrorism suspects, including at least one American citizen, had been launched. Compared to these spectacular transgressions, Holder's announcement was tame, its stakes low. But it captured something of vital importance: it is the quiet decisions, the individual judicial rulings and laws and executive orders—generally fashioned by well-meaning people, often in the plain light of day but overlooked for their homeliness, their implications lost in the weeds of their small details—that make possible the fiascoes, the follies, and the excesses that turn governments into the enemies of their constituents. For every Cheney mongering fear and nurturing paranoia, there are many officials quietly going about their business—drafting legislation, writing legal opinions, arguing in court—thinking they are doing the right thing but failing to grasp that in their wish to protect the country, they are in fact betraying it. And in no part of government has that betrayal by accretion, the death of liberty by a thousand cuts, been more momentous, or more disturbing, than in the institutions of justice—the courts, the laws, and the Justice Department.

THERE IS PERHAPS NO SENTIMENT more American than the suspicion of governmental power. From the time Jefferson declared King George III the enemy of life, liberty, and equality, American law and justice have attempted to embody Aristotle's notion of a society where laws existed "free from passion." A country of "laws, not of men," as John Adams put it, was designed to replace the arbitrary determinations of kings and priests. This native distrust of governmental authority has dominated our politics and political culture since the founding period. Underlying it is a certainty that a government unchecked will inevitably turn into a tyranny. A government restrained by laws that follow logically from unswerving principles to which the governed had consented and which were then enforced fairly and uniformly was our best hope for preserving order, securing freedom, and upholding justice. The rule of law was our best protection from tyranny.

The Constitution, especially the Bill of Rights, reflects both this suspicion and this hope. Its framers were preoccupied with the question of how to give government just enough power to hold us together. Their answers have proved to be imperfect; controversies surrounding the interpretation of our founding documents increasingly seem to tear us apart. Many of these conflicts concern the nature and scope of our rights—whether we have a guarantee of privacy, for instance, or whether the right to bear arms trumps the power of the state to regulate them. But some of them concern the functions of government itself, especially its ability to compromise the rule of law in times of emergency. Adams's Alien and Sedition Acts, Lincoln's suspension of habeas corpus, Roosevelt's internment of Japanese Americans, Truman's attempt to shut down a steel strike during the Korean War, Nixon's use of surveillance against antiwar protestors—all are examples of actions taken by presidents who chafed at the limitations imposed on their power by the Constitution, who saw the rule of law as an obstacle to carrying out their duties to protect the country.

The farther these executive actions recede into the past, the more ignominious they seem. That should tell us something: the rule of law enshrined in the Constitution may be imperfect and at times inconvenient, but it is indispensable. We allow our government to flout it at our own peril.

But what about times when these restrictions on governmental power seem to put us in danger? The calculation seems inconclusive. After all, if there's a ticking time bomb and the man in front of an interrogator knows where it is, why shouldn't Cheney's injunction to use "any means at our disposal" prevail? If there are terrorists who want to blow up our bridges and who talk to one another on cell phones, then why not monitor everyone's phone calls to find them? What good is the Constitution if the Capitol or the White House is in ruins and the citizenry is afraid to go to a football game?

These are deeply troubling questions. They do not have definitive answers, but history does at least show that we need to be very cautious about indulging our fears. And the people with the power to answer these questions and to turn those answers into policy have shown a disturbing lack of caution. They have consistently favored the power of the government over the limitations imposed by the Constitution. Over and over again, in public and in secret, in courtrooms and in prisons here and abroad, lawmakers and presidents and judges and lawyers and generals and bureaucrats have chosen to privilege security over the rule of law. Some, like Cheney, have usurped the instruments of power to take on more power, to undermine the rule of law, and to take away rights from the rest of us. And ironically, much of this usurpation has been carried out by lawyers massaging and distorting and sometimes just plain disregarding the laws they were supposed to uphold.

The appetite for compromise has continued through the two most recent two-term presidencies. At the center of this juggernaut were federal courts that approved of the ongoing detention of prisoners not charged with any crimes and that denied defendants access to lawyers or, claiming secrecy, to exculpatory or mitigating evidence. They stood by as defendants found themselves deprived of a trial because the evidence against them had been obtained through torture— a double win for the advocates of torture. On constitutional issues they were passive as well, deferring to the government with rare exceptions on the grounds that security is a matter for the executive branch, not the judicial.

Some individuals have resisted, including Edward Snowden, who revealed the National Security Agency's (NSA's) secret domestic spying program and who, for his efforts, lives in exile in Russia under threat of prosecution. Other dissenters have been ignored, ostracized, or bypassed. Lawyers within the Department of Justice (DOJ) have seen their objections to the new regime turned into laws and policies that only gave it stronger legal cover. Some members of Congress have objected, such as Senator Patrick Leahy (D-VT), who used his chairmanship of the Senate Judiciary Committee to challenge the incursions into privacy, the abuse of the separation of powers, and the overreach of law enforcement. However, their attempts to restrain the security state have mostly come to naught, as have the Obama administration's thwarted attempts to close the prison at Guantánamo Bay. Some, such as FBI agent Ali Soufan, refused to participate in the rogue policies. Others, made aware of the surveillance and torture programs, voiced their concerns, fought in minimal ways, and finally left government. Nongovernmental organizations, including the American Civil Liberties Union, have fought doggedly against the excesses but began to see success only in the wake of Snowden's disclosures; their objections to assassinations, detentions, denials of due process, and torture have gone largely unheeded by courts. In the few cases in which policies were rolled back, such as the use of torture, their architects were left unpunished.

Lawyers who seek to challenge policies such as drone killings have been hampered by the Kafkaesque requirement, upheld by courts, that the legal rationales they wish to challenge remain secret. Bureaucrats have fashioned cosmetic changes to the programs brought to light by leakers, giving them the appearance of legality without actually altering the content. A court designed to prevent law enforcement agencies from abridging defendants' rights on the grounds of national security has turned into a court that facilitates those efforts. Throughout government, agencies have abandoned their mission in the name of security, aided and abetted by lawyers and judges all too eager to capitulate to leaders convinced that fear must guide policy. Rather than upholding the rule of law, federal courts and lawyers have weakened it. Rather than protecting citizens from government excess, they have protected government excess from citizens' objections—and, in some cases, citizens' knowledge. The institutions of justice, caught up in the war on terror, have gone rogue.

The groundwork for rogue justice was laid in the days and weeks after 9/11, and the new laws and policies to which it gave rise have proved nearly impossible to dislodge. In implementing the new regime, the White House and a group of lawyers led by Deputy Assistant Attorney General John Yoo ignored some of the most sacred principles of American democracy and law, including the rights to freedom from imprisonment without due process and from cruel and unusual treatment while in detention, the right to privacy, the right to free speech, and the overarching right to freedom from passion in favor of the rule of law. And the damage is lasting. Even after the rogue policies were discovered and exposed, the few people inside and outside government who sought to rein them in fell short of the goal. To this day, the government continues to overreach in the name of keeping the nation safe.

There remains some reason to hope. By the late spring of 2015, the efforts of those inside and outside government began to coalesce and to reap rewards. President Barack Obama and the wider executive branch released a series of documents and reports—on torture, on surveillance, and on targeted killings—that directly exposed the claims to national security based on extralegal and illegal policies as false and unsubstantiated. Warrantless surveillance yielded no information leading to the prevention of attacks; neither, it turned out, did torture, according to the massive, multiyear government studies. Then in May 2015, an appeals court decision and legislation combined to outlaw the NSA's mass surveillance program.

These victories were small, but they may lead to a more law-abiding notion of security, one that reflects the historical confidence in America's law, its courts, and its system of justice. As we near the end of the Obama years, the remaining distortions of law and excesses of power may slowly recede. On the other hand, they may be woven so seamlessly into the way the nation is governed that we will forget there was ever a time when fear did not guide policy or weaken the principles upon which the nation was founded. In chronicling these events, I hope to leave a reminder of just how fragile American justice really is and how much it depends on facing fear with courage.

PART I

NEW RULES

CHAPTER 1

Justice at War

Attorney General John Ashcroft spent the morning of September 11, 2001, on a Gulfstream jet, heading to Milwaukee to celebrate Library Day with schoolchildren. He never made it to the event. As soon as the jet landed, a black-clad SWAT team surrounded it and hovered, weapons at the ready, as the plane was refueled and prepared for the return journey to Washington, DC. He made it out just in time—air travel in the United States would soon be suspended—and joined other top government officials at the White House early the next morning to meet with President George W. Bush, who had returned from his own Library Day event in Florida.

Ashcroft was seated between CIA director George Tenet and Secretary of Defense Donald Rumsfeld. He could feel the president's eyes on him. "Don't ever let this happen again," Bush said.

"I took it personally," Ashcroft later wrote. "From that moment forward, I devoted myself to an intense, sometimes secret war with a mission many people thought was impossible: stopping terrorists from striking again on American soil."

Although the president had been looking directly at him when he gave this command, Ashcroft wasn't entirely sure that it was intended for him. But regardless of whom Bush was holding accountable for the previous day's events, everyone in the room probably felt some version of Ashcroft's sense of responsibility and mission. The attack had caught them all off guard. They had failed in their duty to protect the country. Each of them now had to figure out what had gone wrong under his or her watch, how to correct it, and, above all, how to prevent a catastrophe like 9/11 from ever happening again.

Ashcroft's Justice Department, especially its storied law enforcement and investigative wing, the Federal Bureau of Investigation, had a unique role in this reckoning. The FBI and the lawyers under Ashcroft's command would not only have to ferret out and round up those responsible for the attacks; they would also have to stop those who might be planning something similar. This was not a task for which Ashcroft was directly prepared, either by experience or by temperament. As a governor and a senator, he'd focused on domestic issues, carving out a place for himself as a Christian conservative opposed to abortion, desegregation, and big government. As he had told Larry King in February 2001 during a discussion of gun control, "We've got enough laws on the books. I think what we need is tougher enforcement." It was enough for lawyers and investigators to step in after people had committed crimes, at which point, he said, "we should nail them." Seven months after he talked to King, it was clear that this approach would not suffice when it came to terrorism.

When he returned to his office after the White House meeting, Ashcroft assembled his top deputies. They were being deployed in the war on terror, he told them. They would have to peer into the future and beyond the nation's borders in order to do their new job: keeping the country safe.

———

ROBERT MUELLER'S FIRST FULL DAY on the job as FBI director was September 10, 2001. He hadn't even found the bathrooms in his new headquarters when the planes hit the buildings in New York and Washington. But he was plenty oriented to the job of combating terrorism—certainly more so than his boss. Princeton-educated, worldly, a decorated Vietnam Marine veteran, and a prominent prosecutor, Mueller had told the Senate committee vetting his nomination to the FBI post in the summer of 2001 that "the major threat that we have, and the threat that the Bureau needs to worry about the most, is terrorism."

Yet as Mueller recalled for a 2012 gathering of Harvard Business School students, one of his very first meetings with President Bush after 9/11 didn't go very well. He was in the Oval Office describing to Bush and Cheney his agents' efforts to piece together an account of who the conspirators were, how they had carried out their attacks, and what their connection was to Al Qaeda and Osama bin Laden, when Bush interrupted him: "Stop it! What you're telling me the bureau is doing is what you've been doing for a hundred years; my question for you today is what is the bureau doing today to prevent the next terrorist attack." The president, Mueller said, asked him that same question every day for the next four years.

What the bureau had been doing for a hundred years, or at least for the previous decade or so, clearly hadn't worked. As Ashcroft told Congress on September 25, the attacks revealed "a total breakdown in our intelligence, one that cannot be excused and must never be forgotten." Mueller, Ashcroft, and others had immediately begun to investigate how the bureau had missed the signs that a terrorist attack was imminent. This wasn't the first time the FBI had had to investigate itself. Less than a year earlier, in February 2001, it had arrested one of its own agents, Robert Hanssen. Hanssen had been spying for the Russians for years without being caught. High-profile failures like these had led investigators to ugly conclusions about the health of America's premier law enforcement agency. Internal communications were, as one report put it, rife with "human error, compounded by antiquated and cumbersome information technology systems and procedures." There was no networked computer system for research and information sharing; field agents were reduced to consulting public libraries to obtain information. Relationships among the various sections of the agency were "dysfunctional" and "broken," which led to repeated failures to communicate. The bureau was cripplingly short on able translators.

Sometimes the consequences of the disarray were only minor, if embarrassing. Ashcroft, for instance, was forced to postpone Timothy McVeigh's execution in the wake of a disclosure that the FBI had failed to provide evidence to McVeigh's defense team, a lapse that turned out to be the result of disorganization. But sometimes they were devastating, as in the case of Wen Ho Lee, a Los Alamos scientist suspected of transmitting nuclear secrets to China—"allegations of espionage as significant as any the United States Government is likely to face," as the official report on the debacle put it. But, the report concluded, the "FBI's . . . investigation of Wen Ho Lee, in virtually every material respect, was deeply and fundamentally flawed." The agency failed to make the Lee case a priority. It assigned an overworked, underexperienced agent to it and then denied him resources. Information got tangled up in bureaucratic webs. Supervisors ignored the case. In the meantime Lee, who had indisputably downloaded nuclear secrets onto a flash drive and who had been caught on wiretap promising a captured spy that he would find out who had turned him in, languished in solitary confinement for nine months, becoming a civil liberties cause célèbre. In the end, he pleaded guilty to just one of the fifty-nine counts on which he had been indicted, received an apology from the judge, and then went on to write a book called *My Country Versus Me*, in which he argued that he had been a victim of racial profiling.

If the FBI's logistical and informational infrastructure was too dysfunctional to nail the bad guys, it certainly wasn't up to the task of finding out in advance who they were and what they were up to and then preventing them from committing crimes. Running an effective intelligence operation required competent data collection, skilled analysis, and timely exchange of massive amounts of information, and the FBI, by its own reckoning, had failed miserably at all three.

Turning the FBI around was a daunting task, but at least Mueller and Ashcroft got along, which is more than you could say for their predecessors, Louis Freeh and Janet Reno, whose mutual dislike erupted into open hostility in the aftermath of the Waco siege and shoot-out. And in Mueller, Ashcroft had a man who was motivated not only by a sense of duty and patriotism but by the kind of institutional loyalty that can make a person even more dedicated. The FBI's intelligence failures had initially led to proposals for a new agency dedicated to domestic intelligence, an idea that would gain steam in the years to come. In February 2003, for instance, Senator John Edwards (D-NC) called for the creation of a Homeland Intelligence Agency to "replace FBI units that failed to uncover the September 11 terrorists and still cannot find suspected al Qaeda operatives in the United States." A domestic intelligence agency was also on the 9/11 Commission's radar, and White House officials were considering it throughout the early post-9/11 years. None of these proposals gained much traction, but Mueller took the fact that the subject was under discussion as a cue to put in motion several programs designed to maintain the FBI's hold on domestic intelligence. Mueller was successful, though the threat of domestic intelligence agencies would linger for several years. When the 9/11 Commission finally issued its report, it noted that its recommendation to keep domestic intelligence at the FBI was valid only if the bureau "can do the job."

Mueller met these challenges by setting up new programs that would focus on intelligence collection both at home and abroad, with more resources, better technology, and an expansion of intelligence functions already in place. But some of the hurdles were not the result of internal disarray; nor could they be fixed directly by Mueller. They were the result of the suspicion of governmental power woven into the Constitution, and especially the Fourth

Amendment's guarantee against searches and seizures. The framers had prevented the state from forcibly entering people's homes and sifting through their papers and effects—precisely the kind of power that a law enforcement agency bent on ferreting out "evildoers" and stopping them might like to have. But Congress could pass laws that pushed against the boundaries of the Constitution and let the courts sort out whether they were permissible. That was just what Mueller needed, and for this he was dependent on his boss, who would have to persuade legislators to give the FBI more power to expand its intelligence capabilities.

Within two weeks of 9/11, Ashcroft had done exactly that. On September 25 he appeared before the Senate Judiciary Committee with a sobering message: "I regret to inform you that we are today sending our troops into the modern field of battle with antique weapons." But there was good news, too, he said. In the two weeks since the attacks, the DOJ had assembled a twenty-one-page proposal for a so-called Anti-Terrorism Plan that would provide "new tools to fight terrorism." The bill was called the Uniting and Strengthening America by Providing Appropriate Tools Required to Intercept and Obstruct Terrorism Act of 2001—a title whose first letters spelled out USA PATRIOT. The acronym was awkward, to say the least, but as Ashcroft explained, it described "the true nature of the battle": stop terrorism before it could start. The name was also excellent public relations; it was impossible to imagine anyone but a traitor objecting to a *patriot* act.

The act amended 108 preexisting criminal justice statutes and created nine new ones, changes designed to equip the country's law enforcement agencies with new weapons to fight the intelligence battles of the war on terror. Agents could now search telephone and email records, get access to individual and corporate financial data, and search homes and businesses—all expanded powers that reduced the protections of the Fourth Amendment. Some activities, such as wiretapping, still required court orders, but the act made those orders much easier to obtain. It also allowed for the indefinite detention of immigrants suspected of having ties to terrorist groups—not only to prevent them from committing violence but also to make them available for interrogation. In short, the Patriot Act privileged intelligence collection over constitutional protections.

In case members of Congress objected to this turnabout, Ashcroft was ready with some explanations. The new approach to search and detention was necessary, he told them, because "our fight against terrorism is not merely or primarily a criminal justice endeavor. It is a defense of our nation and its citizens." In sum, Ashcroft explained, "We cannot wait for terrorists to strike to begin investigations and to take action. The death tolls are too high, the consequences too great." This approach would not suffice when it came to terrorism, he continued: "We must prevent first, prosecute second."

"Of course," he assured lawmakers, the FBI and other law enforcement officials would exercise their new powers with "careful regard for the constitutional rights of Americans and respect for all human beings." Ashcroft did not say exactly how he intended to square that restraint with warrantless searches of Americans and indefinite detention of foreigners held in custody without access to the federal courts. But then again, he didn't really have to. The country was still in a state of panic, and questioning the need for strong action seemed naïve at best and dangerous at worst. Only one senator, Russ Feingold (D-WI), and sixty-six representatives voted against the bill, and on October 23 the Patriot Act, the most significant reshaping of Americans' relationship to the power of their government at least since the Alien Act of 1918 (or perhaps ever), became the law of the land. Suspicion of governmental power—a tendency of many conservatives—had given way to a hope that a powerful government could keep the country safe by preventing future attacks.

OF ALL THE PROVISIONS OF the Patriot Act, a section that would make it easier for intelligence and law enforcement agents to talk to one another was of particular significance to the top officials of the Justice Department—especially Michael Chertoff, the head of its Criminal Division. Chertoff, a former federal prosecutor under US Attorney Rudolph Giuliani, was the senior on-duty official from Main Justice—the Justice Department's headquarters—working at FBI headquarters on the morning of 9/11. He spent the following days poring over files, trying to figure out how such a large operation had escaped notice. He came across one file that was so disturbing that he sprang from his chair and rushed into Ashcroft's office. "John," he said, "you won't believe this."

Chertoff handed his boss a memo—a report from an FBI agent who had written, "This is a guy who could fly an airplane into the World Trade Center." The guy in question was Zacarias Moussaoui, a thirty-three-year-old French citizen of Moroccan descent. In early August 2001, Moussaoui had shown up at the Pan Am International Flight Academy in a suburb of Minneapolis, seeking time on the school's 747 simulator. Clarence Prevost, the flight instructor who first brought suspicions about Moussaoui to the FBI's attention, said that it wasn't only the hundred-dollar bills Moussaoui used to pay the $8,300 training fee that got his attention; it was also the fact that despite the fifty or so hours he'd spent on lessons in a single-engine plane, Moussaoui had failed to get a pilot's license; that once seated at the simulator, he clearly had no idea what he was doing; and that when Prevost asked him if he was Muslim, the otherwise genial student flared up and yelled, "I am nothing!"

Prevost, a retired commercial pilot, alerted his bosses. "We don't know anything about this guy," he told them, "and we're teaching him how to throw the switches on a 747." At first, they dismissed Prevost's concerns and reminded him that Moussaoui was a paying customer. But the next day, perhaps heeding Prevost's warning that "we'll care when there's a hijacking and the lawsuits come in," they contacted the FBI office in Minneapolis.

Agents soon discovered that Moussaoui had overstayed his visa, and on August 16, 2001, he was jailed on an immigration charge. From discussions with French intelligence officers, the FBI quickly determined that he was affiliated with Islamic terrorists, including Bin Laden. The bureau moved to obtain a warrant to search Moussaoui's computer, which had been seized during his arrest, but the supervising agent at FBI headquarters refused to pursue it. To the agents in Minneapolis, his resistance was infuriating and inexplicable and based on trivial concerns, such as his worry, later recounted by Minneapolis agent Coleen Rowley, that the French information "only identified Zacarias Moussaoui by name and [the supervisor] did not know how many people by that name existed in France." (A check of the Paris phone book turned up no others, but this did not convince the Washington office, either.) The agents did finally get their warrants—weeks later, in the first hours after the attacks.

Moussaoui's computer proved to be a trove of information about the hijackers and their plans. Had it been opened when Rowley and her Minneapolis colleagues wanted, the disaster might have been averted.

Immediately after the attacks, Chertoff and Ashcroft had claimed that the FBI had had no warning of them. Now it was clear that an unmistakable clue had been in their possession for nearly a month and that more information was in the head of a man they had in custody. A single, seemingly arbitrary decision by a single agent in Washington had kept from the bureau information it could have used to thwart the hijackers.

Word would soon leak out to the public about the Moussaoui file, especially that prescient comment about his ability to fly into the World Trade Center. The FBI would be under scrutiny once again, this time for failing to "connect the dots." Critics lambasted the bureau for its sloppy handling of the investigation, as if human error or poor communication were to blame. But to those on the inside, it appeared that the trouble emanated from a little-known outpost of the justice system, housed within the same building in which Ashcroft had his office: the Foreign Intelligence Surveillance Court (the FISA Court, also known as the FISC). This court had the power to issue a warrant that would have allowed Moussaoui's computer to be searched even in the absence of strong evidence that it held material relevant to criminal activity. It was in the course of trying to persuade his Washington supervisor to request such a warrant that a Minneapolis FBI agent had written the ominous message about Moussaoui's piloting skills. But the FISC judges had never heard that warning, or anything else about Moussaoui, because the FBI had never brought it to them—in part, it seemed, because at the time of Moussaoui's arrest, relations between the court and the bureau had broken down. A FISC judge had accused the FBI of routinely lying in the affidavits used to obtain court orders, and agents had become unwilling to stick out their necks by approaching the court for the warrants it could issue. Fear of bureaucratic reprisal, it seemed, had prevented the bureau from breaking the biggest terrorism case ever to come its way.

THE FOREIGN INTELLIGENCE SURVEILLANCE COURT came into being in 1978, another troubled time for America's "intelligence agencies." In 1975 the Senate Select Committee on Intelligence Activities, headed by Senator Frank Church (D-ID), began the largest congressional inquiry into America's intelligence agencies since the Second World War. The inquiry was a response to "allegations of substantial, even massive wrong-doing" that had surfaced in the aftermath of the Vietnam War and the Watergate scandal. The Church Committee found many of these allegations to be true. Intelligence agencies had attempted to assassinate foreign leaders, plotted coups overseas, and spied extensively on civilian populations at home. Under director J. Edgar Hoover, the FBI had been a central participant in the wrongdoing, especially through its COINTELPRO initiative, which, starting in 1956, attempted to gather information on and undermine groups deemed (primarily by Hoover) to be subversive. FBI agents infiltrated groups ranging from the NAACP to the Ku Klux Klan, attempting to foster internal squabbling and ultimately to discredit them. They spied on Robert

Kennedy and Martin Luther King, Jr.; Hoover called the latter "the most dangerous Negro in America" and sent him a letter threatening to publicize an extramarital affair in hopes that it would persuade him to kill himself. They smeared "enemies" in the press. They broke into dissidents' homes, induced local cops to beat them, and had them jailed on trumped-up charges. They opened mail and tapped phones without warrants. And they coordinated their activities with other intelligence agencies, especially the CIA, while keeping them secret from the rest of the country, including large portions of the government.

"The intelligence agencies are a sector of American government set apart," the Church Committee reported (while noting how uncooperative they had been with its inquiry). "Intelligence work is a life of service, but one in which the norms of American national life are sometimes distressingly distorted." The people who conceived and executed these programs, the committee wrote, might think they had the nation's best interests at heart, but as Justice Louis Brandeis wrote, "experience should teach us to be most on our guard to protect liberty when the Government's purposes are beneficent." Hoover and other "men of zeal, well-meaning but without understanding," Brandeis warned, posed "the greatest dangers to liberty." They had to be reined in without also threatening their intelligence-gathering mission, and that, the committee concluded, was the job of Congress.

In 1977, thirteen months after the Church Committee released its final report, Senator Edward M. Kennedy (D-MA) introduced the Foreign Intelligence Surveillance Act (FISA) in the Senate. The bill called for the creation of a court whose judges, appointed from the federal bench by the chief justice of the Supreme Court, would rule on requests from Justice Department lawyers for surveillance of people suspected of spying for foreign powers. The lawyers would not have to show probable cause that a crime had been committed, the usual standard for obtaining a criminal warrant; they would only have to persuade the judge that there was some reason to believe that the target was an agent of a foreign power hostile to the United States. And while the existence of the court would be public, if quiet, its proceedings would be held in secret.

To ensure that investigators could not exploit FISA's lower standard of probable cause as a workaround for a regular criminal warrant, the act separated intelligence investigations from criminal investigations. Under the Clinton administration, Attorney General Janet Reno turned a strict interpretation of this requirement into firm policy, establishing the "FISA wall," which forbade the secret court to authorize information-gathering activities related primarily to criminal matters. The FBI could get permission from a FISA court to tap a suspect's phone or to obtain his or her tax records but only to collect intelligence and not primarily to launch a criminal investigation of any sort; intelligence had to be the "primary purpose" of the surveillance or search. If the investigation did reveal evidence of criminal activity, the investigators could turn the wiretap transcripts over to their colleagues on the criminal side, but suspected criminal activity could not be the primary purpose of a FISA wiretap.

On paper this system might have worked perfectly. But in real life it did not, in large part because the integrity of the wall depended on people whose interests sometimes—perhaps often—lay in breaching it. FBI agents prepared the factual information the FISA Court received before issuing a decision and enforced those decisions after surveillance had been authorized. FISC judges, already aware of agents' temptation to misrepresent facts in order to get lawyers to approve their applications, began to hear about instances in which they had been misled. Specifically, the judges began to suspect that the searches and surveillance they authorized were "being used sub rosa," as a court opinion later put it, "for criminal investigations."

Under pressure from the FISA Court, the Justice Department launched an internal investigation, and in September 2000 "the government came forward to confess error in some 75 FISA applications related to major terrorist attacks"—an "alarming number," wrote Judge Royce Lamberth, the chief FISA Court judge at the time. Lamberth was being kind by calling them "errors." As the opinion made clear, they were really lies intended to abuse FISA's leniency to get around the rigors of the Constitution. Agents had distorted facts that would have disqualified them from receiving the court's approval for a warrant. After the confession, FBI agents discovered that the court no longer took them at their word. The court took action to tighten up the "'wall' procedures," including introducing a requirement that multiple agents at every level of the FBI would now have to sign off on, and thus take responsibility for, statements made to the court. One agent was barred from submitting an application to the FISA Court ever again. If FISA had formerly been a rubber stamp for the FBI's requests (it had denied only one in its twenty-three years of existence), it would be so no longer.

WHEN COLEEN ROWLEY HEARD FBI director Robert Mueller assure the nation that the FBI had had no advance warning of the attacks, she tried frantically to get in touch with him. She had no reason to think he was aware of the Moussaoui file and the incendiary material it contained, but as she explained in a letter to Mueller, she feared that once word of the case got out, "this statement could easily come back to haunt the FBI." When she didn't hear back from him or any FBI officials, and when Mueller did not modify his remarks, she thought her message had failed to penetrate the bureaucracy. But weeks later, following the first press reports about Moussaoui, the agency continued to profess no advance knowledge; she concluded that "someone, possibly with your approval, had decided to circle the wagons."

"I don't know how you or anyone at FBI Headquarters, no matter how much genius . . . you may possess, could so blithely make this affirmation without anything to back up your opinion except your status as FBI Director," Rowley wrote. "I think your statements

demonstrate a rush to judgment to protect the FBI at all costs."
She was, it seemed, willing to risk sacrificing her FBI career for her
principles.

But before she accused her boss of malfeasance, Rowley offered
an analysis of the failure. She explained that at first she had wanted
to get a FISA warrant for Moussaoui's apartment. She had known
that if she tried first to get a criminal warrant and failed, any subsequent attempt to get a FISA warrant could contribute to the appearance that the FBI overused "less-demanding intelligence methods"
for obtaining warrants—a sensitive subject, given the recent dustup
between Lamberth and the bureau. So she went the "other route,"
only to find that her supervisors in Washington "almost inexplica-
bly" proceeded to "throw up roadblocks and undermine Minneapolis's by now desperate efforts to obtain a FISA warrant." They
brought up "ridiculous questions" (which Rowley did not specify)
and failed to tell her that the Phoenix FBI office had been reporting on suspected "Al Qaeda operatives" who had sought training
at flight schools. Finally, on August 28, 2001, after the Washington
agent in charge of the case had once again "deliberately undercut"
her FISA effort—this time by withholding information about Moussaoui's foreign contacts and activities—her unit chief informed her
that there was not "sufficient evidence of Moussaoui's connection to
a foreign power."

In her letter, Rowley didn't say whether she thought the Washington agent was making a good faith effort to meet the stringent
requirements recently laid down by the FISA Court or merely avoiding all the new paperwork (or, for that matter, merely acting resent-
fully in the wake of the rebuke from higher-ups), but the letter made
clear what Ashcroft and Chertoff—and many others inside the
government—must have been thinking at the time: the FISA wall
was an obstacle to preventing terrorist attacks.

One way to surmount this difficulty was to enhance the Justice
Department's involvement with intelligence protocols and laws and
to improve, where possible, the communication between intelligence

agents and criminal investigators. For his part, Mueller started an analysis section inside the Counterterrorism Division and the FBI and created an Office of Intelligence, which eventually became a full-fledged Directorate of Intelligence whose authority spanned the entire FBI. With the increase in intelligence work, training in FISA and sensitivity to the FISA wall would have to become more pervasive as well.

But there was a more direct way to address the problem, one that in the wake of the Moussaoui embarrassment seemed increasingly appealing: eradicating the wall entirely.

CHAPTER 2

The Problem

E ven before 9/11, Department of Justice lawyers were surveying the FISA wall and wondering how to renovate it. In early 2001 the FBI was reeling from the FISA Court inquiry and subsequent crackdown. If the court was going to start rejecting requests for surveillance orders for the first time in its twenty-three-year history—even as every day seemed to bring new terrorist threats—the DOJ worried, investigations would be threatened, and the country's safety would be put at risk. The task of removing the restrictions seemed more and more urgent.

The natural man for the job was David Kris, the thirty-four-year-old associate deputy attorney general. The son of two Viennese-trained psychoanalysts, Kris had studied philosophy at Haverford College and gone on to attend Harvard Law School, where he was a classmate of Barack Obama's. Soon after graduation he began to publish law review articles, one focusing on terrorism prosecution. He emphasized the need for stronger rules to protect defendants' rights in international terrorism cases, warning that "when the nation's ire is provoked," as it was bound to be in cases of terror- ism, "democratic bodies may follow passion rather than reason" and pass laws that would compromise constitutional protections during prosecution.

Kris had come to the DOJ after several years working as a federal prosecutor in the DC district court. He served under Eric Holder, the deputy attorney general in the Clinton administration, and stayed on when George W. Bush came into office. While at Justice, he'd continued to pursue his interest in questions about terrorism and the law. He'd come to the conclusion that the Church Com- mittee had been correct to try to strike a balance between national security and citizen rights, and that while the FBI and the NSA had to be reined in, they still needed some method by which to moder- ate constitutional guarantees—by, say, getting a warrant to search a computer without showing probable cause—in order to protect the country from terrorism and espionage. FISA, he thought, had struck that balance, but that didn't mean it couldn't be improved.

Kris was particularly concerned with the FISA wall, which he thought had created more problems than it had solved. It hamstrung investigators, kept evidence out of the hands of prosecutors until too late, and prevented prosecutors who might turn up informa- tion relevant to counterintelligence from helping out in espionage investigations. In a perverse way, too, it actually compromised civil liberties: by keeping the criminal side of the DOJ separate from the intelligence side, the FISA wall diminished defendants' access to evidence and thus took away one of the important checks on pros- ecutorial power. "From lawyer access," he once told a congressional committee, "comes lawyer oversight."

What was true of the wall was true of FISA in general. Its at- tempt to have it both ways—to protect civil liberties even as it tried to work around them—had led to a slow and laborious process of review and negotiation. The man in charge of this process was James Baker, counsel at the DOJ's Office of Intelligence Policy and Review (OIPR). Here Baker found himself sandwiched between judges and

FBI agents eager to gain FISA Court approval for their wiretapping requests and the court itself. Because of the secrecy of the matters coming before the court, Baker had to play his own devil's advocate, representing the interests of the potential targets as well as the interests of those who wanted to target them. So he moved slowly and deliberately, conveying to his colleagues that he took his multiple conflicting roles seriously. "He *was* the wall," one of them later said.

Early in 2001, before the terror attacks, Deputy Attorney General Larry Thompson gave Kris a green light to conduct a review of FISA procedures. Neither man was enamored of the restrictions imposed by FISA, but they both knew that Congress and the courts were unlikely to sanction the complete removal of the wall. So they settled for telling agents that when an intelligence investigation turned up criminal activity, notification of their colleagues on the other side of the wall "is *mandatory* and is to be followed by the FBI absent a specific exemption" from top officials at the department. Agents would also have to report monthly to those officials on their activities in order to determine if there was information they ought to share. Not only could they stop worrying (assuming they had in the past) about whether FISA allowed them to talk to other agents, they now had no choice but to clue them in.

Still, compared to what the two men wanted, this change was a minor tweak, and Thompson would later regret stopping short. "We knew something was broken," he said. We were "too timid, too cautious. . . . If only we'd been a little more aggressive, a little more sure-footed, a little less afraid of breaking china." He recalled the immense regret he had felt as he rode to a secure bunker on 9/11, listening to Baker on the phone with a FISA Court judge, asking for authorization for the immediate removal of the FISA wall on an emergency basis, which he got. Four days later the FISA Court suspended the wall to give investigators a freer hand in looking into the possibility of further impending attacks.

Still, Thompson, aware that "two guys unilaterally couldn't just take down the wall," had succeeded in sending a signal to anyone

paying attention: lawyers high up in Justice had their eye on the
FISA wall and were willing to test its strength. Perhaps they could
take out only a brick or two right now, but they were scouting for
ways to knock it down completely and grant FISA's powers to any
law enforcer who needed them, congressional and judicial reservations notwithstanding.

EVEN IN THE IMMEDIATE AFTERMATH of the deadliest
terrorist attack ever to take place on American soil, lowering the FISA
wall was a delicate operation. It raised constitutional questions that
had never been answered (or even, in some cases, asked), and some of
its implications, like extending the ability to conduct surveillance without a criminal warrant to more people under looser conditions, were
potentially incendiary. So even as he gained a mandate to take further
steps to reduce the separation between intelligence and criminal investigations, Kris had to proceed carefully. For guidance, he turned to another DOJ lawyer, John Yoo, in the Office of Legal Counsel, the group
responsible for providing opinions on the legality of such policies.

Yoo, a thirty-four-year-old lawyer, had emigrated as a child to the
United States from South Korea and had gone directly from Yale
Law School to work in Washington. Soft-spoken, sure-footed, and
preternaturally calm even in stressful circumstances, Yoo had risen
quickly through Washington's elite legal circles, clerking for Federal
Circuit Court Judge Laurence Silberman, a conservative DC insider
and member of the Federalist Society, an organization of conserva-
tive lawyers, who had been appointed by President Ronald Reagan.
He went on to clerk for Silberman's close friend and associate on the
Supreme Court, Clarence Thomas.

Yoo and Kris shared some characteristics. Less than a year apart
in age, both were raised in upper-middle-class suburbs, and both
graduated from one of the nation's best law schools. Both had psychoanalysts as parents; Yoo's had been trained in South Korea. Both
had written about national security before coming into government

service. Both were considered exceptionally bright, even among their Ivy League peers. Both had entered the DOJ through the Attorney General's Honors Program, designed to bring the best and brightest into government service.

But Kris and Yoo were different in ways that perhaps neither of them appreciated when Kris asked for Yoo's guidance. Not only were they at different places on the political spectrum—Kris a pragmatic Democrat who was comfortable serving administrations on both sides of the aisle, Yoo a staunch conservative—they also had different allegiances. Kris was a philosopher, interested in making sure that the interpretation of laws upheld the original ideas and intent of the legislators who wrote them. Yoo was an ideologue, a believer that the law can and should be used to advance a particular agenda. Unlike Kris, Yoo was a daily visitor to the White House, where he met with the president's legal staff—an arrangement common for lawyers in Justice's Office of Legal Counsel—but Yoo kept the details of these meetings mostly to himself, rarely sharing them with colleagues or even with his boss. If Kris's client was the US government, Yoo's was the Bush administration.

The question Kris brought to Yoo was of the greatest consequence, but it pivoted on the smallest word in the English language. FISA authorized the lowering of Fourth Amendment protections only when "the purpose" of the proposed search or surveillance was the collection of foreign intelligence. This standard was the foundation of the FISA wall, the guarantee that the limited license the law granted to the government to circumvent the Constitution in special circumstances would not become a ticket that any law enforcement agent could punch at any time for any purpose. But what would happen, Kris wanted to know, if the law were changed to require foreign intelligence to be only "*a* purpose" of the search or surveillance? If the FISA Court granted permission to an agent who said that intelligence was only one of several purposes of the proposed activity, would it be in violation of the Fourth Amendment?

Yoo's answer drew on another similarity between himself and

Kris. Both believed that the Constitution is not a suicide pact, that its absolute language of "shall" and "shall not" must give way under certain circumstances. The Fourth Amendment ensures that "the right of people to be secure ... against unreasonable searches and seizures" and that "no warrants shall issue, but upon probable cause" and with particularity as to "the place to be searched, and the persons or things to be seized." But sometimes government, in order to uphold its mission to defend the nation, had to be flexible in its understanding of the Constitution. And Yoo had an agenda that went beyond balancing, as he put it in his memo to Kris, "the government's interest against the individual's Fourth Amendment interests."

Yoo had written his undergraduate thesis at Harvard on presidential power in the nuclear age. He had argued that Eisenhower, Kennedy, and Nixon had succeeded in protecting American hegemony during the Cold War by promoting an expansive notion of the power of the executive branch. Presidential power remained Yoo's focus after law school. By the time he arrived at the Justice Department, he had already published five law review articles on the subject.

Yoo was among the large group of conservative lawyers, many of them Federalist Society members, hired into both the DOJ and the White House by the Bush administration. One of the most prominent was David Addington, Vice President Dick Cheney's counsel and longtime adviser, who came into his office fiercely determined to strengthen and expand the powers of the executive branch—in particular, the president's office (which, in Addington's reading, included the vice president). Having a man of Yoo's intelligence and training inside the DOJ—which had always been seen as one step removed from the interests of the White House, its decisions and policies seemingly less tainted by politics—was, as Addington's counterparts put it, a godsend, a gift from heaven, one they were exceptionally lucky to have.

Even before Kris approached Yoo with his question about lowering the FISA wall, Yoo had had a chance to help Addington fashion a legal rationale establishing the supremacy of the executive. On

September 18, 2001, Bush signed into law the Authorization for Use of Military Force (AUMF), which granted the president the right to use "all necessary force and appropriate force" against those responsible for the 9/11 attacks and against those who "harbored such organizations or persons." It also allowed him to do whatever he deemed necessary to "prevent any future acts of international terrorism against the United States." The law took the place of the declaration of war required by the Constitution, but rather than simply declaring war, it granted the president broad power to act in the name of national security—even if that meant diluting the Constitution's checks on presidential authority in the name of keeping the country safe.

Yoo had been one of the authors of the AUMF, and only a week after it passed, he drew on it to justify an unprecedented expansion of executive power. Kris had unwittingly given him the opportunity to do so by asking the *the* vs. *a* question. That answer was simple enough in Yoo's mind. "'A' purpose" searches would obviously not exclude "'the' purpose" searches, he wrote in his memo, so those would continue to fall within the law. As for the "'a' purpose" searches, it would be up to FISA Court judges to determine whether a prosecutor was asking for an unreasonable exception to the Fourth Amendment—as they would have to, for instance, if "criminal investigation constitutes an overwhelming purpose of the surveillance."

Yet according to Yoo, it would not necessarily violate the Constitution to give judges some leeway, to allow them to balance the criminal purpose against the intelligence purpose of a particular warrant, rather than force them to consider only investigations for which intelligence was the primary purpose (or, as had clearly been happening for years, to pretend that this was the case). Yoo reasoned that Kris's proposal merely acknowledged what 9/11 made clear and what the AUMF provided justification for: that "the current situation, in which Congress has recognized the President's authority to use force in response to a direct attack on the American homeland, has changed the calculus of a reasonable search." The amended law, according to Yoo, would not contradict or even dilute the Fourth Amendment. It would "simply allow the Department to apply for FISA warrants up to the limit permitted by the Constitution, as determined by the FISA court." In other words, substituting *a* for *the* would just make the judges do the math and determine whether, in the new environment, the search was reasonable.

But Yoo did not stop there. Nearly half of his thirteen-page memo was devoted to the question of whether the fuss about warrants was necessary in the first place. When a judge, FISC or otherwise, signed a warrant, he or she was certifying that the proposed search was within the bounds of the Constitution. But, Yoo reminded Kris, a warrant was not the only mechanism for determining reasonableness. "A warrantless search can be constitutional," he wrote, " 'when special needs beyond the normal need for law enforcement make the warrant and probable cause requirement impracticable.' "

Here Yoo was quoting a Supreme Court decision on whether a school district had the right to subject student athletes to random drug tests. The Court had determined that indeed it did, because the government's legitimate interest in keeping students off drugs outweighed the invasion of students' privacy. And if drug-free kids were a "special need," then what about "exigent circumstances such as a potential threat to the safety of law enforcement officers or third parties"?

Here, Yoo went on, there was a long tradition arguing that in such cases, the powers of the president were vast. From Alexander Hamilton, who opined in the Federalist Papers that "there can be no limitation of that authority which is to provide for the defence and protection of the community," to the Fourth Circuit Court's 1980 assertion that "the needs of the executive are so compelling in the area of foreign intelligence, that a uniform warrant requirement would . . . 'unduly frustrate' the President in carrying out his foreign affairs responsibilities," there was a clear line of jurisprudence establishing that "a warrant is not required for all government searches." Surely, Yoo concluded, "[i]f the government's heightened interest in self-defense justifies the use of deadly force, then it certainly would also justify warrantless searches." Self-defense now included prevention, and prevention created needs that previously did not exist. This was the new calculus, and it would be years before Americans outside this small circle of advisers discovered just how different it was from the old one.

YOO'S ARGUMENT ABOUT WARRANTLESS SEARCHES was bookended by his consideration of Kris's amendment, and in the conclusion of his memo, he did not even mention warrantless searches; he only reiterated that replacing "the" with "a" didn't appear to violate the Constitution. It was a deft and bold move, arguing, in the course of defending a law designed to prevent warrantless searches, that the law itself was unnecessary—and offering a rationale for subverting it.

Clever as it might have been, Yoo's argument that the president had vast powers to abrogate long-standing protection of citizens was not subtle. David Kris could not have missed it or failed to recognize its expansiveness. Kris did eventually challenge Yoo's opinion on the legality of warrantless searches—but not (at least not publicly) until 2006, after the first revelations of the NSA's electronic surveillance program, when, in a widely circulated paper, he suggested that the program, and Yoo's rationale for it, exceeded the president's constitutional authority. But in the chaotic aftermath of the 9/11 attacks, Kris remained focused on his main goal—the inclusion in the Patriot Act of a lowered FISA wall—and did not publicly object to Yoo's piggybacking his views about the Fourth Amendment onto an arcane discussion of semantics.

Yoo's brief gave Kris enough confidence in the constitutionality of his amendment to go before the Senate Select Committee on Intelligence on September 24 and urge the senators to leave it in the Patriot Act. He was mostly successful. Section 218 of the act that passed into law a month later required that FISA warrants be granted for "a significant purpose," not for "a purpose," as Kris had originally proposed. Still, the act made it easier for law enforcement and intelligence agents to share information about their investigations even as it secured broader latitude for prosecutors to help bring cases before the FISC—just as Kris and Thompson had wanted. It wasn't immediately clear how the judges would weigh the balance between intelligence and criminal purposes when requests for warrants came before them, but they would soon have ample opportunity to figure it out. Applications to the FISC increased from 932 in 2001 to 1,228 in 2002, and additional OIPR staff were hired to process them.

Even without seeing the Yoo memo, Anthony Romero, the director of the American Civil Liberties Union (ACLU) and a man whose job is to worry about constitutional rights, recognized that the changes to FISA had profound implications for civil liberties. When the act came up for a vote, the ACLU sent a letter warning senators that the bill contained "measures that would . . . lead to large-scale investigations of American citizens for 'intelligence' purposes." By allowing "intelligence authorities to by-pass probable cause requirements in criminal cases," the act would invite exactly the kinds of violations that the FISA wall had been designed to prevent.

In a speech delivered in Cleveland the week after passage of the Patriot Act, Romero delineated the ways in which the act posed a threat to civil liberties. Official hand-wringing about balancing civil liberties against counterterrorist efforts amounted to no more than "lip service," he said. Under Section 215, the Patriot Act had given the FBI director the ability to ask a FISA Court judge for authority to sweep up large quantities of data from "books, records, papers, documents, and other items" belonging to people who might be related to terrorist activity anywhere in the world. And those people did not have to be serving a foreign power, as FISA originally required. Now investigators needed only to state that the records it wanted were somehow related to an investigation that was somehow related to terrorism. This amounted, Romero said, to issuing "blank warrants" that didn't even have to "specify the phone to be tapped or require that only the target's conversations be eavesdropped on."

The act also extended to the Internet the authority that law enforcement already had to request records of phone calls from telecommunication companies so long as they were "relevant to an ongoing criminal investigation." But as Romero pointed out, Internet records reveal information that phone numbers do not, such as the sites a person has visited. And since the act also lowered the FISA wall, virtually any FBI investigator, from the criminal or the intelligence side, could avail him- or herself of this new power. Taken together, Romero told his audience, these measures gave law enforcement officials "expanded power to invade our privacy, imprison people without meaningful due process, and punish dissent."

The ACLU has always had an influential but limited constituency, and in the climate of fear that had taken hold after 9/11, it was easy enough to dismiss Romero as naïve about the dangers of terrorism, or worse. But by March 2002, John Ashcroft had instituted a policy that confirmed Romero's fears. In a memo spelling out his understanding of the Patriot Act, he declared that it "allows FISA to be used *primarily* for a law enforcement purpose"—a far cry from what Congress was trying to prevent by changing Kris's "a purpose" to "a significant purpose." Now the foreign intelligence purpose could be tenuous and need not be certified by intelligence officers. Nor did law enforcement agents need to establish anything more than "the possibility of a criminal prosecution" to "exchange a full range of information and advice"—including, of course, all the information swept up under Section 215. Indeed, Ashcroft went on, the FBI was now *obliged* to provide anything turned up in a foreign investigation to criminal investigators. Now domestic FBI agents could direct investigations, order wiretaps, collect phone records, monitor email, and otherwise pry into the lives of just about any Americans they wanted—and all without warrants or any other of the due process guarantees required by the Constitution.

The FISA wall hadn't merely been lowered in Ashcroft's new guidelines. It had been obliterated, and with it whatever modicum of restraint remained among investigators, other than that which the agents and lawyers themselves chose to exercise. Even in the best of circumstances, that would be an unreliable check on power, especially given their determination to carry out the president's edict to prevent another terrorist attack. But these weren't the best of circumstances. Lawyers and agents had been issued a blank check, which would pay substantial dividends in the future.

ACTUALLY, THEY WERE ALREADY RELYING on the wall's disappearance. Even as he was exploring the niceties of constitutional law for David Kris, John Yoo was writing another memo. This one was kept secret—from Kris and almost everyone else in the Department of Justice, from Congress, and, of course, from the American people. Its contents remain largely classified, and the 407-page report on the surveillance program it helped launch, released fourteen years later, is full of redactions, but one thing is clear: Yoo was not wrestling with a question like Kris's, about whether a proposed change to the law was constitutional. He was instead justifying a decision that had already been made, creating constitutional cover for an abridgement of civil liberties unprecedented in American history.

On October 4, 2001, as the inspector general's report would eventually reveal, President Bush issued a top secret edict, declaring that "an extraordinary emergency existed permitting the use of electronic surveillance within the United States for counterterrorism purposes, without a court order." The full scope of the initiative launched under this reasoning, known as the President's Surveillance Program and code-named Stellar Wind by the NSA, is still unknown. But one of the programs instituted under its auspices, later known as the Terrorist Surveillance Program, intercepted the content of phone and email communications. Another initiated the collection of the metadata—the records of senders and recipients who took part in communications, the origin and destination of those communications, and their length—of many, if not all, American citizens. The reach of these new programs was so vast and unusual that even the head of the NSA, Michael Hayden, felt compelled to remind Addington that "the NSA was not authorized to intercept domestic-to-domestic communications." Years later Hayden told the inspector general that he had informed his staff "to do exactly what [Bush] said and not one photon or electron more." But given the scope of the surveillance, it would appear that Hayden's edict about the photons and electrons had been ignored or summarily dismissed.

Hayden told the inspectors that his reservations about the reach of Stellar Wind were put to rest "by the signature of the Attorney General that the program was lawful." It's not clear if he knew at the time that, at least according to the report, John Ashcroft signed off on the program on the same day he was first made aware of it, and that no one else at the Department of Justice was aware of it at the time. If Ashcroft had any concerns about the legality of Stellar Wind, he dispatched them with haste.

But soon enough John Yoo was attending to the matter, writing his memo justifying the NSA program. His handiwork remains mostly classified; the public version is almost completely redacted. But the inspector general's report makes it clear that he pursued the same line of reasoning he had opened in his memo to Kris, once again arguing that the broadening of executive power was not an unconstitutional infringement of civil liberties. Indeed, given the nature and extent of the emergency, attempts to limit presidential power, even if that meant protecting ordinary citizens from warrantless wiretaps, would be "an unconstitutional infringement on the President's Article II authorities." If Congress had wanted to stop the president from spying on citizens, it would have said so in the FISA laws, Yoo wrote. Because it was silent on the issue, the president was free to do it, no matter what the Fourth Amendment said.

This was not an argument that would survive much scrutiny, and later, other Justice Department lawyers repudiated it. They might

have done so even earlier but for the fact that Yoo was the only lawyer in the Office of Legal Counsel—and one of two lawyers at Justice other than the attorney general—who knew about Stellar Wind
early on. (OIPR head James Baker was read in, according to a later
report, in January 2002.) But the White House wasn't interested in
a debate over legal nuance. The point of the legal advice wasn't to
guide them in determining which policies were legal but, rather, to
provide plausible cover for the policies they wanted to impose. That's
what executive power meant to the lawyers at the White House and
to John Yoo at the Justice Department: the authority to do what they
thought needed to be done in the name of security, and then to shape
the interpretation of the law to make it legitimate.

Yoo's memo supporting Stellar Wind came out on November 2,
2001, one week after the Patriot Act was already signed into law.
Less than two months had passed since the terrorist attacks, but in
the name of preventing future catastrophes, policies had been implemented, laws written, and legal opinions rendered that dramatically
changed the balance of powers among the branches of government
and between the government and its citizens—in both cases, elevat-
ing the presidency to a status that was arguably beyond any it had
ever enjoyed. Much of this work had been done behind closed doors;
some of it remains secret to this day.

It wasn't the first time a president had been allowed to wield extraordinary power during a time of crisis. But Lincoln's suspension
of habeas corpus and Roosevelt's internment of Japanese Americans during World War II were responses to wars against known
enemies. The work of Yoo and his allies in the White House, on the
other hand, was in service to an undeclared war being waged not on
a particular enemy but on an idea, terrorism, which, like most ideas,
is probably impossible to eradicate. The policies fashioned in the
early days after the 9/11 attacks, a time of unprecedented fear, had
no natural life span. The expansion of governmental power would
last as long as there was reason to think that someone somewhere
might be plotting a terrorist act. To advocates of executive power like

Addington and Cheney and Yoo, this was the silver lining around the cloud of dust that still rose from the remains of the World Trade Center. Soon enough this rogue operation would spread beyond the executive branch and into the courts, beyond merely surveilling American citizens and toward detaining, torturing, and eventually killing them.

CHAPTER 3

A Pawn in
Their Game

On December 1, 2001, Frank Lindh received an email from his cousin Tommy. "Look at this. Could this be John?" Frank took a look at the grainy image and drove to his ex-wife, Marilyn's, home. Together they peered at the picture. A few facts were attached: the person in the photo was apparently born in DC in 1981. Just like their son, John. Frank had been following the news about Afghanistan and had heard about the recent uprising of prisoners there. But it had never occurred to him that John could be in Afghanistan. They hadn't heard from him for seven months, ever since he'd gone off into the mountains of Pakistan. Still, the more they looked, the more they began to think it was possible the man in the picture was their son, and soon they would see another, much clearer image, this one broadcast on CNN. There was no mistaking it: it showed their twenty-year-old son, named for John Lennon, lying atop a gurney, naked, his face blackened, his shoulder-length dark brown hair matted and filthy-looking; he was writhing in pain.

Neither Frank nor Marilyn had seen John in the last twenty-two months. He had been away for most of the previous four years, studying Islam in Yemen and Pakistan, or so they thought. John had converted to Islam when he was sixteen, inspired, he said, by watching *Malcolm X,* the Spike Lee biopic. He'd become a regular at the mosque near the family home in Marin County, where, after years of homeschooling, he was a student at an alternative high school. He adopted a couple of new names—Suleyman al-Lindh and Suleyman al-Faris—and then, at the age of seventeen, left for Yemen. He returned briefly to California, then went back to Yemen and from there to Pakistan, where he enrolled in an Islamic school, or madrassa.

In June 2001 John left Pakistan for Afghanistan to join the Taliban, motivated, he later said, by "an obligation to assist what I perceived to be an Islamic liberation movement against the warlords who were occupying several provinces in northern Afghanistan." The Taliban were not yet an official US enemy; the mujahideen from which the Taliban emerged had been an ally during the decade when Afghanistan fought the occupying Soviet forces, and after the Russian withdrawal in 1989, they were no longer of strategic interest to the US government—at least not until, in the aftermath of 9/11, they were branded a terrorist organization and became a target of a military campaign to overthrow their rule, on the grounds that they had provided cover and support to Al Qaeda.

In Afghanistan, the US military allied itself with a local enemy of the Taliban, the Northern Alliance. One of its commanders was General Abdul Rashid Dostum, a man with a reputation for extreme brutality—according to one story, he had once killed a captive by having him tied to the tread of a tank and crushed. On November 25, Dostum cornered a group of hundreds of Taliban fighters. Three hundred and thirty of them were taken to Qala Jangi prison, on the outskirts of Mazar-i-Sharif. There they were questioned by American interrogators, including a CIA agent named Johnny "Mike" Spann. One of the captives, Spann learned, spoke English. He went over to him. "All I want to do is talk to you and find out what your story is," he said. The man did not respond. "You believe in what you're doing here that much, you're willing to be killed here?" When the man failed to answer, Spann snapped his fingers in front of his face. "Hey! Wake up!" he said. The man continued his silence. Spann ordered the Northern Alliance soldier holding the man to pull his hair back off his face. "You got to talk to me," he said. Another CIA agent approached. "The problem is," the second agent said, loud enough for the man to hear, "he's got to decide if he wants to live or die, and die here."

After more fruitless attempts to get answers, the CIA agents had the man pulled to his feet and returned to the brigade of prisoners. Before they could question him again, the prisoners rioted. In the ensuing daylong skirmish, Spann was shot dead—the first American killed in the new war. The rebelling prisoners took up a position in the prison basement. Northern Alliance guards under Dostum's direction poured gasoline into the basement and ignited it. When that did not force out the prisoners, they flooded the basement with cold water from a nearby irrigation canal. Finally, after seven days in the basement, the eighty-six prisoners who had not been shot to death, burned alive, or drowned surrendered.

The mysterious English speaker was among the survivors. At six feet tall, he had managed to keep his head above the rising water while others drowned. Still, he'd sustained a bullet wound to his right thigh, and according to a US medic, he was "malnourished and in extremely poor overall condition."

The Americans finally determined that his name was John Walker Lindh and that he was an American citizen from California. They took him to Sheberghan, a hospital and prison three hours away. There he encountered another American, one who would accidentally seal his fate. A journalist and veteran war reporter working for CNN, Robert Pelton chanced upon Lindh among the wounded prisoners. In return for Pelton's promise to obtain medical attention, Lindh agreed to an interview. From his hospital bed and in obvious pain, he told Pelton that he'd been attending a "simple training camp" in Afghanistan.

"And did you enjoy the jihad? I mean, was it a good cause for you?" Pelton asked.

"Definitely," Lindh replied.

Frank Lindh saw this interview. So did the rest of America. John quickly became the target of public outrage. Here finally was a captive in the war on terror, someone whose face could be put before the American public as an enemy caught and awaiting punishment. And he spoke English! True, he was not a mastermind or ringleader of 9/11. In fact, he had not been involved in 9/11 in any way. But he had voluntarily enlisted with the enemy, he *enjoyed* being a jihadi, and the events that led to his capture had also resulted in the death of an American. Rudolph Giuliani accused him of treason. Hillary Clinton called him a traitor. *Newsweek* branded him the "American Taliban," a nickname that stuck. But while he was being found guilty in the court of public opinion, a battle was raging inside the Bush administration over what exactly should be done with John Walker Lindh. Was he entitled to constitutional protections? Or should he be subject to the new regime, the one in which the campaign for prevention already had a pass to trump the Bill of Rights?

FOR THE PENTAGON, THE CIA, and the other agencies blindsided by 9/11, Lindh's presumed intimate knowledge of Bin Laden, Al Qaeda, and the Taliban was the most compelling consideration. If prevention was the priority, then Lindh had to be considered an intelligence asset first and a criminal defendant second. Prosecutors could nail him, of course—but only after his valuable knowledge had been extracted.

Michael Chertoff, who as head of the DOJ's Criminal Division was in charge of federal prosecutions, expected that Lindh would be prosecuted in federal civilian court despite the fact that he had been captured on the battlefield. The American Taliban was, after all, an American, and the courts had demonstrated their ability to try and convict terrorism defendants. Chertoff understood the need for intelligence collection, but he also believed that using the criminal justice system to convict and imprison suspected terrorists was its own powerful form of disrupting terrorist networks and incipient plots, an important tactic in prevention.

The White House, however, had already decided on its preferred course. In the weeks before Lindh's capture, lawyers there had been drafting a policy decreeing that detainees in the war on terror would be held in military custody and tried—if they were to be tried at all—by military courts. This move was necessary, the order said, "to protect the United States and its citizens, and for the effective conduct of military operations and prevention of terrorist attacks."

John Yoo had helped White House lawyers draft the new policy— a fact unknown to his boss, Attorney General John Ashcroft. "You've got to be kidding me," Ashcroft said when he found out. He was enraged not only at Yoo's failure to clue him in but at the policy itself, which he knew would diminish the role of his department in handling terrorism cases. The attorney general immediately went to the White House to argue that the federal courts were the appropriate venue for trials of foreign terrorists.

Ashcroft had precedent on his side. Prior to 9/11, suspects in terror attacks had been successfully prosecuted in the federal courts. Omar Abdel Rahman (the Blind Sheikh), accused of a plot to blow up New York City landmarks; the perpetrators of the 1993 World Trade Center bombing; and the men who had blown up the US embassies in Nairobi and Dar es Salaam—all of them had been tried and convicted in federal courts, as recently as 2001. But Ashcroft failed to make any headway against David Addington, White House counsel Alberto Gonzales, and other administration officials, all of whom threw their support behind the military trials.

As an American citizen, Lindh was not subject to the new decree, but that didn't stop administration officials from trying to figure out how to extend it to him. Some suggested simply amending it to include citizens. Others proposed expanding the court-martial system to civilians like Lindh. But Ashcroft promised the president that his prosecutors would level harsh charges against Lindh, including some related to the death of an American, Mike Spann. The White House agreed not to place Lindh in military custody. In February 2002, Lindh was indicted on ten counts, including conspiracy to commit murder, charges that carried a life sentence. The trial would take place in federal court, in the Eastern District of Virginia, ten miles from Washington. Lindh's case would become the first test of how the criminal justice system in the post-9/11 era would handle terrorists, and of how far the government was willing to bend justice in order to convict them.

DAVID KELLEY WAS A MAILMAN'S son who had worked as a cop on eastern Long Island while attending evening law school classes in New York City. While still in law school, he secured an internship in Manhattan's Southern District, where Rudolph Giuliani was then US attorney and Michael Chertoff head of the Criminal Division. Hardworking and determined, Kelley remained nearby after graduation, eventually landing a full-time position as an assistant US attorney in Manhattan—one of the most prestigious jobs a young lawyer could hope for.

As a prosecutor, Kelley had helped with the investigation into the 2000 bombing of the USS *Cole,* which had killed seventeen US soldiers and wounded thirty-nine others. He had been a member of the team investigating the bombings of the US embassies in East Africa and had helped in the prosecution of the conspirators in the first World Trade Center bombing. He arrived in Washington in the early morning hours of September 12 with the dust from the World Trade Center "still on his shoes," and immediately took a leadership role in the 9/11 investigation. He was still in DC when the Lindh case broke.

Michael Chertoff knew that Kelley was familiar with prosecuting Al Qaeda members. He would know which charges to bring, what evidence to present, how to frame the narrative for a jury, and how to direct a criminal proceeding to a swift and decisive conclusion. So he was confident that Kelley was the right man to take on the Lindh case.

The new job came with significant problems, most of them stemming from the circumstances of Lindh's capture. As the trial neared its start date of August 26, 2002, James Brosnahan, the San Francisco lawyer hired by Frank Lindh to represent his son, filed a motion to suppress the statements Lindh had made in CIA custody—statements that provided the bulk of the government's case against him. Those statements, Brosnahan argued, were extracted under conditions that made the evidence obtained legally questionable.

Lindh's poor treatment, as Brosnahan's motion made clear, had not stopped at Qala Jangi or at the hospital in Sheberghan. On December 7, after five days of interrogation by the military, Lindh was transferred to Camp Rhino, an American forward operating base in southern Afghanistan. Army photos from Rhino show Lindh naked, dirty, and duct-taped to a gurney, his eyes covered with a blindfold emblazoned with the word *shithead*. A couple of days later he was finally given some clothes—a thin hospital gown—and carried on his gurney out of the windowless, unheated shipping container in which he had been held and into an interrogation room. "He was sleep-deprived, malnourished, hungry and in pain," as Brosnahan's cocounsel George Harris wrote to the court, "with a bullet and shrapnel still lodged in his body." When the blindfold was removed, Lindh found himself facing FBI agent Christopher Reimann, an armed guard behind him. Immediately, Reimann read Lindh his Miranda rights, informing him that he had the right to remain silent when being interrogated and the right to an attorney. "Of course," Reimann added, "there are no lawyers here."

Neither, to Lindh's knowledge, was there a lawyer in San Francisco; Reimann neglected to mention Brosnahan, despite the fact that the attorney had informed Donald Rumsfeld, John Ashcroft, and many other Bush administration officials that he was on the case. Lindh had been brutalized and humiliated, if not tortured outright, and he'd been deprived of his constitutional rights as a US citizen. Nearly everything Lindh had told interrogators from the time of his capture until he signed a confession (with a bullet still lodged in his leg) on board a navy ship on December 14 should be considered "fruit of the poisonous tree" and inadmissible in court, Brosnahan argued. The suppression hearing was scheduled for mid-July. It was to be the first of dozens like it, in which the power of prevention-minded investigators would be weighed against the rights of defendants.

Kelley tracked down the interrogators. They all swore they had adhered to the standard rules of conduct and had not coerced any evidence from Lindh. He questioned Lindh's doctor about details of his treatment that Brosnahan had raised in his motion to suppress, including the failure to provide Lindh with intravenous fluids or to remove the bullet from his leg. His response—that it was preferable for the dehydrated Lindh to take the fluids by mouth, and that since the bullet "wasn't going anywhere," the surgery should occur in a better place than a filthy prison or makeshift hospital—satisfied Kelley. Kelley lined up twenty witnesses ready to testify for the government's side of the case.

But there was no doubt that Lindh had been in pain throughout his questioning, that there were photos documenting his pathetic state, and that some of Lindh's incriminating statements had been made before he had been advised of his rights. Kelley also knew that there was virtually no evidence to support the accusation that Lindh had conspired to kill Spann, which was the emotional center of the case and the charge most likely to capture the jury's interest (and result in severe punishment). And while Kelley was assembling his rebuttal to Brosnahan's motion, the media were spinning the emerging details of Lindh's treatment into a narrative bound to elicit sympathy among Americans: that Lindh wasn't a happy jihadi so much as a lost and beleaguered soul, an earnest if misguided kid who had turned up in the wrong place at the wrong time. Even President Bush, perhaps unwittingly, evoked sympathy for Lindh, whom he referred to as "that poor fellow."

Any prosecution has its risks, but in this case the stakes were particularly high. Kelley considered offering a plea bargain: he would drop the charge of conspiring to kill Spann in exchange for Lindh's guilty plea on somewhat less serious counts and for his continued cooperation with the government in its quest for information about Al Qaeda.

This proposal did not please Donald Rumsfeld. According to Kelley, the secretary of defense wanted the government to take Lindh to trial because trials usually led to longer sentences than plea deals. But no one, including Rumsfeld, wanted more details of Lindh's treatment at the hands of the military to come into public view, as they would have to at a suppression hearing. Security—in this case, the security of the government's secrets about the way the military and the CIA had handled Lindh's interrogation—suddenly took precedence over sending a message. Furthermore, as Kelley pointed out, officials believed Lindh still had information to provide about Al Qaeda and about the handful of men with whom he was arrested and who were now being held at the recently opened military prison at Guantánamo Bay.

Late into the night before the hearing, Kelley prevailed. Lindh would plead guilty to aiding the Taliban and to carrying explosives in the commission of a felony. Rumsfeld got his severe, although not draconian punishment—a twenty-year term, with no possibility of parole (although good behavior could cut it down by eighteen months)—and Lindh was spared the prospect of a trial before a jury of people traumatized by 9/11 who might send him to prison for the rest of his life. As a condition of the plea bargain, Lindh was forbidden to speak publicly about his case for the duration of his sentence.

ON JULY 15, 2002, THE TWENTY-ONE-YEAR-OLD Lindh stood before Judge T. S. Ellis III, his head and face shaved by the Bureau of Prisons. "I plead guilty," he told the judge. "I provided my services as a soldier to the Taliban last year from about August to December. In the course of doing so, I carried a rifle and two grenades. I did so knowingly and willingly, knowing that it was illegal." It was a decision he now regretted. In twenty tear-filled minutes, Lindh read his statement aloud to the courtroom. "Had I realized then what I know now about the Taliban," he said, "I would never have joined them." But any harm against the United States was inadvertent: "I went to Afghanistan because I believed it was my religious duty to assist my fellow Muslims militarily in their jihad against the Northern Alliance." He might have been a willing jihadist, but he had "never understood 'jihad' to mean anti-Americanism or terrorism. I condemn terrorism on every level, unequivocally. . . . Bin Laden's terrorist attacks are completely against Islam, completely contrary to the conventions of jihad, and without any justification whatsoever. . . . I have never supported terrorism in any form, and never would."

It was an equitable deal, even if it left Lindh's family aching. Given the toxic atmosphere of public condemnation, led by the officials who had publicly declared him guilty before the plea, Frank Lindh felt it was "almost miraculous." But the deal's implications went well beyond the fate of John Walker Lindh. The lawyers from both sides, the judge, and Lindh himself had, without meaning to, helped the rogue elements within the White House, and especially within the Department of Justice, avoid a full and public reckoning. The threat of aggressive prosecution had led to a deal that prevented the systematic dismantling of constitutional protections from coming to light at trial, even as it procured John Walker Lindh's silence for twenty years. Firsthand stories of prisoner abuse, coercive interrogation, and disregard for due process would remain out of the public record. The Lindh prosecution proved for the moment Ashcroft and Chertoff's claim that the courts could handle terrorism prosecutions. But it also revealed what they had not yet fully contemplated: that in every trial lurked the possibility that the public would hear the details of the government's abuse of prisoners and discover just how far from traditional American ideals, and the Constitution, justice had strayed.

CHAPTER 4

Tearing Down
the Wall

On September 10, 2002, Solicitor General Theodore Olson stood before a panel of three judges in a steel-encased secure room. The room, in the Department of Justice building on Pennsylvania Avenue, had been built especially for FISA hearings, but on this day it was being put to a different use. Olson was addressing the FISA Court of Review (FISCR), a panel of three judges that was meeting for the first time in the twenty-four-year history of the statute. The meeting, like all FISA Court proceedings, was held in secret.

Olson was at the hearing to oppose, on the government's behalf, a decision the FISA Court had made that May. The memo Ashcroft had sent to FBI director Robert Mueller and other top department officials in March had demolished whatever remained of the FISA wall, but before the new policy could go into effect, the FISA Court still had to be willing to accede to it. At the May hearing, held in the same cloistered courtroom, David Kris had argued before a panel of seven judges that the court needed to understand the new normal.

The new policy wasn't just an expedient way to address the 9/11 failures, he told them, but a legitimate reading of the legislation that had created FISA. Congress had surely not intended to impede national security, Kris argued; Janet Reno, who had institutionalized the strict notion of the wall as impermeable, had made a mistake, and the court had been going about its business incorrectly ever since.

On May 17, 2002, the FISA judges responded to Kris's argument with a decision written by Judge Royce Lamberth. Patriot Act or not, he declared, the law continued to require that "law enforcement officials shall not make recommendations to intelligence officials concerning the initiation, operation, continuation or expansion of FISA searches or surveillances." After all, Lamberth reasoned, "if criminal prosecutors direct both the intelligence and criminal investigations . . . coordination becomes subordination of both investigations or interests to law enforcement objectives." Similarly, if the attorney general or other department officials ran intelligence investigations or otherwise made those missions an integral part of criminal law enforcement, they would be violating the letter and the spirit of FISA—and especially Congress's explicit attempt to minimize the program's potential to infringe on constitutional rights by requiring the separation of prosecution and intelligence. Kris had expended "considerable effort justifying deletion of that bright line," Lamberth wrote, "but the Court is not persuaded."

The Justice Department challenged Lamberth's decision, which brought Ted Olson to face the review judges in September. "It's a potential matter of life or death," he told them. The words were particularly meaningful coming from Olson, whose wife, Barbara, had been on the flight that crashed into the Pentagon almost exactly one year earlier. She had called her husband just moments before she died, a story that still resonated in Washington circles. "Three thousand lives were taken from us that day," Olson continued, "because the resources that we have been given to protect us from such acts either did not work or were not being used effectively." Olson placed some of the blame on FISA. The wall had stood in the way of investigators; indeed, if someone wanted "to make it difficult for us to detect and prevent another September 11th," he said, maintaining the FISA wall would be the perfect way to do it.

In attendance at the hearing were two men who wanted the wall removed—David Kris and Larry Thompson—and two who wouldn't have minded if it were but who seemed intent that its continued existence would not present an impediment their secret system of justice, John Yoo and David Addington. Presiding was Laurence Silberman, a Reagan appointee who had been associated with some of the more notorious political scandals of the late twentieth century. During the 1980 election, he participated in a meeting with Iranian representatives that allegedly resulted in the "October Surprise" delaying the release of the US hostages in Iran until after Reagan became president. (Silberman maintains that the Iranian offer to delay the release of the hostages was rejected.) He was also associated with early efforts to impeach Bill Clinton, and was on the panel of circuit court judges who overturned the conviction of Oliver North for his participation in the Iran-contra scheme, with Silberman voting to reverse.

Silberman was often mentioned as a candidate for top legal positions, including Supreme Court justice and attorney general, but his influence was visible in another way: through the clerks he had mentored who had then gone on to positions of power. John Yoo, Olson deputy Paul Clement, Patriot Act author Viet Dinh, and numerous Supreme Court clerks had graduated from Silberman's informal academy of conservative jurisprudence. Occasionally, at national security meetings, Silberman's clerks would look around the room, pause, and acknowledge aloud to one another the number of Silberman clerks who were present. Silberman was also one of Olson's close friends. When Olson remarried in 2006, the judge flew out to Napa County to perform the ceremony. Both were deeply involved in the Federalist Society, which Olson had helped found in 1982.

This hearing, like all FISA Court proceedings, lacked an advocate for the opposition. The closest equivalent was an amicus brief filed by the ACLU (and another by the National Association of Criminal Defense Lawyers) over Silberman's objections. The ACLU pointed out that FISA warrants did not require their targets to be notified, as was the case with conventional court-ordered surveillance. That meant not only that targets could not challenge their surveillance in court, but also that, as in the days of Nixon's COINTELPRO, citizens might be the subject of government-held dossiers they did not know existed. Ashcroft's policy, the brief warned, was an "audacious reinterpretation of FISA" that amounted to an "end-run" around the Fourth Amendment. "Neither the text of FISA as amended by the USA Patriot Act nor twenty years of judicial interpretation supports this result," the brief argued. FISA, it reminded the court, "does not authorize surveillance whose primary or exclusive purpose is law enforcement." Nor could national security serve as a rationale for diluting constitutional protections: "The notion that a search or surveillance may be justified simply because the government invokes the rubric of 'national security' flies in the face of the most basic principles of American constitutional democracy."

Owing to the novelty of the proceedings, the decision to accept amicus briefs was made late in the process, in fact after the hearing, which might be why the judges did not seem to have their arguments in mind as they questioned Olson. The solicitor general, often speaking directly to Silberman, reiterated the message Ashcroft had sent in his memo, and in testimony to Congress weeks after the attacks of September 11. By contradicting Ashcroft, he argued, the FISA Court was obstructing efforts to "accomplish the vital and central purpose for which [FISA] was created . . . the protection of the United States and its citizens from attack and from international terrorism." Maintaining the wall, Olson told the court, would be like forbidding a surgeon and an anesthesiologist from discussing the status of the patient upon whom they were operating. He urged the court to let prosecutors out of their "dreadful box" for the sake of the country. Reverence toward the restraints imposed by the Constitution needed to be put aside in favor of keeping the nation safe. Business as usual was no longer an option.

EARLIER IN THE SUMMER, SENATOR Patrick Leahy (D-VT), chair of the Judiciary Committee, had gotten wind of the fight over the wall and had written a letter to the FISA Court in July asking for clarification about Ashcroft's new rules and procedures. When he learned the date of the September hearing, he scheduled a hearing of his own for the next day to discuss the fate of the FISA wall. The press had also heard about the skirmish. A couple of weeks before the FISCR and Judiciary Committee hearings, *The New York Times* published an editorial on the subject. "The public needs to know more about how the government is prosecuting the war on terror," the paper proclaimed.

At the hearing, Leahy reminded the Judiciary Committee of the reasons that FISA had been created. This was a subject on which he could speak with authority: he'd been in the Senate when the law was passed in response to the Church Committee report. "FISA was originally enacted in the 1970s to curb widespread abuses," which included the illegal "bugging and wiretapping of Americans" by presidents and FBI officials alike. The Constitution had been violated, and the executive branch had gone unchecked in its power grab, he recalled, and FISA had been part of the response: a law that preserved the ability to gather evidence while protecting citizens from intrusion.

The history lesson given, Leahy went on to discuss the status of FISA after 9/11. Here again he was an authority; he'd been a major participant in the writing of the Patriot Act, especially the sections that addressed surveillance. Congress had not intended "to fundamentally change FISA from a foreign intelligence tool into a criminal law enforcement tool," he said. Their aim was "to improve coordination between the criminal prosecutors and intelligence officers, but we did not intend to obliterate the distinction between the two, and we did not do so." He'd been relieved, he said, that the FISA Court had remained true to this intent by rejecting Ashcroft's reading of the Patriot Act in May.

Leahy's colleagues chimed in with similar concerns. Senator Dianne Feinstein (D-CA) recalled that the Senate had intended "to lower the bar slightly but not entirely." Under Ashcroft's new policy, "the administration need not show any purpose of gathering foreign intelligence in any investigation involving national security." Russ Feingold (D-WI), the only senator who had voted against the Patriot Act, accused the Justice Department of "abuse . . . of the language of the bill," adding that the potential for this kind of "unreasonable interpretation" was "just the reason I could not in the end vote for the USA PATRIOT Act." Richard Durbin (D-IL) said the Department of Justice "has abused the faith entrusted them with this change in the FISA law." Even Charles Schumer (D-NY), typically known as a law-and-order type, argued that "DOJ's powers shouldn't be unfettered. If we blur the line too much between criminal investigations and foreign intelligence gathering, the Fourth Amendment may get tossed out with the bath water."

Kris was the first witness at Leahy's hearing. He rehashed the argument Olson had made at the FISCR hearing the day before. "What is at stake here really is the Government's ability effectively to protect this Nation against foreign terrorists and espionage threats," he said. "And I don't . . . mean to be melodramatic about it, but the truth is that when we confront one of these threats, whether it be a terrorist or an espionage threat, we have to pursue an integrated, coherent, cohesive response to the threat. We need all of our best people, whether they be law enforcement personnel or intelligence personnel, sitting down together in the same room and discussing . . . the best way to neutralize this threat."

"Is this saying that for twenty years the courts have been deciding these things wrongly? . . . I mean basically what you are trying to do is change twenty years of a way of doing things," Leahy asked.

Kris answered simply: "Yes."

LEAHY AND HIS COLLEAGUES COULD do no more than register their dismay at this change of course. On November 18, 2002, the FISCR released the only opinion on the matter that counted. In a forceful opinion written by Silberman and echoing Kris's brief almost verbatim, the FISCR declared that the FISA Court had erred when it rejected the Ashcroft policy. Its action was reversed, and the policy was implemented. As Kris put it, "Legally, the wall came down that day." No longer did national security investigations, with their lower standard for obtaining a warrant, need to be cordoned off from criminal investigations. The decision was final; only the government could appeal, which it was not about to do, and the Supreme Court turned down without comment the ACLU's attempts to push it further.

It was a brilliant accomplishment for Kris and his allies, one with vast implications. Not only had the court granted law enforcement a freedom from constitutional restraint previously reserved for foreign intelligence, it had also gone beyond Kris's argument in the same way Yoo's memo on surveillance had. It opened the door to legalized warrantless surveillance. Silberman's opinion had rested in part on a 1980 case—*Truong Dinh Hung v. United States*—in which the Fourth Circuit ruled that warrantless wiretapping leading to the conviction of a Vietnamese spy had been legal. Because the case involved foreign intelligence surveillance, the court reasoned, prosecutors did not need to show probable cause of criminal activity to obtain a criminal warrant. According to Silberman, this meant that "the President did have inherent authority to conduct warrantless searches to obtain foreign intelligence information" when national security was at stake and that FISA "could not encroach on the President's constitutional power" by limiting that authority. Just as John Yoo had used a memo about *the* versus *a* to build a rationale for warrantless surveillance, Silberman was using an opinion about policy to establish a legal basis for the government to spy on its citizens, despite what the Constitution said.

THE FISCR DECISION GAVE ASHCROFT'S prosecutors permission to use tactics that would have been unthinkable just a year earlier. But it also created a difficulty: even if those tactics were legal under FISA and yielded evidence of a suspect's guilt, the new emphasis on intelligence collection affected the prioritization of criminal prosecutions for terrorism suspects; the intelligence value of investigations stood to take precedence over the incapacitation value of a prosecution. In addition, sources and methods stood the chance of being revealed. The tension between trials, with their transparency requirements, and counterterrorism, with its demands for secrecy, thus put prosecutors in a delicate position, one that the decision helped to clarify. They were to pursue prevention even at the cost of prosecution. In this sense, they had been conscripted into the war on terror.

The decision had another subtle but profound effect. It not only diminished, by removing the wall, the role of the FISA Court in maintaining civil liberties; it also signaled that judges were willing to take the urgency of the nation's fight against terrorism, or at least the Bush administration's view of it, as reason to back away from longstanding precedent regarding due process. The Department of Justice now had at least one court on its side. To be sure, it was an obscure court, one with unusual practices and a limited jurisdiction, but it was nonetheless an important cog in the machinery of justice. And the federal judges who presided over it had signaled that they would not stand in the way of the DOJ's crusade to reorganize itself around prevention. Soon enough, partly under the direction of David Kris, national security and law enforcement would become even closer. And going forward, the courts would struggle to maintain their role in jurisprudence related to the ever-expanding war on terror.

CHAPTER 5

The Twilight Zone

When he said goodbye to his wife and family in Egypt early in May 2002, Jose Padilla did not know he would not be seeing them again for a very long time, perhaps ever. When he boarded his Chicago-bound flight in Zurich, he did not know intelligence agents from both Switzerland and the United States were following him onto the plane. Nor did he know he'd been under investigation for months, based on allegations leveled by a man the CIA had fingered as one of Al Qaeda's top operatives, or that FBI agents were waiting for him in Chicago, ready to take him into custody, or that he would soon disappear from his family, his friends, his lawyers, and any traces of the justice system that, as an American citizen, he'd known for the thirty-one years he'd been alive.

Padilla was well acquainted with being on the wrong side of that system. He'd been a hotheaded kid who, at fourteen, had kicked a man in the head as he lay dying from a knife wound inflicted by Padilla's fellow gangbanger, an act that earned him five years in juvenile detention. He'd been out only a year or so when a road rage incident ended with a pistol shot, three felony counts, and more time in prison, where within a few months he'd assaulted a guard. But none of that could have possibly prepared him for what was to come after the FBI picked him up at O'Hare, flew him to New York, placed him on the high-security floor of the Metropolitan Correctional Center, and told him he was being detained not for a crime but as a material witness to the 9/11 attacks.

Donna Newman wasn't prepared either. A veteran defense attorney practicing in Jersey City, she was no stranger to the criminal justice system or to representing clients assigned to her for no other reason than that she was next on the list of lawyers whom federal courts could call upon to represent indigent clients. Throughout May and early June she met with Padilla a dozen times, but there wasn't much she could do for a man who had yet to be charged with anything; material witnesses could be held initially for thirty days and, if a judge approved it, for another two months.

"We thought he'd be willing to talk," a federal prosecutor working in Washington on post-9/11 terrorism investigations told me. But as the thirty-day period drew to a close, he had not, and Newman geared up to fight the government's request to extend his detention. The hearing was scheduled for June 12, but two days before, as Newman was on her way to pick up a client for a meeting, her phone rang. On the other end was Assistant US Attorney Eric Bruce, calling from Manhattan. David Kelley, Newman recalls, was with him for the call. "Your client is no longer here," Bruce told Newman. He couldn't tell her where Padilla had been taken or how long he'd be there or any other details. "Your client," he explained, "is now an enemy combatant pursuant to the laws of war."

IN THE NEWS CONFERENCE ANNOUNCING Padilla's arrest, held via Skype from Moscow, John Ashcroft would make it clear that the prisoner wasn't even subject to the laws of war. "I am pleased to announce today a significant step forward in the War on

Terrorism," he said. "We have captured a known terrorist who was exploring a plan to build and explode a radiological dispersion device, or 'dirty bomb,' in the United States." Padilla, whom Ashcroft called by his Muslim name, Abdullah al-Muhajir, was "an enemy combatant who poses a continuing threat to the American people and our national security."

In calling Padilla an "enemy combatant," Ashcroft was signaling a new policy, one that drew on yet another John Yoo legal opinion. In January 2002 Yoo had advised the president that Al Qaeda and the Taliban were "non-state actors" and members of a failed state, respectively, and thus those captured fighting for them were not actually prisoners of war. They were therefore not entitled to the international protections guaranteed to prisoners by the laws of war, protections that included humane treatment, freedom from humiliating and degrading treatment, and sentencing or execution "without previous judgment pronounced by a regularly constituted court."

Newman wasn't immediately certain what it meant that Padilla had been given this designation, but she was sure that whisking him away to an undisclosed location for unspecified purposes was an obvious case of government overreach. "It was Constitution 101," she recalled. "You can't just steal a client away from a lawyer and disappear him. That only happens in the Twilight Zone." But Eric Bruce had sounded sure of himself, and he'd told her about the case the government was relying on—United States v. Quirin. After picking up her client in New Jersey, Newman explained that they had to stop at the library on their way to the meeting. What she read there could not have given her comfort, for the case had not ended well for a pair of US citizens designated as enemy combatants by a president.

In 1942 two groups of Nazi saboteurs had come ashore from submarines onto beaches on Long Island and in Florida, four from each boat. The Long Island group was discovered by a local cop. They fled, but two of them, one of whom was a US citizen, turned themselves in shortly afterward. They told the FBI that the men had planned to destroy military facilities and industries in the United States. All eight, including a second US citizen, were eventually captured and placed in military custody. Convicted after a month-long trial before a military commission, they were sentenced to death. A week after the conviction, six of them, including one of the US citizens, were executed; the other two, the cooperators, had their sentences commuted and were eventually deported to Germany.

Even as he was defending the men, their court-appointed lawyer was arguing that they should not be tried by a military commission. They had not been captured on the battlefield, they were not soldiers, and the courts of the United States were functioning even though the country was at war. The men should be released from military custody, he argued, and tried in civilian courts. But the Supreme Court disagreed. In a ruling issued just before the trial ended, it declared that the men were unlawful combatants, which meant that they could be detained and tried by the military, but not under the terms reserved for prisoners of war. They were entitled, in other words, to the protections of neither laws of war nor the US Constitution.

Newman scrambled to get her client out of the Twilight Zone. She filed a writ of habeas corpus, claiming that Padilla was being unlawfully detained, and she called habeas experts at universities around the country to ask for advice. She pored over journal articles about military commissions and detention under the laws of war. She talked to Frank Dunham, one of the lawyers representing Zacarias Moussaoui, who had been indicted in federal court in December 2001, asking for guidance on how to get Padilla freed from military custody. She phoned Ashcroft and the White House to register her protest about Padilla's treatment. How was it possible that a US citizen had been "seized" by the government? she wanted to know. No one called her back.

Dunham had made his opinion clear to *The New York Times.* "This is the model we all fear or should fear," he told reporters. "The executive branch can arrest an American citizen here and then declare him an enemy combatant and put him outside the reach of the courts. They can keep him indefinitely without charging him or giving him access to a lawyer or presenting any evidence." Yoo's memo, coupled with the power granted in *Quirin* to treat citizens as unlawful combatants, had apparently given government lawyers grounds to believe they had unlimited power to deny Americans their constitutional rights—not only their Fourth Amendment protection from searches and seizures but also the right to a fair and speedy trial, granted in the Fifth and Sixth Amendments.

Yoo's analysis had bearing on Padilla's case in another way, although neither Newman nor the vast majority of Americans could have known that at the time. He had advised the president that unlawful combatants were not only outside the reach of the Constitution; they were also beyond the protections afforded by the Geneva Conventions, the international code requiring that prisoners of war "in all circumstances be treated humanely" and forbidding "violence to life and person, in particular murder of all kinds, mutilation, cruel treatment and torture" and other "outrages upon personal dignity, in particular humiliating and degrading treatment." But as international law expert Gabor Rona explains, the memo depended on categories that had been tailor-made to fit Yoo's purpose. "The US invented 'unlawful enemy combatant,' 'unlawful combatant,' and 'enemy combatant,'" he said, "in an effort to avoid the strictures of the Geneva Conventions applicable to armed conflict." The United States wanted "to avoid the strictures of domestic law and international human rights law. Simply by calling [the detainees] by a new and different name, they were falsely able to avoid the consequences of international law." On February 7, Bush had ratified Yoo's opinion in a memo to his national security cabinet officials, announcing that "none of the provisions of Geneva apply to our conflict with al Qaeda in Afghanistan or elsewhere throughout the world." It would be years before the rest of the world found out what Bush and his advisers already knew—that agents of the United States of America were using the Yoo memo to provide legal cover for torture. But torture was already at issue in the Padilla case, and it reduced even further what appeared to be the already infinitesimally small likelihood that he would get a fair trial.

Abu Zubaydah was captured in Faisalabad, Pakistan, on March 28, 2002. The CIA quickly identified him as one of the top three or four members of Al Qaeda. (It emerged years later that he was merely a facilitator for the group.) In US custody, Zubaydah, who had suffered several bullet wounds in the gunfight that led to his capture, was taken to Thailand, the location of one of the "black sites" where the CIA had begun questioning its prisoners in the war on terror. Among the interrogators was FBI special agent Ali Soufan, to whom Zubaydah, questioned in a makeshift hospital room in a CIA safe house, immediately disclosed a trove of useful information, including details about an impending attack that, says Soufan, the United States was able to avert. Whisked back to the hospital when medics predicted Zubaydah wouldn't be alive by morning, the interviews continued. Within days, Soufan had elicited the name of the mastermind of the 9/11 attacks: Khalid Shaikh Mohammed, whom the CIA would capture in Pakistan a year later and send to a black site in Poland.

But several days later a new CIA team arrived. That team included a psychologist and a polygraph specialist, who announced that they wanted to "do something new." They would "force Abu Zubaydah into submission," they told Soufan, by making him "see his interrogator as a god who controls his suffering."

"Have you ever conducted any interrogations?" Soufan asked the psychologist.

"No, but I know human nature," he answered.

Zubaydah, still recovering from his wounds, was taken from the hospital. Thrown into a cell, he was stripped naked, bombarded nonstop with loud rock music, deprived of sleep, and then questioned by the CIA interrogator under the guidance of the psychologist. Soufan, increasingly uncomfortable with the CIA's techniques, was able to interview Zubaydah again—insisting that he do it when the CIA's tactics were not actively in play—and to elicit more information, including a new name: Jose Padilla, who, he said, was planning to set off a "dirty bomb" in a metropolitan area in the United States. But as the CIA continued to ratchet up its techniques, Soufan requested to leave, refusing to "stand by" while abusive, humiliating, and painful techniques were used. FBI director Robert Mueller supported Soufan's decision. "We don't do that," he said, referring to the CIA's tactics in Thailand.

Soufan was, and remains, skeptical of Padilla's capacity to carry out the operation Zubaydah claimed he was planning. "While Padilla was a committed terrorist set on trying to harm America," Soufan later wrote, "he was a brain transplant away from making a dirty bomb." For Soufan, Padilla's value was that he might lead them to other terrorists plotting to harm the United States—but only if he were free and unaware that he was being followed. Soufan, along with one of the top FBI counterterrorism officials in the United States, would have preferred to see "who met up with him in Chicago."

But Soufan lost that battle and, with it, not just the opportunity to follow Padilla to other, possibly more important, terrorists on US soil. He also lost the ability to conduct the interrogation in a way that would serve a civilian prosecution. Coercion like that being exercised by the CIA was not only morally problematic; it was also legally problematic, raising the same issue the Lindh prosecution had to confront: coerced statements make for tainted evidence. Of course, tainted evidence is a problem only if you're considering prosecution in criminal court. And while the Bush administration hadn't quite made up its mind about whether to charge Padilla with a crime, it was already clear, as the interrogation of Zubaydah and many prisoners to come indicated, that pursuing the kind of justice practiced in our criminal courts was not high on the priority list of the rogue lawyers dedicated to changing the contours of American justice in the name of national security.

DESPITE ALL THE DISCOURAGING NEWS, Donna Newman went ahead with her habeas petition demanding Padilla's release. She presented it to Southern District of New York judge Michael Mukasey, who had signed the material witness warrant for Padilla. Mukasey, who would later become President Bush's third attorney general, had presided in 1995 over the case of Omar Abdel Rahman, known as the Blind Sheikh, the Egyptian cleric who was convicted and sentenced to life in prison for a plot to blow up the United Nations and other New York City landmarks. The Blind Sheikh trial had alerted Mukasey to the personal perils that could come with prosecutions of Islamic terrorists: after a death threat, Mukasey had been assigned a security detail that was still in effect at the time of Padilla's habeas case and would last until 2005.

Mukasey scheduled the hearing for July 31, 2002. In hearing the case, he became the first federal judge to address in open court proceedings the constitutional issues raised by the government's aggressive approach to the prevention of terrorist attacks. The government sent five lawyers to New York for the hearing. Among them, and leading the argument, was Deputy Solicitor General Paul Clement. It was rare for so high-ranking a lawyer to argue a case outside the Supreme Court, let alone to appear at a pretrial hearing. It was clear that the government was deeply invested in the outcome.

While the FISC and FISCR judges had had to grapple with the Fourth Amendment implications of the government's counterterrorism policies, Mukasey's job was to consider whether Padilla's treatment was in accordance with the Fifth and Sixth Amendments, which protect citizens against undue deprivation of liberty and guarantee them the right to know the charges against them and to have a lawyer. The question before Mukasey was in one way technical and limited: Could Padilla challenge his detention in court? But behind it lay a much deeper question: Could the president order a citizen to be detained as an enemy combatant, the term the administration was now using exclusively to describe the detainees? His answer, and the way he conducted the hearing, would also help to clarify the place courts would occupy in the rapidly changing national security landscape.

Newman was smart and hardworking and had the moxie to accuse the president of the United States of ordering what amounted to the kidnapping of a citizen. But she had little experience with the media and the public spotlight, and as a litigator she was no match for the silver-tongued Paul Clement. Clement had graduated summa cum laude from Georgetown's School of Foreign Service and magna cum laude from Harvard Law School, where he was Supreme Court editor on the *Harvard Law Review*—a résumé that suited him perfectly for arguing difficult, high-profile cases before demanding judges. (Indeed, he would eventually emerge as the government's leading defender in 9/11-related litigation.) Newman needed to bring on a lawyer with experience handling complex terrorism cases. New York criminal defense attorney Andrew Patel thus joined her as cocounsel at the direction of Judge Mukasey. Patel had a background in terrorism litigation, having represented El Sayyid Nosair, a central defendant in the 1995 Blind Sheikh case, which like many of Patel's cases had come before Judge Mukasey.

At the hearing, Newman and Patel addressed the big questions raised by the case. Was it really legal for the government to deprive a citizen of the constitutional rights to counsel and due process? Could the president really order an American citizen to be pulled out of the federal court system and placed in military custody?

Meanwhile, Clement focused on legal technicalities. Did Newman have the authority to file a habeas motion for Padilla? Was New York the proper venue for a hearing about a defendant now being held at a naval brig in South Carolina? Wasn't the commander of that brig the proper target of the habeas petition, rather than Rumsfeld, to whom Newman and Patel had directed it? When Clement did address the substantive issues of the case, he argued that the president indeed had a right to declare an American citizen an enemy combatant, just as Roosevelt had done in the Quirin case.

Mukasey's ruling fully pleased neither side. He backed Newman and Patel on the technical questions, ruling that their client did indeed deserve a habeas hearing, reasoning that under a 1971 law known as the Non-Detention Act, US citizens cannot be detained except pursuant to an act of Congress. A habeas petition required a lawyer, and Padilla was entitled to the legal counsel promised by the Sixth Amendment. Newman and Patel, Mukasey ruled, were the appropriate lawyers. He also agreed that Rumsfeld was the ultimate custodian of Padilla and the rightful target of the habeas petition, and New York the right court for the lawsuit.

But on the issue at the heart of the case, Mukasey deferred to the government. "Whether or not a war has been declared," he ruled, "the laws of war . . . apply." That meant that "the President . . . has both constitutional and statutory authority to exercise the powers of Commander in Chief, including the power to detain unlawful combatants," he wrote. "It matters not that Padilla is a United States citizen captured on United States soil." In the words of Donald Rumsfeld, whom Mukasey quoted approvingly, the national interest was better served by "find[ing] out everything [Padilla] knows so that hopefully we can stop other terrorist acts" than by following the normal course of indictment and trial on criminal charges. It was much more important to "prevent [him] from rejoining the enemy" than to give him due process or even to punish him as the law might demand.

In accepting Clement's argument, Mukasey also ratified the claims about executive power that lay behind it. During war, he explained, the courts were expected to defer to the executive branch and to Congress. In war more than in peace, the job of the judiciary was to stand back and let the public decide if their leaders had made the correct decisions through "the less didactic but nonetheless searching audit of the democratic process" called elections. As Judge Silberman had done in his FISCR ruling, Mukasey had given his imprimatur to the government's position that unprecedented dangers justified, and perhaps even demanded, unprecedented presidential powers.

THE PRESIDENT AND HIS MEN had gotten much of what they wanted from the judiciary: an acknowledgment that the nation was at war, an agreement that it could treat a citizen as an enemy combatant, and a ratification of the expanded role of the executive branch. But they were convinced that the threat posed by terrorism granted them powers even beyond what Mukasey had ordered. In fact, it seemed that they intended to directly defy his ruling, at least insofar as it required them to allow Padilla and his lawyers to meet— something that had not happened since he'd been whisked away into military custody. The government refused even to begin to negotiate the terms of such a meeting, explaining that "no conditions could be set that would protect the national security." And they indicated that they were going to seek "reconsideration" of Mukasey's order that Padilla be granted access to his lawyers.

After the decision, Paul Clement traveled to the New York courthouse to tell Mukasey that the White House was defying his ruling because it was so erroneous that he ought to retract it. Clement's colleagues at the Department of Justice considered the trip a "suicide mission," and indeed Mukasey was not amused. Clement's argument, he said, was nothing but "pinched legalism." More to the point, Clement's claim that his decision was part of a "continuing dialogue" was ridiculous. The ruling was "not a suggestion or a request." It was an order from one coequal branch of government to another.

But it didn't matter what Mukasey or, for that matter, the Constitution said. As James Comey, the US attorney for the Southern District of New York at the time and the future director of the FBI, put it in a letter to Mukasey, "There is no possibility that any consultations with Padilla's counsel will result in agreed terms of attorney access." Access to Padilla "poses a danger to the national security of the United States," Comey argued, while his "interrogation will promote public safety." The country was at war, so the government could do as it pleased, with or without court approval. By the time the White House finally officially appealed the Mukasey decision in the spring of 2003, its defiance had inadvertently strengthened Padilla's case—so long, that is, as a court considered him entitled to due process. While Newman and Patel fought to acquire the security clearance needed to obtain unredacted versions of the allegations against their client, and to get the access to him ordered by Mukasey, Padilla was being held in solitary confinement in a dark cell—conditions that were known to cause hallucinations, panic attacks, and paranoia and can lead to permanent mental illness and incapacitation.

The White House's intransigence and its extravagant claims about wartime powers, Padilla's treatment and the abrogation of his rights—all these were at issue when the case found its way to the Second Circuit Court of Appeals, which meets in the Thurgood Marshall US Courthouse near ground zero in New York. Once again Clement argued the government side, while Newman and Patel had added an expert appellate lawyer to their team, Stanford professor Jenny Martinez.

"Never before in this nation's history has the President been granted the unilateral authority to imprison indefinitely and without trial an American citizen seized in a civilian setting on U.S. soil," Martinez told the three judges hearing the case. "Your Honors, the Constitution allows him no such power." She reminded them of what Mukasey had ruled: that under the 1971 Non-Detention Act, it was illegal to imprison a citizen without an act of Congress. "The President seeks an unchecked power to substitute military rule for the rule of law, wherever and whenever he wants," she said. He claimed the prerogative to wield that power "without Congressional authorization, without review by the courts when they're open and functioning." This, she concluded, was "inconsistent with a free and democratic society."

Judge Rosemary Pooler, a Clinton appointee, seemed sympathetic to Martinez's pleas. "Why isn't the traditional plea bargain, which the government knows how to do, why isn't that the way to get information from someone who has it . . . rather than keeping him incommunicado in a brig?" she asked Clement. After all, prosecutors routinely traded leniency for information. As Pooler pointed out, that would have been the constitutional way to go about doing things.

"If the executive branch wanted to limit itself to one intelligence gathering tool and close another," Clement answered, "it could have done that and avoid [sic] this question." But this executive, he continued, "did not want to take any tools off the table." The president was going to push the envelope, but the proper response of the courts, according to Clement, was to defer to the executive branch, as they traditionally had when it came to issues of intelligence.

The court of appeals did not agree. After affirming that Padilla's lawyers could file the habeas brief, that Rumsfeld was the proper respondent, and that New York was the right jurisdiction for the suit, it overturned Mukasey's decision on the constitutional issue: "The President does not have the power under Article II of the Constitution to detain as an enemy combatant an American citizen seized on American soil outside a zone of combat." National security could not be used as a one-size-fits-all rationale for expansive presidential powers. Indeed, the courts had rejected such claims in the past— most notably when the Supreme Court overturned Harry Truman's order that striking steelworkers in Youngstown, Ohio, return to work on the grounds that their labor was essential to the Korean War effort.

That case, *Youngstown Sheet & Tube Co. v. Sawyer,* was one that John Yoo, in his memos justifying indefinite detention, torture, and the removal of the FISA wall, had ignored in favor of the precedents that supported his case. This wasn't the only implicit rebuke to the government's reasoning, which echoed Yoo's thinking. In overturning Mukasey's holding that the need for intelligence-gathering trumps constitutional protections, the appeals court's opinion also rejected the idea that the Authorization for Use of Military Force was an adequate substitute for the congressional authorization required by the Non-Detention Act. Congress, after all, had gone to the trouble of crafting a joint resolution to explicitly authorize the president to deploy the military under the AUMF, the opinion pointed out. It was unlikely that it would "at the same time leave unstated and to inference something so significant and unprecedented as authorization to detain American citizens under the Non-Detention Act."

Neither did the AUMF allow the president to usurp one of the judiciary's most essential functions: dispensing justice to American citizens accused of crimes while preserving due process of law. The government had a number of options to choose from. At any time "it could transfer Padilla to appropriate civilian authorities who can bring criminal charges against him." It could hold him as a material witness. But whatever it did, the opinion declared, "Padilla will be entitled to the constitutional protections extended to other citizens."

Finally, the judiciary had stood up to the White House. Meanwhile, in another courtroom, this one in Virginia, another case was under way that would pit the two branches of government against each other over questions of secrecy, detention, and the costs of the war on terror to the rule of law.

CHAPTER 6

Defanging
the Courts

B y the end of 2001, Zacarias Moussaoui had emerged as the White House's best hope for making good on the president's promise to bring the 9/11 hijackers to justice—at least if the courts were going to render the justice. He was the only alleged conspirator known to have survived who was in US custody. His computer had yielded incriminating evidence, notably a phone number that led to a known Al Qaeda figure who had wired $14,000 to him in August 2001. And then there was that note Michael Chertoff had discovered in the days following the attacks, the one that characterized Moussaoui as someone who could fly a plane into a building—a piece of information that had come to embody all the failures that had led to the disaster. A successful prosecution of Moussaoui could perhaps salvage the tattered reputation of America's law enforcement apparatus and soothe a nation (and a White House) filled with fear and bent on vindication.

But as straightforward as the case seemed, it would soon become entangled in the disarray—at the White House, in the Department of Justice, and in the courts—that was beginning to overtake the government's attempt to reckon with 9/11. The infighting between the intelligence and law enforcement communities began with the question of where Moussaoui should be tried. Shortly after his arrest, he'd been taken out of the custody of the Immigration and Naturalization Service and placed into the hands of the federal court in New York City—a jurisdiction with a proven track record of successful terrorism prosecutions. But Chertoff, then still head of the DOJ's Criminal Division, wondered if the Eastern District of Virginia, where John Walker Lindh had been convicted and sentenced, might not be a better choice.

Chertoff decided to make each of the possible jurisdictions—the Southern District of New York and the Eastern District of Virginia, home to the World Trade Center and the Pentagon, respectively—compete for the trial by making a case for itself. New York prosecutors sent in a two-hundred-page memo offering a history of their district's experience in handling high-profile terrorism cases. The Virginians' brief was shorter and focused on their expertise in handling the classified information involved in the espionage cases they often heard. The Virginia court also boasted a reputation for speeding cases along, which had earned it the nickname "rocket docket," and for being friendly to the death penalty—or at least friendlier than its northern rival, which had not ordered an execution since 1954. And its location, a Metro ride away from downtown Washington, made the court convenient for Chertoff and his prosecutors.

Chertoff favored Virginia and, especially with the death penalty on the table, it proved an easy sell to Ashcroft and the White House. He offered the New York office an olive branch: the prosecution would be a joint effort between its prosecutors and those in Virginia. Together they would seek to convict Moussaoui of six counts, including conspiracy to kill Americans in the 9/11 attacks. Four of the charges carried the death penalty.

But before it could begin, the new team had to compete for

jurisdiction with another rival. The specifics of the military commissions called for by President Bush had not yet been spelled out, but that didn't stop members of Congress or media pundits from demanding that Moussaoui be their first case. "If we will not try Zacarias Moussaoui before a military tribunal, a non-citizen alleged to be a coconspirator in the attacks that killed 4,000 Americans—who will we try in a military tribunal?" asked Senator Joe Lieberman (D-CT). Senator Carl Levin (D-MI), chair of the Armed Services Committee, agreed, declaring that when it came to the Moussaoui case, "the glove [the military commissions] fits so perfectly here."

"Every day," David Raskin, a prosecutor on the Moussaoui team, told me, "the specter of the military commissions hung over the case . . . threatening to end [it], particularly in its earlier days." Ultimately, the Justice Department prevailed and saw the Moussaoui case through—but not before it had profoundly altered the legal landscape of the war on terror.

THE BURDENS IMPOSED BY THE Constitution on the courts it establishes under Article III were apparent as soon as the Moussaoui proceedings got under way in January 2002—not least because Moussaoui was an expert at using those rights to create chaos. He refused to stand up when the judge in the case, Leonie Brinkema, entered the courtroom. He seemed to pay little attention to the proceedings, preferring to mutter prayers or stare into space when others had the floor. He was prone to outbursts, at one time calling the attorneys assigned to him, including Dunham, "a horde of blood sucker[s]" and refusing to consult with them.

Sometimes his behavior backfired, as when he tried to plead guilty (which he did repeatedly) and the judge turned him down on the grounds that she couldn't determine whether he was competent to make that decision, or when she had taken the extraordinary step of having him fitted with a "stun belt" that would, at the touch of a marshal's finger on a remote control, shock him into submission, at the cost of his bowel and bladder control. But sometimes Moussaoui seemed to mock the system by turning its strengths into weaknesses, as when a prosecutor rose to object that one of those standby defense lawyers was badgering Moussaoui. And always he got the last laugh, departing the courtroom every day with an imprecation—sometimes shouting a standard-issue jihadi refrain ("God curse you, America") but other times showing a canny command of American popular culture, as when he cried out that his trial was a "cyberlynching" or sang "Burn in the USA" to the tune of the Springsteen hit.

He might only have been trying to break the monotony of arcane legal argument. According to Joshua Dratel, one of the country's leading criminal defense attorneys and an expert consultant for the defense, the Moussaoui case "involved more pretrial appeals than any case on record." Like the Padilla case, it brought lawyers and judges into mostly uncharted waters whose navigation proved to be slow and treacherous—and irresistible to ambitious, clever, and dedicated lawyers. Much of the wrangling was over the same problem that had threatened to derail the Padilla and Lindh cases: the question of what evidence could be introduced at trial.

When they first undertook the Moussaoui case, the prosecutors believed that the biggest challenge would be introducing information and evidence, much of which was classified, without revealing sources or otherwise compromising national security. But as they began to approach trial, they realized they faced a new challenge. The prosecution was unwilling and, as it turned out, unable to accede to defense lawyers' requests for witnesses to take the stand. They were unable even to disclose where they were located and, in the event they were identified, to produce them in court. They were among the "high-value detainees" the White House had only recently been acknowledging. Unknown to the public at the time, these were captives held in secret at CIA black sites scattered around the globe, where, as John Yoo had advised the Bush administration, they could be questioned without regard to domestic or international legal codes—tortured, in other words.

When the DOJ officials and lawyers knew about these policies is not entirely clear. According to CIA lawyer John Rizzo, Chertoff was at a meeting where the subject of "enhanced interrogation techniques"—as the Bush administration had decided to label a series of new and physically and psychologically abusive methods—came up. Michael Chertoff left the meeting where the subject of an "advance declination of prosecution" for the enhanced interrogation techniques came up, refusing outright to grant such immunity and departing as soon as he could—to attend a Sheryl Crow concert. Soon enough the lawyers, along with the rest of the world, would know that the detainees in question were Ramzi bin al-Shibh, who would have been among the 9/11 hijackers but for his failure to get a visa; Mustafa al-Hawsawi, who had handled the money end of the 9/11 operation; and Khalid Shaikh Mohammed, its alleged mastermind. Officially that was all the prosecutors knew, and from the beginning of the trial they claimed that they were unable to produce the witnesses because they could not wrest them from the control of the CIA, which was in charge of interrogating them. So the Moussaoui trial would bring into play yet another constitutional right: the Sixth Amendment's guarantee that a defendant be allowed to face his accuser in court.

LEONIE BRINKEMA WAS FIFTY-EIGHT WHEN the Moussaoui case landed in her courtroom in late 2001, sixty-three when it ended. She managed to maintain control, sometimes subtly (she responded to Moussaoui's refusal to stand by having him enter the courtroom at exactly the same time she did, so he'd have to be on his feet) and sometimes forcefully, as when she entered a not guilty plea over Moussaoui's objections. But it was never easy—not only because of Moussaoui's erratic behavior but also because of the legal questions the case elicited. "In the annals of criminal law," she said when it was all over, "I don't know if there has ever been a case with this many significant problems."

Early in the proceedings, Zacarias Moussaoui requested that Ramzi bin al-Shibh, who had apparently told interrogators that Moussaoui was among the 9/11 conspirators, be made available to testify. That was at least arguably Moussaoui's right under the Sixth Amendment, which ensures that hearsay does not become evidence, or a trial a parade of uncontested accusations. But as much as the White House wanted to demolish the wall between intelligence and law enforcement, it also wanted to be able to throw up a fence when it needed to. And it decided that it needed to when it came to witnesses against Moussaoui, including Bin al-Shibh—a position reiterated defiantly even after Brinkema sided with the defense and ordered the government to present them.

But Brinkema was not going to let the government off completely. In January 2003 she ordered that the three witnesses—Bin al Shibh, Hawsawi, and Khalid Shaikh Mohammed—be examined and cross-examined on video. It was an attempt at compromise to break the stalemate, relieving the government of the obligation to bring the witnesses to the courtroom in person, while satisfying the defendant's request for direct testimony. As the Fourth Circuit later summarized, Brinkema argued that "Moussaoui and the public's interest in a fair trial outweighed the Government's national security interest in precluding access to the enemy combatant witness."

Prosecutors countered that they would be willing to provide a summary of Bin al-Shibh's statements to interrogators, an offer that Brinkema refused outright. This was a death penalty case, she reasoned. With Moussaoui's life on the line and his ability to confront his accusers already compromised, the court needed to grant the fullest possible presentation of evidence on his behalf. She had reviewed the classified evidence and determined that the testimony in question could prove exculpatory to a jury. Bin al-Shibh's testimony in particular, Brinkema thought, might "undermine the Government's contention" that the defendant's acts directly resulted in the attacks of 9/11. The prosecutors refused to back down. Continuing to defy the judge's order for depositions, they appealed her ruling to the Fourth Circuit Court of Appeals.

Michael Chertoff argued the case on June 4, 2003. It would be his last case as a federal prosecutor; he had been appointed to the federal appeals court bench. "We are fighting a war unlike any other," Chertoff told the three judges. "This is really a battlefield in the minds of some of the top operatives of al Qaeda." And those were devious minds, minds that could turn a deposition into "another weapon for achieving their ends." Chertoff wasn't clear on just how Moussaoui or the witnesses would accomplish this goal, but he insisted that to grant the defendant the right to cross-examine his accusers was to put the levers of power into the hands of people who could use them to "cause irreparable harm to ongoing efforts in the war with al Qaeda."

But Chertoff had his eyes on a much larger prize than preventing the courts from playing into the enemy's hands. Focusing on Bin al-Shibh, he told the judges that before they could decide whether to order the depositions, they had to decide if the witness was even within the prosecution's reach. He was, after all, being held by the military—or at least by "the military in the legal sense." And the military was under the command of the president, which meant, Chertoff argued, that he was unable to compel Bin al-Shibh's testimony.

Judge William Wilkins asked Chertoff what he meant by "military in the legal sense."

"I mean anybody who is operating in the executive branch under the president's power as Commander-in-Chief." The president, he was arguing, could grant his wartime powers to whomever he saw fit. Intelligence agents and FBI agents, prosecutors, civilian interrogators—all of these had apparently been conscripted into the war on terror and given the unprecedented power the president was claiming: to detain people indefinitely, to hold them incommunicado, to prevent them from facing their accusers, and, as it would turn out, to torture them.

THREE WEEKS LATER THE FOURTH Circuit punted. The appeal had been premature, it ruled. The Moussaoui case would have to go further forward before the circuit court could weigh in. It sent the case back to Leonie Brinkema.

The judge wasted no time in moving the case along. She ordered the video depositions once again. The prosecution refused to comply. In response, Brinkema took the death penalty off the table. If the prosecution wanted to execute Moussaoui, she declared, then they were going to have to extend to him the maximum rights of a defendant. And if the government was not going to allow Bin al-Shibh's testimony, then it would have to forgo not only the death penalty but "any argument or . . . any evidence suggesting that the defendant had any knowledge of or investment in the September 11 attacks." She concluded that to allow such testimony "would simply be unfair." Bin al-Shibh's testimony could potentially prove exculpatory—excluding it meant that it would be difficult for Moussaoui to fairly defend himself against charges related to 9/11. As the judges of the FISA Court had when confronted with Ashcroft's attempt to remove the wall, Brinkema refused to defer to the demands of the White House.

And as they had in the FISA case, the president's lawyers did not give up. After Brinkema's ruling, the case was ripe for appeal, and this time it was Paul Clement who took the helm for the prosecution. In early December he appeared before the same three judges who had heard the earlier version of the case. Clement picked up Mukasey's argument that it wasn't even within the prosecution's ability to produce the three key witnesses against Moussaoui. In fact, Clement said, "we would like to get" Bin al-Shibh just as much as the defense would. But the members of the "military in a legal sense" were unwilling to part with the prisoners. Indeed, the prosecution wasn't even sure where the witnesses were—although they knew they weren't in the country, because if they had been, say, in the Charleston brig, then indeed the military would have to produce them, in accordance with the Sixth Amendment right to compulsory process, which gives the defendant the right to call witnesses located within the geographical jurisdiction of the United States. And the fact that the witnesses were in the Twilight Zone in the first place wasn't the prosecution's doing, either. The defense had mistakenly "lump[ed] the executive branch together," but in fact it was not monolithic. The FISA wall might have been removed, but barriers remained, at least when it was convenient.

At least one of the judges, Roger Gregory, wasn't buying it. "You have control over the alien witness" Bin al-Shibh, he said, and by not producing him, the prosecution was impeding the "search for truth" that is the "purpose of our courts."

"We do have to have an independent judiciary," Gregory added, "not answering to the executive. . . . We have to ensure fair trials." But Clement was asking the court to take the president's word that national security concerns were more important than Moussaoui's rights, that to protect the country, his trial would have to be a little less fair—though not unfair enough to warrant Brinkema's decision to disallow the death penalty. "Nothing guarantees a perfect trial or a perfect truth-seeking process," Clement told Gregory. But, Clement assured the court, Moussaoui would not be deprived of his access to witnesses forever. Once he'd been convicted, Clement said, and the trial entered its penalty phase—in which a jury would be asked to decide if Moussaoui should be executed—then "the information would go before the jury."

"I wouldn't necessarily call it a remedy," Clement conceded, but at least when it came to the life-or-death question, the calculus changed enough to allow the jury to know what the witnesses would say—or at least some of it. At the penalty phase, summaries of the witness accounts, though not videos or transcripts, could be made available to the defense. It was even possible that the defense could have a say about how the information was presented in court.

But there was also no guarantee that the interrogators would get around to asking them, or that they would be able to extract an answer, or that their account of the answer would summarize it accurately. As Moussaoui's lawyer pointed out, this made the prosecution "the architect of the defense" and turned the trial into a "fool's game." And the court agreed. In April 2004 it ruled that the trial jury should hear what the witnesses had to say and that Moussaoui should have a chance to respond. But that response was not going to come in the form of a cross-examination. Instead, he would have to settle for summaries prepared by the prosecutors based on reports from the intelligence community. The court was satisfied that this truncated version of due process was sufficient to allow the prosecution to seek the death penalty.

The defense had won the ability to gain access to the witnesses who could plausibly speak, it seemed, against its client without the chance for cross-examination. If so, the victory only ensured that he would face the death penalty, even as it established a legal precedent for whittling away at the Constitution. The Supreme Court refused to hear Moussaoui's appeal of the Fourth Circuit decision, and a month later Brinkema accepted Moussaoui's guilty plea. Her attempt to secure Moussaoui's rights thwarted, a year later Brinkema presided over the death penalty phase of his trial.

By that time, however, the Fourth Circuit had been forced to modify its opinion. For the court had discovered that the prosecutors had been misinformed and had passed that information along in court. As it turned out, the CIA had been asking questions of the witnesses all along. But the problems were bigger than that. In the months after they issued their opinion, the judges had learned that the Justice Department itself had been instrumental in the mistreatment of detainees, having crafted the opinions that made it possible in the first place.

CHAPTER 7

The Justices
Weigh In

John Walker Lindh wasn't the only American being held at Qala Jangi prison when the riot erupted. Like Lindh, Yaser Hamdi was a Taliban foot soldier who had been brought in by the Northern Alliance in the early days of the American invasion. When he surrendered to American forces, Hamdi, who had been born in Louisiana but grew up in Saudi Arabia, identified himself as a citizen. They did not believe him, so while Lindh, who was not of Arab descent, had been placed immediately in a US prison, Hamdi had been sent to Guantánamo. Two months later, he was transferred to the brig at Norfolk Naval Station in Virginia and held there as an enemy combatant.

By the time his case made it to the Supreme Court, on April 28, 2004, Hamdi had joined Jose Padilla in the lockup at Charleston, South Carolina, where both were held in solitary confinement. Like Padilla, Hamdi had been to federal court (or at least his lawyers, acting on his behalf without ever meeting him, had), arguing that the president did not have the right to detain him indefinitely without charges or access to a lawyer, and he'd won from Judge Robert Doumar what Padilla had won from Michael Mukasey: an order for a habeas corpus hearing. Doumar further commanded the government to produce more evidence corroborating the need for Hamdi's ongoing detention than the sketchy, secondhand summary, submitted by prosecutors, of what unspecified witnesses had told unnamed investigators. But Doumar was an Eastern District of Virginia judge, while Mukasey was from the Southern District of New York, so the government's appeal went to a different court: the more conservative Fourth Circuit. And unlike the Second Circuit Court of Appeals, which had upheld Padilla's right to contest his imprisonment in federal court, the Fourth Circuit ruled that Hamdi's detention was legal. The district judge had erred, the Fourth Circuit judges ruled: to grant the habeas corpus request was to interfere with the president's power to conduct a war. The conflict between the two courts had given lawyers for both men a reason to bring a case to the Supreme Court.

The Hamdi and Padilla cases weren't the only matters before the justices that month. Also at issue was the detention of fourteen noncitizen enemy combatants held at Guantánamo, whose lawyers were demanding a habeas hearing—a case known as *Rasul v. Bush*. A week earlier the Court had heard arguments about the question underlying all these cases: whether the president had the right to detain people, citizens or not, for as long as he wanted, for reasons that could remain secret, and without leveling charges against them. It was a question lawyers and civil liberties advocates had been asking for nearly three years. But it was in many ways an ancient question, the same one that had been on the minds of the British aristocracy in 1215 when they confronted King John at Runnymede: Just how much power does the sovereign power have over the bodies of his citizens or those in his custody? It was, in other words, a question fundamental to the democratic tradition, one that was answered by the Magna Carta and ultimately by the US Constitution.

If the question was familiar, so were the people addressing it:

Deputy Solicitor General Paul Clement for the government; Moussaoui's lawyer Frank Dunham, who was there representing Hamdi; and Donna Newman, Jennifer Martinez, and Andrew Patel, in court for Padilla. As per the rules of Supreme Court arguments, each side would be given thirty minutes for each case. Three hours in total for all three cases would determine the future of American detention policy in the war on terror.

Hamdi's case was the first up. "When it comes to U.S. citizens," Frank Dunham began, "you don't simply detain them. You prosecute them, like they did with John Walker Lindh." He told the justices it was unheard of for the government to keep an American citizen in detention outside the court system. "We have never authorized detention of a citizen in this country without giving him an opportunity to be heard," he said. In his brief, Dunham had referred the justices to a case from the Civil War, *Ex parte Milligan*, in which the Supreme Court ruled that trying citizens by military tribunal where civilian courts were still operating was unconstitutional. Hamdi, Dunham complained to the justices, "hasn't been able to look at the facts that have been alleged against him and give any kind of explanation as to his side of the story." Congress was needed to authorize this kind of detention, and until such legislation was passed, he argued, executive detention was just plain unlawful.

Clement's position was the same one the executive branch had been taking since 9/11: that extraordinary times demanded extraordinary measures, and that to grant a defendant normal rights amid such peril was to put the country at unacceptable risk: "No principle of law or logic requires the United States to release an individual from detention so that he can rejoin the battle against the United States." Justice Ruth Bader Ginsburg interrupted Clement. She pointed out that criminal charges also kept people away from the battlefield—both before and after trial. Why couldn't Hamdi, like Lindh and Moussaoui, be held pending trial, be tried in court, and if found guilty, be sent to prison?

Clement explained that some enemy combatants, Hamdi and

Padilla among them, were of such "paramount intelligence value" that access to lawyers and the court system was inadvisable. After all, the "first advice" an attorney would give to a client "would certainly be to not talk to the Government." That, Clement argued, would "interfere with the intelligence gathering process." In wartime—and Clement repeatedly reminded the court that there were currently ten thousand troops in Afghanistan—interrogators have to have the ability to deal with detainees "to get intelligence to prevent future terrorist attacks."

But, Justice John Paul Stevens countered, couldn't access to a lawyer help, rather than obstruct, intelligence efforts? In criminal cases, the defense attorney often plays the role of explaining to the defendant the benefits of cooperating with prosecutors by reassuring the defendant that the government will hold to its promise to reduce the number or severity of charges or seek a more lenient sentence in exchange for information. "Have you considered the possibility," Stevens asked Clement, "that perhaps a lawyer would have explained to this man that if you do give some information, you won't have to stay here incommunicado for two or three years? That might be a motivation to talk."

Clement allowed that this was possible. In fact, he told Stevens, "it has occurred to us ... that in some circumstances with some individuals, the best way to get them to cooperate and provide information is to give them a lawyer." But the determination of who actually deserved that right should be made by "people whose job it is to make these judgments"—which in the post-9/11 era was, he was implying, no longer courts but interrogators considering national security. If Hamdi wanted to protest his captivity, it was his interrogators and not his lawyer or a judge to whom Hamdi should make his protest. The court did have a "continuing but modest role" in deciding whether or how long someone could be detained, Clement conceded, but it was up to the president to declare when the war that necessitated these abridgements of rights was over.

The nation's solicitor general was arguing that his own office and that of the justices before whom he was arguing—indeed, the whole judicial apparatus—needed to surrender some of its traditional power, especially when it came to putting a check on the president. This idea, as Dunham told the justices, had chilling implications. If the president "can impose indefinite executive detention on anybody that he thinks is necessary," he argued, "then we could have people locked up all over the country tomorrow without any due process, without any opportunity to be heard."

But Clement insisted that the president did not owe the enemy any of these rights—not under the Constitution, not under the Authorization for Use of Military Force, and not under the Geneva Conventions. None of these, Clement told the Court, applied to enemy combatants, especially those of high value. As Olson had argued to the FISA Court, and Clement in the Moussaoui and Padilla cases, this was a war unlike any other. Now that the World Trade Center had been destroyed, the Pentagon damaged, and three thousand people killed, everything had changed. What once might have been precious—rule of law, restraints on sovereign power, an independent judiciary—was now a liability.

THE ARGUMENTS AT THE SUPREME Court that day were familiar enough. The interests of security had to be weighed against the interests of civil liberties, and the president was the best person to make that calculation. The courts were too wedded to law and tradition, and too naïve to the scope and nature of the danger, to have more than a modest role in the outcome. But there was something new in the colloquy, something even more disturbing than depriving citizens of their due process rights.

The justices were probing the limits of the new powers claimed by the president when Justice Stevens posed a question: "Do you think there is anything in the law that curtails the method of interrogation that may be employed?"

Clement answered without hesitation. "The United States is a signatory to conventions that prohibit torture and that sort of thing," he said. "And the United States is going to honor its treaty obligations." Besides, Clement added, the people whom he was suggesting we all—citizens, justices, and soldiers alike—needed to trust in the new wartime order had made a judgment: "the last thing you want to do is torture somebody."

Perhaps it was the chilling ambiguity of this comment, or the reports that had been appearing in the press in the past year or so about America's "brass-knuckled quest for information" from Al Qaeda suspects, or about alleged mistreatment of detainees at Guantánamo, or about the Afghan prisoner somehow beaten to death while in US custody, or maybe it was the duct tape and gags and hoods showing up in press photos, or just the fact that Clement had volunteered the word *torture* in response to Stevens's more circumspect "method of interrogation." Whatever the reason, Justice Anthony Kennedy took it upon himself to return to the subject of the treatment of detainees when the argument shifted away from Hamdi and to Padilla, and to the question of what exactly Padilla's rights as a defendant were. Could we punish him summarily? Shoot him? Kennedy wanted to know.

Clement told the justice we could not, at least not once he had been subdued and captured.

But, Justice Ruth Bader Ginsburg pressed on, "if the law is what the executive says it is, whatever is necessary and appropriate in the executive's judgment ... and it leads you up to the executive, unchecked by the judiciary ... what is it that would be a check against torture?"

The prospect of court-martial for war crimes, Clement told the Court, would deter a would-be torturer.

But what if "it's not a soldier ... but it's an Executive command?" Ginsburg asked. "Suppose the executive says mild torture ... will help get this information?" With the courts out of the picture and Congress not consulted, "What's constraining? ... Is it just up to the good will of the executive?"

Clement acknowledged that "executive discretion in a war situation can be abused" but added that the courts had ruled that this "is not a good and sufficient reason for judicial micromanagement and overseeing of that authority. You have to recognize that in situations where . . . the Government is on a war footing," he continued, "you have to trust the Executive to make the . . . quintessential military judgments."

It was the second time that day that Clement had urged the court to defer to the executive branch, to knowingly relinquish its prerogative to judge whether the law demanded it to restrain the president. And the justices were not surrendering quietly. Now Justice Stephen Breyer jumped in. "Why isn't the appropriate force . . . what we would call ordinary criminal process?" he asked. "Now, maybe there is an answer to that in your vision. I want to find out your vision of what's supposed to happen here and why."

Clement did not spell out his vision, at least not his vision of the system that would replace the ordinary criminal process. Instead, he spelled out a vision of a prisoner who was not only guilty of a war crime but in possession of "information that could be used to prevent future terrorist attacks." In that case—and since to Clement the battlefields of the war on terror were the minds of Al Qaeda operatives, this was potentially every case—"the military ought to have the option of proceeding with him in a way that allows [them] to get actionable intelligence to prevent future terrorist attacks, and should not be forced into a choice where the only way they can proceed is to proceed retrospectively to try to punish him for past acts." Jurisprudence, in other words, was mired in the past. Only military interrogation—the harsh nature of which Clement did not limit in any specific way in his remarks—could address the future, and judicial micromanaging could only bog down this crucial part of the war effort. In military strategy, in the exercise of force at home, in indefinite detention, in the use of torture, the court—precedent and law notwithstanding—should get out of the way.

The deep antidemocratic undertones of Clement's answers were not lost on Padilla lawyer Jennifer Martinez. She stayed focused on the immediate issue—Padilla's ongoing detention—to remind the Court that this was the same issue "that our Founding Fathers were concerned about . . . where the king had locked up citizens." What the president was arguing went against not only the Founding Fathers' vision of the rule of law but the history that gave rise to the idea that centralized power was inherently suspect and always in need of restraint. "Never before in the nation's history has this Court granted the President a blank check to do whatever he wants to American citizens," she said. "Even in wartime, especially in wartime, the Founders wanted to place limits on the ability of the executive to deprive citizens of liberty."

By the time arguments closed for the morning, American justice had passed a new threshold. Clement had not only said that the president could violate criminal law, the law of war, the Eighth Amendment, and various international accords and treaties if he thought it was necessary; he'd also turned the president's power grab into a legal doctrine. A skeptical but still listening Supreme Court had heard the nation's own lawyer proclaim that it should disregard an eight-hundred-year-old tradition of rule of law, not to mention years of restraining the president, and that it should yank out one of the cornerstones of post-Enlightenment politics—the obligation of governments to uphold the dignity of their citizens—in favor of a government run by a president vested with the authority to do whatever he deemed necessary to protect the country. In peacetime, the Court was an institution to which the president could defer, and the nation would remain safe. In war, especially a war where the battlefield was in the enemy's mind, the Court's scruples and deliberateness and skepticism were a dangerous luxury, one the country could not afford. In this respect, the justices of the Supreme Court were no different from the rest of the citizenry: if we wanted to be safe, we should just let the president be, as he claimed, the decider.

DONNA NEWMAN, THE FIRST OF Jose Padilla's many lawyers, remembers that after the Supreme Court session she and her family spent the car trip from Washington back to New Jersey complaining bitterly about the government's outrageous claims. Once home, they turned on the television and found that things were worse than she had thought.

On the night of the Supreme Court arguments about Hamdi and Padilla, the same day that justices inquired directly into whether the United States was torturing prisoners, the CBS news show *60 Minutes II* broadcast a series of pictures from Abu Ghraib prison in Iraq. They showed six of what would turn out to be hundreds of images: images of naked human bodies stacked in a pyramid; a man cowering naked before dogs set to attack him; a detainee on the floor in a pool of blood, a dog threatening him; a man, hooded and attached to wires; and the smiling thumbs-up grin of a young private. Newman was infuriated. "We all were," she said. "How could Paul Clement have had the audacity to stand up and say those things? Those bald-faced lies?"

Subsequently, Clement's colleagues, "liberal and conservative" both, insisted that he had been kept in the dark—that he had not known about the administration's reliance on torture to elicit information from detainees—and had not been lying.

But Clement didn't outright deny that there was torture. He never said the government wouldn't torture people. He said it would be the "last thing" it would consider. He said that it would be against international treaties. He even said that a "binding treaty" would "constrain the actions of the executive branch." But he did not say what would happen if the prisoners in question were considered residents of uncharted legal territory or if the president were unbound.

Soon enough, that story would emerge—first about Abu Ghraib, then about the prisoners close to the high-profile cases like those of Hamdi and Padilla. The early disclosures made it seem as if the perpetrators were just a few undisciplined soldiers or maybe the military staff overseeing the prison. But evidence would soon come into the public view that the president's lawyers had determined those treaties inapplicable to the war on terror, and that if he deemed it necessary to torture prisoners in order to probe the battlefield in their minds, he could. And it was all perfectly legal—at least it was in the opinion of the rogue force in the White House and the Department of Justice that was working behind the scenes to make it so.

For now, however, the president was going to have to act without the help of the Supreme Court. In June 2004, even as the Abu Ghraib story was filled in, especially by reporter Seymour Hersh, the Court was preparing to rule on the Hamdi and Padilla matters. On June 28 it released its decisions in the two cases, as well as *Rasul v. Bush,* the case concerning the indefinite detention of prisoners at Guantánamo. Hamdi could file a habeas petition. Rasul and the enemy combatants in Cuba could challenge their detention in federal courts, even if they were noncitizens held abroad. Padilla could ask a district court in South Carolina to take up his habeas writ. In all three cases, in short, the Court ruled that the president did not have the powers that he was claiming to hold prisoners in a Twilight Zone.

"A state of war is not a blank check for the president," wrote Justice Sandra Day O'Connor in her majority opinion in the Hamdi case. "Habeas corpus allows the Judicial Branch to play a necessary role in maintaining this delicate balance of governance," she continued, "serving as an important judicial check on the Executive's discretion in the realm of detentions." War or no, the Court was not going to relegate itself to the modest role Clement had ascribed to the courts.

Justice Antonin Scalia would have preferred a different decision. "Today, the Court springs a trap on the Executive," he wrote in his dissent from the *Rasul* ruling. In "subjecting Guantanamo Bay to the oversight of the federal courts, even though it has never before been thought to be within their jurisdiction," it was expanding its own power, not merely refusing to shrink away from it. It was not, in other words, the president's power grab that had to be resisted but the judiciary's.

But Scalia's was a lonely dissent. The Supreme Court had responded to Clement's argument that its role was limited by reasserting its broad powers and in the bargain chastising the executive branch for overstepping its bounds. It was a setback for the expansive national security agenda of the executive and a reassertion of constitutional protections that had been under assault. But the Court's victory would prove to be short-lived.

PART II

AGENTS OF CHANGE

CHAPTER 8

Legal Cover— Uncovered

The justices of the Supreme Court were not alone in having misgivings about the president's power grab. Even some executive branch officials were wondering if the White House had gone too far. One Justice Department lawyer in particular found himself deeply disturbed by some of what his predecessors, colleagues, and friends had done, leading him to question their legal competence and even doubt their moral integrity.

Jack Goldsmith thinks he was an "improbable choice" to head the Office of Legal Counsel (OLC), the DOJ section responsible for providing advice and counsel to the president. Most of his career had been spent in the university rather than in politics. Just forty, he'd been a law professor, most recently at the University of Chicago, with a focus on the relationship between US and international law, when he became special counsel to the Pentagon's top lawyer in the fall of 2002. There, he advised the military on Guantánamo, military commissions, and the occupation of Iraq. "I hadn't even sought the OLC job," he wrote in a memoir of his ten-month stint in the position. But his Pentagon boss recommended him for the position, and in October 2003, six months before the Abu Ghraib revelations, he was hired.

Goldsmith was not the first choice for the job, at least not from the White House's perspective. They had wanted John Yoo, who, as an assistant in the OLC, had been working closely with them since 9/11, an integral part of the "War Council," as its members called themselves, that included Cheney's lawyer David Addington and White House counsel Alberto Gonzales. But even as it gave Yoo power, this group did not ingratiate him with Ashcroft, especially because Yoo had not always consulted him before giving the White House his advice. Yoo, it seemed, was taking his orders from Gonzales and Addington rather than from the attorney general himself, and when the White House recommended Yoo for the OLC post, Ashcroft seized the opportunity to remind everyone who was the real boss, telling White House chief of staff Andrew Card that Yoo was "not competent" for the job. Yoo recommended Goldsmith for the post and soon left Washington to teach at the UC Berkeley School of Law. In his interview for the job, Goldsmith recalled, Ashcroft seemed focused on a single issue: "keeping the Attorney General in the loop."

Goldsmith managed to assure Ashcroft of his loyalty. But he was friends with Yoo, he'd clerked for Anthony Kennedy alongside Gonzales's top aide, and he'd been a team player at the Pentagon, so David Addington must have been surprised when Goldsmith, soon after taking office, informed him that he didn't think the exemption the White House had claimed from the Geneva Conventions for enemy combatants would apply to civilians captured in Iraq and considered terrorists. Whatever crimes they had committed, Goldsmith reasoned, they were citizens of a sovereign country and thus entitled to the protections of international law. To treat them otherwise was to court international scorn and to leave the people making and carrying out the orders susceptible to prosecution for war crimes.

Goldsmith's analysis perplexed Gonzales, who said that he didn't understand "how terrorists who violate the laws of war can get the protection of the laws of war." And it infuriated Addington. "The President has already decided that terrorists do not receive Geneva Convention protections," he informed Goldsmith. "You cannot question his decision." The president had apparently also decided that anyone he designated as a terrorist was a terrorist and thus subject to whatever treatment he saw fit to authorize.

It was clear from the start that while Goldsmith was a staunch supporter of the war on terror, he was not going to massage the law into a shape that would give legal cover for the activities the White House was seeking to carry out. The rule of law had to come first. He would limit his analysis to "legality, regardless of what morality may indicate, and even if harm may result," as he had done with the Geneva Conventions question. He would not, in other words, be the War Council's man at Justice. He would not be their John Yoo.

WHEN HE TOOK OVER THE OLC in October 2003, Goldsmith knew Yoo as a colleague, a squash partner, and a fellow traveler in conservative legal circles. He didn't know him as the legal architect of America's torture policies until about six weeks later, when Patrick Philbin, the lawyer who had taken over from Yoo when he left for Berkeley Law, alerted him to a Yoo memo that was, in his words, "out there." As Goldsmith later wrote, Philbin "was not squeamish about pushing the President's power to its limits. He was a longtime friend of Yoo. . . . Any worries he had about flaws in OLC's post 9/11 national security opinions were informed and credible."

So Goldsmith dug—first into the memo Philbin had pointed to, then into others Philbin had flagged. What he found alarmed him. Some of the opinions that guided counterterrorism policy, including detention and treatment of prisoners, were "deeply flawed: sloppily reasoned, overbroad, and incautious in asserting extraordinary constitutional authorities on behalf of the President." Particularly guilty of these flaws were a series of opinions and letters authored by John Yoo.

The documents concerned questions that had first arisen with the capture of Abu Zubaydah in March 2002. The CIA was sure that he was "the one guy who would likely know when, where, and by whom the next attack would be carried out." But he had not divulged those details yet, and the CIA agents on the scene thought that the FBI's approach was unlikely to succeed. They wanted to kick FBI agent Ali Soufan off the job and turn it over to a new "interrogation specialist" and a "training psychologist," who would "move the interrogations into . . . an increased pressure phase." Here they were climbing out onto a legal limb, and if it snapped off, they might find themselves falling into the category of war criminal—as would the superiors who had given them the orders to turn up the heat. They needed to know exactly what they could do to extract the information. Just how much pressure could the CIA bring to bear on a prisoner in order to stop the time bomb from ticking?

It was the CIA's lawyer, John Rizzo, who brought the question to the Office of Legal Counsel. He might have settled for a promise from the Department of Justice not to prosecute should the interrogation stray into illegal territory, but that was the request Chertoff had refused to grant. So he sought an official opinion from the OLC as to whether the CIA's plans complied with the law. If they did, no one would need immunity, because they would be acting legally.

Rizzo told me that when he approached the OLC, he wanted an honest analysis. "I wanted them to tell us if we had lost our senses," he said. If they had concluded that "a lot of this stuff clearly constituted torture" and thus was off-limits, it "would have been perfectly okay with me, provided the 'no way' was put in writing." Either way, he wanted a buy-in on any decisions about the techniques to be employed, so that when and if the use of harsh methods (or the decision not to use them) came to light, "we would all be in this together, for better for worse." To get the most accurate answer, Rizzo reasoned, he'd have to give an accurate account of what the CIA intended to do to Zubaydah. So "I laid it all out, in graphic detail."

But what is chilling about the details is not how graphic they are. To the contrary, to read Yoo's memo to Rizzo, issued on August 1, 2002, is to behold the sanitizing power of bureaucratic language—not to mention the trouble that looms when legality, regardless of morality or harm, becomes the focus of inquiry. Each of the ten techniques for which Rizzo sought guidance is named (the "attention grasp," the "insult slap," "cramped confinement") and described the way a procurement clerk might describe an order for paper clips. Here is how Yoo summarized Rizzo's account of the method that became most notorious and for which the CIA apparently did not have a bureaucratic name—"a technique called the 'waterboard.'"

In this procedure, the individual is bound securely to an in-clined bench, which is approximately four feet by seven feet. The individual's feet are generally elevated. A cloth is placed over the forehead and eyes. Water is then applied to the cloth in a controlled manner. As this is done, the cloth is lowered until it covers both the nose and mouth. Once the cloth is satu-rated and completely covers the mouth and nose, air flow is slightly restricted for 20 to 40 seconds due to the presence of the cloth. This causes an increase in carbon dioxide level in the individual's blood. The increase in the carbon dioxide level stimulates increased effort to breathe. The effort plus the cloth produces the perception of "suffocation and incipient panic," i.e., the perception of drowning.

Rizzo promised Yoo that this would never go on for more than twenty minutes. He guaranteed that nothing they did would exac-erbate the gunshot wound Zubaydah had suffered in the course of being captured. He assured him that if they put an insect in the tiny lightless box in which they intended to place Zubaydah, it would not really be a stinging bug (as they would describe it to Zubaydah, who "appears to have a fear of insects") but a "harmless insect such as a caterpillar."

It's not clear whether all the sterile language was the CIA's attempt to sell the OLC on the torture program or part of an effort to ensure that history would not be unkind to either agency. What is clear is that Yoo, writing on behalf of the OLC, gave the CIA the green light to torture Zubaydah. Of course, Yoo did not put it that way. What he said instead was that "the interrogation procedures you propose would not violate Section 2340A," the federal law that defines torture.

In Section 2340A, Yoo wrote, Congress had defined torture as "an act . . . specifically intended to inflict severe physical or mental pain or suffering." And none of the techniques in question causes pain "difficult for the individual to endure and . . . of an intensity akin to the pain accompanying serious physical injury such as death or organ failure," as the law demands. "Discomfort," perhaps, or "muscle fatigue," but not severe pain. Even when the interrogator slaps the prisoner in the face, "the slap is delivered with fingers slightly spread"—a technique "designed to be less painful than a closed-hand slap"—and, furthermore, it is delivered to "the fleshy part of the face." When the interrogator slams Zubaydah into a wall, he will roll a towel around his neck to prevent whiplash, and besides, because the wall will be flexible, "the sound of hitting the wall will be far worse than any possible injury to the individual." And when he crams Zubaydah into a box too small to stand up in, even if that might inflict severe pain on most people, "Zubaydah remains quite flexible, which would substantially reduce any pain associated with being placed in the box." Between the CIA's own good intentions and the prisoner's good physical condition, it seems, harsh treatment can be stopped from turning into severe pain.

But what about mental pain? Yoo asks. Here the law tells us the mental harm must be "prolonged" and the result of certain specific acts: the infliction or threat to inflict severe physical pain, the use of drugs "calculated to disrupt profoundly the senses or the personality," the threat of imminent death, or the threat that these acts will be inflicted on another person (presumably a family member or someone else close to the prisoner). None of the techniques Rizzo described meets any of those criteria, Yoo reasoned, except one: waterboarding. "Any reasonable person undergoing this procedure . . . would feel as if he is drowning" or, in the words of the statute, under "threat of imminent death." But does it inflict "prolonged mental harm," as the legal definition requires?

As it happens, there is some data on this question, owing to the more than ten thousand American military personnel who have been subjected to waterboarding as part of their training in how to resist interrogations. And aside from a couple of people who tried to blame their shoplifting and child pornography habits on their training, and one who suffered "an adverse mental health reaction that lasted only two hours," it would appear that whatever mental injury might result from being repeatedly brought to the brink of death by drowning is short and negligible. If, in coming to this conclusion, Yoo considered the difference between being waterboarded by members of your own army who you are pretty sure are not going to kill you and being waterboarded by avowed enemies who have shown you no mercy, he did not say so. He did, however, give waterboarders the ultimate out: even if harm was inflicted, the law required the would-be torturer to have the "specific intent" to inflict pain. Clearly the interrogators were not using the proposed techniques in order to cause their subjects pain but rather as a means to the end of getting information. The CIA, his explanation held, was running not an S&M dungeon but a prison devoted to defusing ticking time bombs.

Much as he was following the legal rules, Rizzo confessed "surprise at some of the techniques that were approved." "No one pushed back," he said, still seeming to wonder about this. "No one." But he wasn't disappointed. The CIA, which had hardly been treating Zubaydah with kid gloves—it had held him in total isolation for forty-seven days—was now free to do what it wanted with him. So was everyone fighting the war on terror, for Yoo's analysis was not for the CIA alone. On the same day he gave the official go-ahead to Rizzo (Ashcroft had delivered the good news verbally a few days earlier), he sent a fifty-page memo and a letter to Alberto Gonzales at the White House. And in March 2003 he sent a similar opinion to the Pentagon's lawyers, authorizing twenty-four techniques for the use of military interrogators.

All these memos, authored by Yoo and signed by OLC head Jay Bybee, reiterated Yoo's conclusion that the techniques in question did not constitute torture. But they put it in terms that Gonzales and his colleagues would like, arguing that the Authorization for Use of Military Force—the order authorized in part by Yoo that gave the president sweeping powers to conduct the war on terror—made these questions moot. A criminal statute such as Section 2340A could not infringe "on the President's ultimate authority" in the conduct of war. This meant that even if Yoo's opinion was someday overturned and the acts it authorized declared illegal, anyone who ordered or carried out the interrogations would, according to their reasoning, be exempt from criminal prosecution on the grounds of self-defense and necessity. His legal analysis could be wrong, and the proposed techniques might be considered not mere brutality but actual torture, but it didn't matter. The president's need for information that could save the nation was more important than his responsibility to uphold the law. Yoo had turned the question about torture into an opportunity to extend his, and the rest of the War Council's, radical reinterpretation of American law.

THE OLC'S JOB MIGHT HAVE been to provide legal advice without regard to morality or harm, but Goldsmith's reading of this mission was far different from Yoo's. To Goldsmith, the OLC's objectivity must be tempered by a calculation of the stakes of its opinions. "The nature of the question informed how OLC should answer," he wrote. "Interpreting the torture law is not like resolving an interagency dispute about regulatory control over a merger." Unlike the effects of a corporate merger on employees or society at large, "the stakes in the interrogation program were unusually high," Goldsmith wrote. National security was important, but so was the US commitment to outlawing torture internationally, "its relations with the Muslim world . . . [its] moral reputation and honor. In this context it was unusually important for OLC to provide careful and sober legal advice about the meaning of torture."

This was, in Goldsmith's view, exactly what Yoo had failed to do. To assert, as he had in his memo to Gonzales, that "any effort by Congress to regulate the interrogation of battlefield detainees would violate the Constitution's sole investing of the Commander-in-Chief authority in the President" was to take an extreme and unprecedented position, one with sweeping consequences for all laws, both military and civilian, governing the treatment of prisoners. In claiming that courts had long established that war granted presidents the power to abrogate laws, Yoo had cherry-picked the cases that supported his position and left out those that did not—like the Supreme Court's ruling in *Youngstown* that the Korean War did not give the president the power to shut down a steelworkers' strike. In striking a "tendentious tone," one that made clear from the beginning that he was arguing in support of a position rather than laying out both sides of an argument, Yoo had written a memo that "lacked the tenor of detachment and caution that usually characterizes OLC work," one that seemed "designed to confer immunity for bad acts." In going beyond Rizzo's question about specific techniques into the definition of torture and the limits of presidential power, Yoo had made arguments "wildly broader than was necessary to support what was actually being done," and in effect handed interrogators (and their bosses) a "blank check." In short, Yoo's work "seemed more an exercise of sheer power than reasoned analysis." Goldsmith was forced to conclude that his friend and colleague had gone about his crucial business with "an unusual lack of care and sobriety."

Goldsmith didn't mean to stop interrogation by the military. "These separately and specifically approved techniques," he wrote, "contained elaborate safeguards." But those safeguards were not in accord with the larger argument made in the memos—the one that gave the president and his men power over the bodies of prisoners (and with it the ability to "maintain, and not without justification, that they were acting on the basis of the OLC's view of the law"). Yoo had moved the line between legal and illegal in a way that seemed transparently political—a gerrymander that Goldsmith thought could threaten the integrity of the Department of Justice and, with it, the confidence of citizens in the attorney general as their lawyer.

There was, in Goldsmith's view, only one option. The torture memos had to be revoked—and with them the presumption of legality for the enhanced interrogation techniques. He started with the most recent one, a Yoo memo from March 2003 written for the Pentagon. Tried and true methods of interrogation, Goldsmith wrote later, were already part of the military manual and had been determined to be in accord with the Geneva Conventions; they were neither brutal nor abusive. But as he informed the Pentagon's chief counsel over the 2003 Christmas holiday, while the techniques were legal, the analysis was flawed and could not be relied upon for any other interrogation methods. He was shredding the blank check issued by Yoo.

The CIA's memos, on the other hand, posed a different problem. Goldsmith wasn't even sure the methods Yoo had authorized were actually legal. It seemed that no one other than Yoo had pondered that question, and his judgment was suspect. "I wouldn't know until we had figured out the proper interpretation of the torture statute, and whether the CIA techniques were consistent" with it. With the reputation of his office and the legal fate of those who relied on its guidance at stake, Goldsmith was reluctant to withdraw the memos before his interpretation of the law was confirmed. Neither did he want to leave the CIA with no guidance at all. So until he could fashion a replacement opinion, he did not want to withdraw the memos.

But the torture question was only one of many urgent conundrums with which Goldsmith and his staff were struggling in the first half of 2004. They had not resolved the future parameters of the interrogation policy when the Abu Ghraib story broke—and with it the story of the torture memos. With each revelation, the scandalous photos became less a record of individual misbehavior than powerful testimony to malfeasance at the highest levels of government, orchestrated by its lawyers. "Every day the OLC failed to rectify its egregious and now-public error was a day that its institutional reputation, and the reputation of the entire Justice Department, would sink lower yet," wrote Goldsmith. The legal analysis was still incomplete, and Goldsmith's staff had not yet come up with a new opinion, but on June 14, a week after the first news stories about Yoo's opinions had emerged, Goldsmith withdrew the torture memos. A parochial concern—the reputation of his office—had motivated what repugnance alone could not. It also spelled the end of Goldsmith's brief tenure at OLC. Exhausted, demoralized, and presumably tired of fighting with the White House, he resigned on June 16.

GOLDSMITH'S RESIGNATION DID NOT SADDEN David Addington, who resented the OLC's meddling. At a meeting in Alberto Gonzales's office during the Abu Ghraib crisis, Addington had taken an index card out of his pocket. It listed all the OLC opinions that Goldsmith had either revoked or modified during his brief tenure. "Since you've withdrawn so many legal opinions that the President and others have been relying on," said Addington, "we need you to go through all of OLC's opinions and let us know which ones you still stand by."

And that was before Goldsmith formally rescinded the torture memos. But Addington wasn't referring only to the question of interrogation. He had also been incensed by Goldsmith's pushback on yet another of Addington's pet projects: Stellar Wind.

It was Patrick Philbin, the lawyer who had first brought Yoo's memos to Goldsmith's attention, who had urged, in November 2003, that Goldsmith be alerted to the program. Philbin was one of the few people outside the White House who knew about Stellar Wind. He also knew about the legal reasoning that supported it—an opinion also authored by John Yoo, in which he argued that the Court's jurisdiction over electronic surveillance for foreign intelligence was "an unconstitutional infringement on the President's Article II authorities." Once again Yoo had used a narrow question about policy as an opportunity for a broad assertion of presidential power.

Philbin had to work hard to convince Addington to let Goldsmith in on the secret. "Prepare for your mind to be blown," he told Goldsmith when he got the go-ahead. And it was. Not, Goldsmith emphasized, because he thought "vigorous surveillance of terrorism" was itself a bad thing, or because he opposed any changes to FISA. "We were at war with terrorists . . . armed with disposable cell phones and encrypted emails," he wrote. The FISA laws had been fashioned long before the Internet revolution, so they were at least outdated and perhaps unrealistic in their demands for the president to seek permission for every last wiretap. Reforming them seemed both necessary and prudent. But reform was not what the White House had in mind. "We're one bomb away from getting rid of that obnoxious court," Addington had told him in February.

The War Council was dealing with FISA "the way they dealt with other laws they didn't like," writes Goldsmith. "They blew through them in secret based on flimsy legal opinions that they guarded closely"—so closely, in fact, that the National Security Agency's own lawyers had not been allowed to see the analysis that had authorized the agency's intelligence gathering. Philbin had made sure Goldsmith saw the opinions, and his response was no more positive than it had been to the torture memos. He concluded that Yoo had once again cherry-picked laws, this time sections of FISA law, to critique; left undiscussed the sections relevant to war; and used specious legal reasoning. In addition, he had made factual errors.

Once again opinions that were deeply flawed had been used to justify activities at the outer edge of legality. And this time the defects
were so severe that, at least in Goldsmith's view, "the presumption
of legality flipped."

Goldsmith insisted that James Comey, the second-highest-
ranking lawyer in the department since December 2003, be brought
in on the secret. Comey met with Ashcroft over lunch. Using the
salt and pepper shakers and silverware on the table, Comey outlined
Stellar Wind to his boss, explaining that the NSA was sweeping up
both content and metadata of phone and email communications on
a wholesale basis and without any FISA oversight. He detailed the
flaws in Yoo's legal analysis. It was the first time Ashcroft had heard
of the program, despite the fact that one of his staff had written
the memo authorizing it. But he seemed anxious to resolve the issue
quickly. "Just fix it," he told Comey.

Meanwhile, Goldsmith and Philbin had met with Addington and
Gonzales to let them know that they had reviewed the legal authorization for the surveillance programs carried out under the auspices
of Stellar Wind and were now recommending that certain parts be
brought to an end. It was a crucial moment; the authorization for
Stellar Wind would expire on March 11, 2004. The White House
lawyers tried hard to convince the Justice Department lawyers that
the wiretapping was necessary to preserve national security, but
neither Philbin nor Goldsmith had ever doubted that. Nor did they
want Stellar Wind entirely dismantled. They just thought portions
of the program, including what eventually became known as the
Terrorist Surveillance Program, should be put on a firmer legal footing. The White House was not reassured. Hedging its bets against
the possibility that the OLC would never find that new rationale, the
president's team arranged a meeting with congressional leaders to
discuss legislation directly authorizing the continuation of the program. The members of Congress had to know this was important to
the White House: Cheney led the meeting.

Time was running short for Stellar Wind, and so was the patience of the War Council, which drafted a reauthorization that could stand in, at least for the time being. Aware that the program, having been exposed to the light of day, needed some form of legal backing, the council looked to John Ashcroft's signature to save it. But there was a new problem: since the day after Comey told him about Stellar Wind, Ashcroft had been in George Washington Hospital with acute gallbladder disease. On March 10 he was still in the intensive care unit. That night he took a call from the White House. His wife, who was at his bedside, relayed the message Ashcroft had gotten to his chief aide: Alberto Gonzales and Andrew Card, President Bush's chief of staff, were on their way over to see Ashcroft. At eight o'clock the aide called Comey, who was serving as acting attorney general while Ashcroft was indisposed. Comey called his own chief aide and told him to scramble his top staff to the hospital. In the car at the time, he told his driver to hit the lights and siren. When he arrived at George Washington, he ran up the stairs to the ICU, his security team in tow. Philbin, Goldsmith, and FBI director Mueller soon joined him. They were in the room, Comey sitting by the head of Ashcroft's bed, when the White House team arrived, bearing an envelope. Gonzales explained that they needed Ashcroft's signature on the reauthorization.

"Attorney General Ashcroft then stunned me," Comey later told a Senate committee. "He lifted his head off the pillow and in very strong terms expressed his view of the matter, rich in both substance and fact." After his disquisition, Comey said, Ashcroft "laid his head back down on the pillow, seemed spent, and said to them, 'But that doesn't matter, because I'm not the attorney general.'" He pointed at Comey.

Card and Gonzales, who knew where Comey stood on the matter, left without talking to him. (In subsequent testimony, Gonzales claimed to have been oblivious to Comey's presence in the room.) But almost immediately Card called Comey and ordered him to appear at the White House right away. Comey refused to comply unless Solicitor General Ted Olson attended the meeting. They met at eleven. In the meantime, Comey had conferred with his staff and told Card that many of them were prepared to resign if Card and Gonzales insisted on renewing Stellar Wind when the Justice Department had determined (and advised them) that it had no legal basis.

Just a few hours later, four trains were bombed in Madrid during the morning rush hour, killing 191 people. At a six a.m. meeting at the White House, Gonzales told Goldsmith that his critique of Yoo's memo was misplaced. But the legal quibble was academic. The president was going to go ahead and renew the surveillance program that very day, with or without the Justice Department's approval.

The next day Bush stopped Comey after the morning cabinet meeting (which he was attending in Ashcroft's place) and asked to meet with him. Comey told the president what troubled him about Stellar Wind, about the Justice Department's attempt to stop its renewal, and about why the president's order to renew it anyway was illegal. Bush was not persuaded. According to *Washington Post* reporter Barton Gellman, Bush told Comey, "I decide what the law is for the executive branch."

"But I decide what the Department of Justice can certify to and can't certify to," Comey replied. "And despite my absolute best efforts I simply cannot in the circumstances. As Martin Luther said, 'Here I stand, I can do no other.'"

But it wasn't theology that convinced Bush that he could not be the decider this time. It was the prospect of losing Robert Mueller, who was waiting for Comey and who, Comey told Bush, was among the Justice Department officials prepared to resign over the matter rather than order his agents to engage in activities the attorney general deemed illegal. With mass resignations would come scrutiny—of the program and of the White House's disregard of the law.

"Just tell Jim [Comey] to do what Justice thinks needs to be done," Bush said to Mueller.

Reconciling the surveillance program with the law (as opposed to the other way around) turned out to be "by far the hardest challenge

I faced in government," Goldsmith wrote. Much of what changed remains classified, but the Justice Department was eventually satisfied that the program was legal, and the FISA Court was ultimately reformed to give the president more flexibility in ordering surveillance. The reformed program would still, for the time being, operate outside the authority of the FISA Court and Congress, but it would be reauthorized every forty-five days by the signature of the president and the attorney general. Future steps remained to be determined. In May, Goldsmith completed a memo in which he found that the program, as reformed, did not violate the Fourth Amendment. He agreed largely with the president's position that the AUMF was an "express authorization to conduct targeted electronic surveillance against al Qaeda and its affiliates," and that to the extent that FISA had been used to limit the president from "directing surveillance of the enemy to prevent future attacks upon the nation," it amounted to "an unconstitutional infringement" on the president's commander-in-chief powers. While he had strongly rebuked Yoo, he ultimately ratified the opinion that constitutional rights could be curtailed in the name of national security.

JACK GOLDSMITH'S RESIGNATION TOOK EFFECT on July 7, 2003. In his ten months at the OLC, he had put what he believed to be two necessary components of the nation's defense on a solid legal footing. Enhanced interrogation continued, only now supported by a limited and more legally strict reading of the law, while substitute memos for those he'd withdrawn and called into question still remained to be written. The surveillance policies survived more or less intact. Both would continue to be revised over the next few years. Occasionally they would surface in the news media—sometimes explosively, as they did years later when Edward Snowden revealed the breadth of the country's domestic spying program in 2013. But even after the departure of John Yoo, the rest of the War Council got largely what it wanted: not exactly a blank check,

but still the ability to treat inmates harshly and detain them indefinitely, and unprecedented power to tap into the private communications of American citizens.

Goldsmith's work—the work that had eventually led to the hospital showdown—accomplished another purpose, one that Goldsmith
perhaps did not intend. He had forced the War Council's disregard
for the Department of Justice, and with it the rule of law, into the
open. A memo written collectively by senior DOJ lawyers summarized what had transpired, outlining the disregard for the law that
had led Goldsmith to resign. The document elicited a response from
Alberto Gonzales (although probably authored by David Addington)
so strong that it came to be known as the Fuck-You Memo. "Your
memorandum appears to have been based on a misunderstanding of
the President's expectations regarding the conduct of the Department of Justice," it said. "While the President was, and remains,
interested in any thoughts the Department of Justice may have on
alternative ways to achieve effectively the goals of the activities authorized by the Presidential Authorization of March 11, 2004, the
President has addressed definitively for the Executive Branch in
the Presidential Authorization the interpretation of the law." Unpleasant as this and the other exchanges were, they at least compelled the administration to openly declare its disregard for the
Justice Department, which until this point it had expressed only
through circumvention and deception. (In the case of the Fuck-You
Memo, it might have all been for show: Gonzales left a voicemail for
the Justice Department reassuring Goldsmith and Comey that he
would be implementing the changes anyway.)

Goldsmith later pointed out that much of his work should have
been unnecessary. After all, if the White House had not treated the
Department of Justice as the enemy, or asked one of its lawyers to
gerrymander the law—if, in other words, it had followed the usual
practices—then "the whole ordeal could have been avoided." The
two sides were really not opposed. Goldsmith's view of what was
permissible under the law was not all that different from Gonzales's,

except for one important matter. Addington and Gonzales were concerned not only with the war on terror but also, and perhaps more centrally, with the extension of presidential power—not just for their president but for all American presidents to come. A strong executive was not simply the means to fight a war; it was an end in itself, and the more the president's men could flex their muscles, the more the rest of the government would back down. That was exactly what Goldsmith and Comey (and even Ashcroft) would not do. That such loyal men would stand up so firmly, and at such risk, against their own colleagues was a good measure of just how far Addington and Gonzales had tried to push their cause.

The standoff might also have alerted the president to what his staff were doing. In their meeting on March 12, Bush told Comey he didn't like the way the question of the legality of Stellar Wind had come up just a day before the deadline. Comey explained to the president that the question had been on the table for months, ever since Goldsmith had flagged it. Comey believed Bush about his being blindsided and was duly shocked: the president's advisers had kept him in the dark.

When he left Washington for a professorship at Harvard Law School, Goldsmith had not ended the troublesome detention and surveillance policies of the Bush administration. But that was not necessarily his intention; what he meant to do, and what he succeeded at, was to make the policies legal, where he could, without recourse to strained and cynical readings of the law. In this sense, his efforts, incomplete when he left, amounted to less heinous and more legitimate policy. Even so, and especially in light of the Supreme Court decisions in the three prisoner detention cases (which followed his resignation by two weeks), his work had shifted the momentum of the legal battle even as it shined a light on the policies that would continue to be debated for years to come. But whether or how much he had succeeded in slowing the rogue elements in the American justice system remained to be seen.

CHAPTER 9

Glimmers of Light

In November 2004 George Bush was elected to another term as president. Whatever the degree to which his administration's detention, torture, and surveillance policies had penetrated the public consciousness, they had not induced voters to reject him. Nor, evidently, had they led him to reconsider the approach the administration had been taking to the justice system—at least not when it came to replacing John Ashcroft. According to one government lawyer, Ashcroft had submitted his resignation as a formality, expecting to be reappointed. Whatever his expectations, he was passed over. The new man in charge of the Department of Justice would be White House counsel Alberto Gonzales, whose loyalty to the president was beyond question. No longer would the president's men have to work around an attorney general who might not share their opinions. With Gonzales at Justice and David Addington, now Vice President Cheney's chief of staff, back at the White House, the new administration was in a perfect position to consolidate the gains of the past four years, continuing to dilute citizens' rights and liberties in favor of national security, and to strengthen the office of the president in the bargain.

Among those who left the administration was James Comey; he resigned in April 2005. One of his remaining tasks was to shepherd to a conclusion the work of Jack Goldsmith, who had never had the chance to write a replacement for the Yoo torture memos he had rescinded. The first part of that job fell to OLC lawyer Daniel Levin, who at the end of 2004 issued an opinion clarifying the definition of torture. Levin began and ended his opinion by asserting that torture, whatever it is, is abhorrent and illegal. He repudiated Yoo's view that severe "pain" and "suffering," both of which enter into the legal definition of torture, are one and the same. " 'Physical suffering,' " he wrote, could rise to the level of torture, even if it did not involve pain that was "excruciating and agonizing"; it only had to be cruel and inhumane. Levin also rejected the idea that a technique had to inflict prolonged mental harm to qualify as torture; severe psychological damage of any duration was enough. He reiterated that the ban on torture was not subject to means/ends analysis. "There is no exception under the [torture] statute permitting torture to be used for a 'good reason,' " he wrote. And he repudiated Yoo's gambit of using this question to provide a legal foundation for unchecked executive power. That discussion, Levin wrote, "was—and remains—unnecessary," so he simply left it unaddressed.

Levin did not address the question of whether individual interrogation techniques qualified as torture under his new and improved definition. That would have to wait until May 2005, when Steven Bradbury, the new head of the OLC, drafted a series of memos on that subject for CIA counsel John Rizzo. If Rizzo anticipated that the new regime at the Justice Department would put an end to the enhanced interrogation program, he need not have worried. Bradbury might have been working with a new definition of torture, but none of the techniques the CIA wanted to use, which now included "dietary manipulation" and nudity (and which still included waterboarding), fell under it. The techniques were designed to induce "shock and drama," and some of them undoubtedly caused pain and suffering, both mental and physical. But in the official opinion of the Department of Justice, to leave a man standing naked (except for a diaper), shackled hand and foot so he could not sleep for 180 hours, or to strap him to a gurney, place a cloth over his mouth, and for two two-hour sessions within a twenty-four-hour time period pour water over the cloth in order to induce the sensation of drowning—this was not torture. It was undoubtedly harsh treatment, but measures had been taken to make sure the suffering was not severe: the diaper would be changed as needed, with due care to avoid skin irritation, and physicians were standing by in case, for instance, the waterboarding got out of hand and the prisoner needed an emergency tracheotomy. Other doctors had defined the "limits that, when combined with careful monitoring, in their professional judgment should prevent physical pain or suffering or mental harm to a detainee." Such treatment did not violate US law, Bradbury concluded, and in a May 30 memo he assured Rizzo that it did not run afoul of the United Nations Convention Against Torture, either.

The work Goldsmith started had made some headway but had fallen short of revoking outright the policies authorized by Yoo's torture memos. Yoo's excesses had been curtailed, and torture had been redefined. Yet what the CIA had been doing all along had once again been pronounced legal, only this time by competent lawyers proceeding with care and sobriety. Doctors and lawyers had signed off on the CIA's interrogation techniques. But with the polished version of the memos came increased confidence that any attempt to prosecute interrogators or officials for war crimes would fail. And all had been done with minimal public outcry and with minimal disruption to the program or threat to national security. Alberto Gonzales was in charge at the Department of Justice, Bush and Cheney were in office for another term, and whatever worries about additional legal scrutiny they might have had after the infighting over surveillance and detention policies had faded. At least inside the government, the rogue programs were no longer secret. They were now officially sanctioned policy.

WHILE THE DEPARTMENT OF JUSTICE was rallying to provide legitimate legal support for detention and surveillance programs, courts were also taking up the questions. In a little noted, although public, proceeding in February 2005, an American citizen named Ahmed Omar Abu Ali was brought from Saudi Arabia to Virginia to stand trial for nine counts, including allegedly plotting to kill the president of the United States and conspiring to hijack and destroy aircraft.

Abu Ali's presence in a Virginia courtroom was itself the result of the still unresolved controversy over prisoners' habeas corpus rights. He had been taken into custody by the Saudis in June 2003 as a suspect in a bombing in Riyadh. (He had been studying theology at the Islamic University of Medina since 2000.) The Saudis notified the United States, and FBI agents interviewed him and searched his family's home in Virginia. No charges were filed at the time, but Abu Ali continued to be held by the Saudis, who, he claimed, tortured him, a fact he told to the FBI when he was still in Saudi Arabia. In the course of his interrogation, he confessed to both the Saudis and the FBI that he was a member of Al Qaeda and was plotting to kill the president. Late in 2004 his family, backed by a human rights organization, filed a habeas writ in federal court. They also sought consideration of Abu Ali's treatment, claiming that the FBI was involved and that its involvement meant that US law—which, unlike Saudi law, prohibited torture—should prevail.

Arguing before District Judge John D. Bates in Washington, DC, the government maintained that the court did not have jurisdiction to consider any of these questions because Abu Ali was being held by the Saudis for a crime committed in their country. Bates disagreed. "The Court concludes that a citizen cannot be so easily separated from his constitutional rights," he wrote, adding that "there is at least some circumstantial evidence that Abu Ali has been tortured during interrogations with the knowledge of the United States." He ordered a hearing that, the government knew, would bring up details about detention and interrogation it did not want in the public view—in particular, the practice of rendition, in which the US used a country with laxer standards to hold a prisoner on its behalf. Its lawyers stonewalled Bates's orders, resorting to what the judge called "highly unusual" tactics. They told him, for instance, that they had a good argument against his ruling, but they couldn't tell him what it was "without disclosing the classified information that underlies it."

But before this issue could come to a head, the government brought Abu Ali to Virginia—not for a habeas hearing but to face criminal charges. The Justice Department had not suddenly remembered its commitment to giving US citizens their day in court, nor had it been moved to spare Abu Ali the harsh treatment of a Saudi prison. Although the prosecutors denied it, the decision was made for strategic reasons. As David Cole, a lawyer for Abu Ali, pointed out, "Only when the government was threatened with having to disclose its arrangements with Saudi Arabia regarding Mr. Abu Ali's detention did it take action, bring him back, and indict him." Because the criminal charges would take precedence over the habeas hearing, the indictment served to avoid the hearing Bates had ordered—and, with it, scrutiny of the role the United States played in the detention of one of its citizens in an overseas prison.

This tactic carried some risk, however. Abu Ali's lawyers argued that FBI agents knew that his confession had been coerced through torture and that he had not been read his Miranda rights. The lawyers wanted the confession suppressed on these grounds, which meant they had to introduce evidence that their client had been tortured. At the suppression hearing, Abu Ali detailed the beatings he'd undergone in his first days of confinement. He also submitted photographs of scars he claimed the beatings had left. The government produced as a witness a dermatologist who disputed that claim, arguing instead that the marks on his back were "pigment discolorations." The judge agreed, ruling that "there is no credible evidence that he was beaten or mutilated." The trial went ahead, and Abu Ali was convicted and sentenced—first to thirty years in jail and then, when the prosecution won its appeal of that sentence as too lenient, to life imprisonment. And the question of torture, at least for now, remained outside the purview of the courts. The gambit had succeeded.

ON THE SAME DAY THAT Abu Ali was convicted—November 22, 2005—Attorney General Alberto Gonzales called a news conference to announce that "dirty bomber" Jose Padilla had been indicted on charges of providing support to terrorists overseas—specifically, Gonzales said, attending a terrorist training camp in Afghanistan with the purpose of attacking the United States. Conspicuously absent from the indictment was any reference to a plot to set off a nuclear weapon in an American city—the allegation on which he had originally been detained. When asked, Gonzales declined to explain why the dirty bomber had not been indicted for plotting to set off a dirty bomb.

The answer was buried deep in the political and legal wrangling over Padilla that had been sparked by the Supreme Court ruling in June 2004 that his habeas petition should be heard in South Carolina rather than in New York. When the case got to the district court in Spartanburg, Donna Newman recalled, "We [defense counsel Andrew Patel and herself] found ourselves in the bizarre circumstance of asking for our client to be charged." The district court ruled in Padilla's favor, but the government appealed, and the case went before the Fourth Circuit Court of Appeals in July 2005. Paul Clement, now the acting solicitor general, went to Charleston to argue the appeal. Padilla was "an al Qaeda–trained operative," he said, "who, while armed with an assault rifle, evaded capture by United States troops on a foreign battlefield, and then after conspiring with senior al Qaeda operatives attempted to return to the United States to carry out attacks on domestic soil." By now this was a familiar argument: Padilla might have been a citizen, but he was also an enemy combatant, and to grant him his rights by releasing him from military custody and placing him in the civilian courts was to jeopardize national security.

In September 2005 the appeals court decided for the government. Padilla, it ruled, "took up arms on behalf of that enemy and against our country in a foreign combat zone of that war" and had "traveled to the United States" to bring that war to "American citizens and targets." Under the AUMF, the president had the power to detain Padilla in order to prevent his "return to battle." But the inevitable appeal to the Supreme Court by Padilla's lawyers threatened to turn the government's win into a loss. The high court could seize the opportunity to declare unconstitutional the detention of an American citizen as an enemy combatant, ordering his release from military custody and diluting the president's power in the bargain. After all, in the Hamdi case, the Court held that the president could not deny due process to an American citizen, even one labeled an enemy combatant. Many observers predicted that it could happen again.

On the other hand, the government could go ahead and charge Padilla in civilian federal court, just as his lawyers had requested, and regardless of the decisions by the circuit and appeals courts. But according to the defense, the prosecution's case was built on "intelligence evidence, not criminal evidence." Most of it had come from Abu Zubaydah and one other detainee who had been tortured (and held in the "black sites" run by the CIA, about which the public was still unaware). A federal indictment based on that evidence would fall apart as soon as Padilla's lawyers challenged its admissibility, and in the process the closely guarded facts about CIA interrogation would come to light. Knowing they were on shaky ground, the government's lawyers pondered their options, at a loss for what to do.

Their best piece of criminal evidence was a partially completed Mujahideen Identification Form, sometimes described as an Al Qaeda application, that allegedly had Padilla's fingerprints on it. The early plan was to use this paperwork to prove his allegiance to Al Qaeda. But then crucial evidence "fell from the sky," as one Justice Department lawyer would later put it. Telephone records obtained under a FISA warrant tied Padilla to two terrorism defendants who were already scheduled to go to trial in Miami—a Palestinian named Adham Amin Hassoun and Kifah Wael Jayyousi, a Jordanian-born American citizen. In the intercepted calls, Padilla appeared to be referencing traveling to a training camp. Padilla, the government now alleged, had been one of many would-be terrorists Hassoun and Jayyousi had recruited to train in Afghanistan. Armed with this evidence, the Justice Department went forward with the indictments announced by Gonzales in November. Padilla was charged with providing material support to terrorists, a crime that covers activities ranging from enlisting as a soldier to providing weapons to using the Internet to recruit terrorists.

But the criminal case could not go forward so long as the Supreme Court was still considering whether to hear arguments about the question of Padilla's detention. If it did, it would be the second time that Padilla had come before the high court on the matter of whether the president could hold a US citizen in military detention. Until the Court made its decision, the criminal case was a moot issue; if Padilla remained in military detention, he was not eligible for criminal prosecution in federal court. The only way for the government to prevent the high court from deciding the detention question was to ask the circuit court judges to withdraw the decision that was under appeal—their ruling that Padilla could be held in military custody—and authorize his transfer to civilian court. Faced with the prospect of losing, government prosecutors tried to knock over the chessboard.

The Fourth Circuit judges were not amused, especially not J. Michael Luttig, its chief judge. He was incensed at the government's request for the court to withdraw a published opinion. It was, he noted in his order denying the withdrawal as well as the transfer of Padilla to civilian custody, an attempt to use presidential power to remove a case of "surpassing importance" from the judicial system by fiat—and at great cost to the respectability of the courts. The government had argued strenuously for "the indispensability to our national security of the President's authority to detain enemy combatants such as Padilla," and the court had lent that argument legitimacy, but suddenly, now that it could come under scrutiny, the same government had "determined that it was no longer necessary that Padilla be held militarily." Apparently the president's power to detain a citizen was not so crucial after all. To "intentionally moot" a case like this was to turn the whole proceeding into a farce. In order to protect its bid for executive power, the White House was willing to make a mockery of the judicial branch of government. And it wasn't just the courts that were besmirched by the legal maneuvering. The government's actions "have left not only the impression that Padilla may have been held for these years, even if justifiably, by mistake," Luttig wrote, but also the impression that when it was expedient to do so, the government would make such decisions without considering the costs to the war on terror generally. This was "an impression we would have thought the government could ill afford to leave extant."

The Wall Street Journal once described Luttig as "the most conservative judge on the most conservative federal appeals court." And his Fourth Circuit had been loyal to the Bush administration, overturning Brinkema's ruling about the Al Qaeda witnesses in the Moussaoui case and again in the Abu Ali case. It had been willing to make exceptions to customary procedures and interpretations of the law to join the administration's agenda of prevention in the war on terror. But in its latest request, the government had apparently gone too far, and for the moment the Fourth Circuit sounded more like the ACLU than like the War Council. Alberto Gonzales objected that Luttig's concerns were "legally irrelevant"—and he had a point, since Luttig was clearly making a larger political argument. But none of that mattered. The Fourth Circuit was not going to withdraw its opinion. The Padilla case would go to the Supreme Court. And until any further steps were taken, his victory ironically meant that he would remain in military custody.

But on January 3, 2006, the Supreme Court handed the Bush administration a victory. Without ruling on the lawfulness of his detention, the justices authorized Padilla's transfer to civilian custody; he had already been indicted in November on three counts, including two material support counts and one count of conspiracy to murder US nationals. He was released from military detention—not, as he thought at the time, to freedom but to the custody of the federal courts in Miami. The Justice Department inherited the burden of bringing the Padilla case to a conclusion (and in sixteen months, he would finally be tried), but in return, the White House evaded further Supreme Court scrutiny of its detention policy.

THE CHALLENGES TO THE RULE of law did not end with the release of Padilla from military custody. The Abu Ghraib scandal had inspired Congress, led by Senator John McCain (R-AZ), to pass the Detainee Treatment Act, requiring interrogators to adhere to a standard of treatment specified in the Uniform Code of Military Justice, which, in keeping with the Eighth Amendment, prohibited cruel and unusual punishment. But it also stripped most US courts of the authority to hear habeas petitions from Guantánamo prisoners, placing all those cases in the DC District Court. Meanwhile, no one at the highest levels of government was held responsible for the scandal, which was blamed on a group of low-ranking soldiers and one general in charge of the prison rather than on the officers and civilian authorities who had allowed (or ordered) the abuse. And while the two biggest terrorism prosecutions on US soil—Padilla and Moussaoui—were finally on track for judicial resolution, prosecutors had ensured that there would be no reckoning with the government's treatment of potential witnesses or of the defendants themselves. The rogue policies might have moved out of the shadows, but as President Bush entered his sixth year in office, they seemed more entrenched than ever before.

CHAPTER 10

Everything
Is Broken

I n early November 2005 *The Washington Post*'s Dana Priest reported that for four years in eight countries, the CIA had been operating "black sites," where, among others, "the top 30 al Qaeda prisoners" were being held. Those prisoners "exist in complete isolation from the outside world," Priest wrote. "Kept in dark, sometimes underground cells, they have no recognized legal rights, and no one outside the CIA is allowed to talk with or even see them, or to otherwise verify their well-being." The pictures from Abu Ghraib suddenly appeared in a different light. The soldiers giving a thumbs-up to prisoners forced to masturbate, the man with electrodes attached to his body, the corpse over which soldiers exulted—these were examples not of guards gone wild but of an officially sanctioned strategy of mistreating prisoners. "It's now clear that abuse of detainees has happened all over," Human Rights Watch concluded, "from Afghanistan to Guantánamo Bay to a lot of third-country dungeons where the United States has sent prisoners. And probably quite a few other places we don't even know about." The allegations lodged by lawyers for Padilla, Moussaoui, and Abu Ali were also transformed by these revelations from outlandish tales told in hopes of gaining legal advantage to plausible accounts of abuse of citizens of the United States, at times at the hands of fellow Americans.

A month after the *Post* broke the story of the black sites, James Risen and Eric Lichtblau of *The New York Times* reported that the National Security Agency, whose job was to conduct foreign intelligence surveillance for the CIA and the rest of the government, was also eavesdropping on Americans, both in the country and overseas, without first obtaining a warrant. The *Times* had known about the program, later revealed to be part of the Stellar Wind initiative, for eighteen months but, Risen and Lichtblau wrote, had held off reporting the story at the behest of the Bush administration. Without naming names, the paper let the American public in on the infighting between the FBI and the intelligence agencies, the arguments between the Justice Department and the FISA Court, and the concerns of legislators, judges, and lawyers that the spying had gone too far. It cited a "Congressional official" who said that when he raised doubts about the program, "people looked the other way because they did not want to know what was going on" and a "senior government official" who said his first reaction when he heard about the program was "We're doing what?"

The secret was out, and soon warrantless wiretapping was the subject of reports in news media across the country. Pundits questioned its necessity and legality, and four days after the Risen story appeared, the ACLU filed a Freedom of Information suit demanding the release of documents relevant to domestic spying. The Bush administration was now scrambling to defend a program it had managed to keep secret for four years. On December 19 the president held a news conference in which he explained that he had "the constitutional responsibility and the constitutional authority to protect our country . . . to effectively detect enemies hiding in our midst and prevent them from striking again." Even "a two-minute conversation between somebody linked to al Qaeda here and an operative overseas could lead directly to the loss of thousands of lives," he added. He told the reporter who asked why he had "skip[ped] the basic safeguards of asking courts for permission" that the FISA process was for "long-term monitoring," but "what is needed in order to protect the American people is the ability to move quickly." Due care had been taken to ensure that the program was limited in scope and reviewed frequently—every forty-five days, Bush said. And he'd asked his lawyers if warrantless wiretapping was legal, "and the answer is, absolutely."

The Justice Department was also scrambling—to reassure not the press or the American people but members of Congress, some of whom, according to the *Times* article, had known of the program all along. Assistant Attorney General William Moschella sent a letter to the House and Senate Committees on Intelligence declaring that the surveillance program provided "an early warning detection system" that had to be kept secret, and off the legislative agenda, lest disclosure through debate "tip off our enemies concerning our intelligence limitations and capabilities." FISA was still an important counterterrorism tool, Moschella assured them, but it could not provide the "speed and agility" the task required.

A month later the Justice Department released a white paper, along with a letter from Attorney General Alberto Gonzales to Senate Majority Leader William Frist (R-TN), detailing the program's legal basis, summing up the ways in which it adhered to constitutional and statutory authorities, and concluding that the president had the right to authorize the activities that Risen had described. Drawing on statutes and principles that were by now familiar—the Authorization for Use of Military Force, for instance, and the removal of the FISA wall—and reiterating the ongoing urgency of preventing another 9/11-like catastrophe, the white paper acknowledged but justified the program's deviation from traditional legal standards. So long as the president had the statutory authority granted by Congress in the AUMF, so long as the program targeted foreign communications, and so long as the emergency continued, the white paper concluded, the surveillance program violated neither FISA nor the Constitution.

THE JUSTICE DEPARTMENT WHITE PAPER wasn't the only one to begin circulating in the aftermath of the revelations about surveillance. On January 25, 2006, David Kris, the architect of the original legal edifice for post-9/11 surveillance reforms, circulated his analysis of the program. Kris, who had left government and was now working at Time Warner, teaching at Georgetown Law School, and writing a textbook on national security law, believed that his arguments about FISA had been taken much further than he had intended and put to uses he had not imagined.

Kris's criticism of the program, and the Justice Department's defense of it, was unstinting. FISA, he wrote "prohibits the kind of electronic surveillance" that the Bush administration had engaged in—namely, dragnet surveillance, in which everyone's data is collected in hopes of turning up a lead—and the Authorization for Use of Military Force did *not* provide grounds for an exception to that finding. Citing FISA's legislative history, including the congressional debates over its passage, Kris concluded that neither FISA nor the AUMF authorized the NSA's electronic surveillance program. Nor could FISA be read as "an unconstitutional infringement of President's constitutional power under Article II," the commander-in-chief clause, as the president's lawyers had long been arguing. To the contrary, the president was claiming powers that the Constitution did not seem to grant. After all, there was nothing to stop Congress from authorizing such a program, and it hadn't done so. That meant that the program was not valid.

This analysis held not only for surveillance but also for the treatment of detainees. In the president's view, courts were not authorized to stand in his way; "the President apparently believes his power to torture is plenary." Connecting torture to eavesdropping, Kris was pointing out what both policies had in common: the Bush administration's preoccupation with the extension of presidential power. Kris's conclusions about the invalidity of the surveillance program were tentative—a game of "blind man's bluff," he wrote. He lacked two essential ingredients for more certainty: legal precedent and factual knowledge. The case law was scant and unsettled, he noted. And what was perhaps more troubling was that "we don't know what the NSA was and is doing."

Secrecy was also a factor in a case initiated by the ACLU. The week before Kris's paper came out, the organization filed suit in federal court for the Eastern District of Michigan, asserting that because its members had to assume their communication with detainees or their relatives was being monitored, the surveillance program was impeding their ability to represent their clients by forcing them to conduct meetings in person. The ACLU also argued that "by ignoring FISA and wiretapping Americans on American soil without a warrant, the President broke the law."

The choice of the Michigan court to hear a case accusing the president of illegal eavesdropping was not arbitrary. In the early 1970s that court had heard the case of three men accused of conspiring to blow up a CIA recruitment center in Ann Arbor. It ordered the Nixon administration to turn over records of wiretaps it had placed on the men's phones—wiretaps that had been obtained without a warrant. The Keith case, as it came to be known, went to the Supreme Court, which upheld the order and ruled that warrantless wiretapping of citizens on US soil was illegal. The ACLU was now returning the issue to Michigan's federal courts.

But the ACLU faced a formidable obstacle. In order to have the standing to sue, it would have to prove that it had been directly affected by the surveillance program. But there was no way to demonstrate this was the case because the program's particulars were secret, and the government was not about to reveal them in order to help the ACLU substantiate its claim. As prosecutor Anthony Coppolino pointed out, that would compromise national security—an argument for which he also did not provide the details.

"Critical evidence is not available in this case," Coppolino said. "The case itself concerns a classified activity." But that didn't mean the ACLU's charges should be believed: "There's nothing to suggest that [the NSA] somehow intercepts a wide swath of communications." Not for the first time, the Bush administration was asking the courts (and by extension the American people) to trust its judgment in matters of national security, to take it on faith that it was not abusing its power and that it had the best interests of the nation at heart.

The ACLU case was heard by Michigan district court judge Anna Diggs Taylor. The first African-American woman on the Michigan court, Taylor had been a federal judge for thirty-seven years and was a protégée of Damon Keith, the judge for whom the Ann Arbor wiretapping case had been named. When she delivered her ruling in August 2006, Judge Taylor remained true to her mentor. She ruled that the government's position—refusing to disclose the details that could bring some resolution to the case—was unacceptable; under Coppolino's logic, it was effectively impossible for anyone to have standing to challenge the program. Secrecy was not the government's trump card, she ruled, but, rather, its weakness. "Because of the very secrecy of the activity here challenged, Plaintiffs each must be and are given standing to challenge it, because each of them is injured and chilled substantially in the exercise of First Amendment rights so long as it continues." The ACLU, in other words, had standing precisely because the government had prevented it from proving its standing. And the surveillance program itself, she ruled, violated the Constitution's separation of powers doctrine, the First and Fourth Amendments, and various federal statutes.

The White House had evidently overplayed its hand. At least one court was not going to stand for a policy that so blatantly disregarded precedent and the rule of law.

EVEN AS TAYLOR WAS DELIBERATING, one other court was reasserting the role of the judiciary in the war on terror. On

March 6, 2006, after four and a half years of motions and appeals, the trial of Zacarias Moussaoui finally got under way in Leonie Brinkema's Virginia courtroom.

The trial was a two-stage proceeding in which an anonymous jury would decide if Moussaoui was eligible for the death penalty for the crimes to which he had pleaded guilty in April 2005 and, if so, whether he should be executed. But it was at least as much about proving that the civilian federal courts were an effective weapon in the war on terror as it was about deciding Moussaoui's fate. This question had taken on a new urgency since the disclosures about black sites and torture. Now that those secrets were out, could a case that depended on testimony obtained through those means be brought to a successful conclusion?

Moussaoui remained an unrepentant defendant, and his penchant for outbursts kept the courtroom on tenterhooks. But Brinkema retained control as the argument unfolded over eight days. The government presented its now familiar case linking Moussaoui to important Al Qaeda leaders, including Ramzi bin al-Shibh, and to the 9/11 attacks. The defense presented statements from other detainees denying Moussaoui's involvement in or knowledge of 9/11 and dismissing Moussaoui as an Al Qaeda wannabe, too incompetent to join its jihad. "Moussaoui managed to annoy everyone he came in contact with," said one of the captured Al Qaeda leaders held by the United States. He "was constantly suggesting operations which the rest of them thought were ridiculous." He "was a problem from the start," Khalid Shaikh Mohammed said, adding that when he did "not want to deal with Moussaoui any longer," he "instructed Bin al-Shibh to break off contact with Moussaoui." But Moussaoui wasn't interested in exoneration. When he took the stand, he once again insisted that he had indeed been involved in the September 11 attacks. "By the time he stepped down three hours later," a reporter wrote, "Moussaoui seemed to have undone more than four years of work by his defense team."

On April 3, 2006, the jury returned a verdict concluding that

Moussaoui was eligible for the death penalty, ushering in the second phase of the penalty trial. In this second phase, known as the mitigation phase, the defense argued that Moussaoui was not responsible for 9/11 and that whatever criminal actions he had taken were largely the result of his abusive childhood. Once again Moussaoui's belligerence undermined his lawyers' attempts to spare his life. "I just wish [9/11] could have gone on the 12th, the 13th, the 14th, the 15th, the 16th, the 17th. We can go on and on," he told the jury. He was determined, it seemed, to make himself a martyr.

On May 3, after seven days of deliberations, the jury was deadlocked on the execution question on all three counts against Moussaoui; a pair of jurors held out on two counts, and a lone juror on the third. When Brinkema handed down six consecutive life sentences the next day, she commented that this was an appropriate sentence, one that would deprive Moussaoui of his much-desired martyrdom. For his part, Moussaoui had one last chance to grandstand. "America, you lost [and] I won!" he cried, and clapped his hands. But the criminal justice system could also declare a victory: a high-level terrorism defendant had been successfully tried in civilian court—one that had had, as Brinkema pointed out at the sentencing, to "work around classification issues that were at one point, we all thought, insurmountable."

DESPITE THE ORDERLY CONCLUSION OF the trial, not everyone was convinced that it had been a success. *The Washington Post*, for instance, criticized the trial as too little too late and bemoaned the four and a half years that it had taken to bring it to a conclusion. "Trials of al-Qaeda figures can test the capacity of the American civilian justice system," the paper opined. "The administration was right that some alternative form of military trial for accused terrorists captured abroad was essential."

But as the *Post* pointed out, the military commissions were not ready to take on this task. Instead of relying on the existing court-martial system, the military had attempted to "design a system from scratch"—a project "it has bungled." Since the opening of Guantánamo in January 2002, only four detainees had been charged in military court, and only one had come to trial. And the commissions were still the subject of litigation. Indeed, even as Moussaoui was sentenced, a decision in the case of another Guantánamo detainee was pending before the Supreme Court.

Salim Hamdan was a Yemeni who joined Al Qaeda, became Bin Laden's driver, was captured in Afghanistan in 2001, and arrived in Guantánamo Bay in March 2002. He had filed a habeas suit in US federal court in April 2004, even before the Supreme Court ruled in *Rasul* that detainees had the right to do so. Hamdan's habeas petition came before the DC District Court, which ruled that Hamdan could not be tried in a military commission unless he was first declared not to be a prisoner of war: "Unless and until a competent tribunal determines that Hamdan is not entitled to POW status, he may be tried for the offenses with which he is charged only by court-martial under the Uniform Code of Military Justice." But the appeals court reversed this decision on the grounds that Congress had authorized the military commissions when it authorized the president to use military force against Al Qaeda. Hamdan was an enemy combatant, and the president could order him to stand trial before a military commission.

Hamdan appealed the circuit court decision to the Supreme Court, which agreed to hear the case. Paul Clement, who in June of the previous year had been confirmed as solicitor general, squared off on March 28, 2006, with Neal Katyal, a Georgetown law professor specializing in national security issues who had volunteered to help the military lawyers designated to represent defendants before the commissions. Over the previous eighteen months, he and the military lawyers had prepared a Supreme Court case challenging the commissions as the proper venue for the Hamdan case.

Hamdan had been charged with only one crime: conspiracy. But conspiracy, Katyal pointed out, was not a violation of the laws of war and therefore could not be taken up by a military commission. "The stand alone offense of conspiracy is rejected by international law, because it's too vague," Katyal explained. Rather than targeting individual suspects, "it allows so many individuals to get swept up within its net." At a minimum, Katyal wanted the Supreme Court to order the Bush administration to determine Hamdan's status as either POW or enemy combatant, as it was required to do under Article 5 of the Geneva Conventions.

But Katyal was also challenging whether the military commissions envisioned by the Bush administration should exist at all. "This isn't a challenge to some decision that a court makes," he said. "This is a challenge to the court itself." It was a subject on which he, along with Harvard's Laurence Tribe, had written an influential paper arguing that the commissions hadn't been authorized by Congress and thus violated the Constitution's separation of powers doctrine. The military commission, he said, "is an *ad hoc* trial in which the procedures are all defined with the President." Katyal was challenging (or perhaps inviting) the Court to recognize its own powers and assert its authority rather than deferring to the executive. It was a confrontation, four and a half years after the fact, with the earliest decisions made in the war on terror and thus with the chain of opinions and policies that had followed.

"This is the President invoking an authority that he's exercised in virtually every war that we've had," Clement told the court. But at least some justices were skeptical. Hadn't Congress, by passing the Detainee Treatment Act, negated the prisoner's right to challenge his detention? Didn't that mean that Congress had "deprive[d] this Court of jurisdiction in habeas cases?" Justice Breyer asked. And how exactly did this differ from simply suspending the writ of habeas corpus?

"My view would be that if Congress . . . stumbles upon a suspension of the writ," Clement replied, "that would still be constitutionally valid." Even if the president's ability to close off habeas proceedings was a by-product rather than the direct aim of a policy, especially a policy addressing the "exigencies of 9/11," the Court should not deny it. The government, he argued, should not "have to say or incant any magic words that they are now invoking their power" but should just exercise it, and if habeas corpus is suspended as a result, then that does not invalidate the law granting that power. Holding prisoners indefinitely, without a designated status, was thus legal in the government's view, so long as it was in anticipation of a trial before a military commission. If that inadvertently resulted in the commander in chief's using the authority to suspend a fundamental constitutional right, that might be an unfortunate coincidence, but it did not make the detention unlawful.

The Supreme Court did not buy this argument. On June 29, 2006, in a decision written by Justice John Paul Stevens, it ruled that Congress had not authorized the military commissions, and in setting them up, the president had operated outside the law. For now, military commissions could not "proceed because [their] structure and procedures violate both the UCMJ [Uniform Code of Military Justice] and the four Geneva Conventions signed in 1949." Even if Hamdan were to be designated an enemy combatant, he would still be in legal limbo, because the nation still lacked a legitimate system in which to try him.

"IN THE WAKE OF THIS Court decision, Congress has a choice," said House Majority Leader John Boehner (R-OH) shortly after the ruling was announced. "We can do nothing and allow the terrorists in U.S. custody to go free or to go into a trial meant for American civilians; or we can authorize tribunals for terrorists, find out what they know, and bring them to justice." In early fall, he brought the Military Commissions Act (MCA) to the floor for debate. It was, according to some Republican lawmakers, the "most important measure" of that session of Congress. The debate, much of it heated, centered in part on whether the law would allow detainees to bring habeas petitions in federal court.

As Congress took up this bill, President Bush held a press conference to urge its passage. As part of his pitch, he acknowledged for the first time the existence of the black sites. "A small number of suspected terrorist leaders and operatives captured during the war have been held and questioned outside the United States, in a separate program operated by the Central Intelligence Agency," he said. The black sites, he continued, have been among "the most vital tools in our war against the terrorists," yielding "vital information necessary to do our jobs, and that's [to] protect the American people and our allies." But he did not plan simply to release the captives once interrogators were finished with them, or to let their crimes go unpunished. That's where the proposed law came in. If "Congress acts to authorize the military commissions I have proposed," Bush promised, "the men our intelligence officials believe orchestrated the deaths of nearly 3,000 Americans on September the 11th, 2001, can face justice."

When he signed the bill on October 17, 2006, the president called the MCA "one of the most important pieces of legislation in the war on terror." The procedures set out by Congress for trying Guantá-namo detainees accorded in part with the Uniform Code of Military Justice but differed in significant ways. They would allow coerced confessions to be entered into evidence, so long as the interrogation that had produced them had stopped short of torture or cruel, unusual, or inhumane treatment. The Uniform Code of Military Justice allowed the defendants the right to a speedy trial, whereas the 2006 MCA did not. It allowed hearsay evidence, such as that which might be provided by the witness to an interrogation. And it denied the judiciary the habeas jurisdiction about which the Supreme Court had been so concerned in the Hamdan case. "No court, justice, or judge," it read, "shall have jurisdiction to hear or consider an application for a writ of habeas corpus filed by or on behalf of an alien detained by the United States who has been determined by the United States to have been properly detained as an enemy combatant or is awaiting such determination." Instead, Combatant Status Review Tribunals—established by the Pentagon shortly after the *Rasul* decision and formalized in the 2005 Detainee Treatment Act—would periodically review each detainee's case and make a determination about his status as enemy combatant.

Any progress the Supreme Court had made in reestablishing the rule of law in the war on terror had now been reversed. The MCA effectively nullified the *Hamdan* decision, making explicit what in Clement's argument before the Court had been only implicit: that the prisoners at Guantánamo—and anyone else the government declared an enemy combatant, including (at least according to some lawyers) US citizens—were not entitled to the protections of US or international law. This abrogation of rights was no longer lurking in the shadows of closely held (and shoddily argued) legal memos; nor was it merely something "stumbled upon." It was now the law of the land.

CHAPTER 11

The Crown Jewels

I n July 2005 Congress reauthorized the USA Patriot Act. Among the new provisions was the creation of the National Security Division (NSD) at the Department of Justice. Its job, according to Senator Pat Roberts (R-KS), chair of the Senate Intelligence Committee, would be to "provide crucial legal services and policy guidance for the operational elements of the intelligence community." Senator Carl Levin (D-MI) promised that the assistant attorney general who would run the office would "play a central role in establishing legal policy for the intelligence community."

The NSD was the first new division in the Justice Department since the Civil Rights Division had been established in 1957. It gathered the department's counterterrorism and espionage units, along with its Office of Intelligence and Policy Review (OIPR), under one umbrella, and it added a Law and Policy Section. The reorganization had been proposed by a committee investigating the intelligence failures that had led to the 2003 invasion of Iraq. Laurence Silberman, the judge who had ruled that the FISA wall should be removed, was the cochair of that committee, and the proposal reflected the same conviction that had driven his ruling in that case: that in a post-9/11 world, national security had to take precedence over other concerns, including, if need be, civil liberties. Removing the FISA wall had opened the way for the intelligence side of the department to talk to the criminal side; the NSD set up shop along the border, taking in offices from both sides. But it was clear which function would take precedence. As the press release describing the new Patriot Act explained, the new division would allow the Justice Department to take a leading role in helping to "prevent another terrorist attack on America." Prevention, as it was understood after 9/11, was largely the work of the intelligence community—which had already had at its disposal a lower bar for eavesdropping and other surveillance.

Some lawyers in the Justice Department worried that creating a free-standing intelligence-oriented division would amount to amassing "barbarians at the gate," as one of them told me, empowered to run roughshod over constitutional protections and to turn the Criminal Division into a "stepchild" of the department, less important than the intelligence-driven tasks of the unit. Nor were the lawyers who focused primarily on intelligence satisfied by the change. The OIPR's head, James Baker, would commemorate the demise of his office by handing out plaques with beginning and ending dates of his leadership at the OIPR to his staff at a farewell meeting. Others thought the barbarians were on the other side of the gate—law-enforcement-minded lawyers who would impede intelligence efforts on civil liberties grounds.

It fell to Ken Wainstein, the first assistant attorney general for national security—and a man who had had experience in both worlds, serving in 2002 and 2003 as general counsel and chief of staff to Robert Mueller as he was increasing the FBI's intelligence capabilities and then as the US attorney in DC—to mediate between these forces even as he tried to build his division from scratch. In addition, he had to consider the ongoing protests by groups like the ACLU over policies such as warrantless wiretapping and prisoner detention. At his confirmation hearing, Wainstein acknowledged the difficulty of the job in front of him, but he assured the Senate Select Committee on Intelligence that he and his staff would work hard "to protect our civil liberties, but also be the ally of the investigator."

Wainstein had a chance to make good on his promise almost immediately. He was sworn in on September 28, 2006, a Thursday. On the following Monday he and Matthew Olsen—the close friend he picked to become a deputy assistant attorney general for the new division and who, as head of the Office of Intelligence, would field FISA applications—received a visit from Vito Potenza, the general counsel of the National Security Agency, and Steven Bradbury, head of the Office of Legal Counsel inside the Justice Department. The men told the newcomers about the Terrorist Surveillance Program (TSP), which was still operating outside the authority of the FISA Court and Congress, reauthorized every forty-five days by the signature of the president and the attorney general.

"These were the cards we were dealt," Wainstein told me. And the TSP was only one hand; the detention and prosecution policies were also on the table, and all three were rife with political and legal trouble. Wainstein knew the TSP in particular needed to be placed on sounder legal footing than a discredited memo by John Yoo, the White House's say-so, and two (admittedly high-ranking) signatures. And after Judge Anna Diggs Taylor ruled that the ACLU could challenge the NSA's TSP, he told me, "we knew it was not sustainable." So he and Olsen set about to improve their hand, or at least to play it better.

Wainstein believed it was possible to return oversight of the TSP to the FISA Court, which the system of renewable signatures had cut out of the loop. He assured David Addington, who by then had also concluded that the rogue program could not be sustained, that the FISA process could be made less cumbersome and more adaptable to new technologies that had made the original FISA legislation, passed in 1978, obsolete. The original law, for instance, did not require a FISA warrant for international phone calls transmitted via satellite, as most of them were in 1978. Because intelligence agents could acquire the call directly from the satellite, the surveillance had not taken place on US soil and thus lay outside the purview of FISA. But three decades later most communication traveled via fiber optic cables, which meant that signals could be picked up in the United States, thus constituting the kind of "electronic surveillance" for which FISA required a warrant. Careful legal work by NSD and Office of Legal Counsel lawyers, Wainstein thought, could remedy problems like these.

Late in 2006 the NSD settled upon a case to take before FISC Judge Malcolm Howard. In addition to a two-page list of phone numbers of Al Qaeda suspects, Howard was asked to approve the monitoring of "facilities" located in the United States, which included the switches and servers that routed communications. With Howard's approval, which came on January 10, 2007, the court gave the NSA the legal authority to do what it had been doing all along: sweeping up large amounts of phone and email data from people in the United States. The order also gave the NSA the power to determine whether there was probable cause to target a facility or an individual. Once the agency made that determination, it was free to proceed without returning to the court, so long as it documented its activities, along with the reason for the surveillance. On January 17 Alberto Gonzales informed the Senate Judiciary Committee of Howard's ruling, assuring the senators that from now on, wiretapping would be "conducted subject to the approval of the Foreign Intelligence Surveillance Court." As a result, he continued, "the President has determined not to reauthorize the Terrorist Surveillance Program when the current authorization expires." Within a few months of its birth, the National Security Division had scored an early victory, bringing the rogue wiretapping policy in out of the cold.

IT WAS A WIN-WIN, AT least on the surface. Though the ruling was not without its detractors—Olsen had to field complaints from the agency that the reporting required by Howard's decision was a "massive effort" that compromised its "speed and agility"—these were minor problems compared with the major victory that had been handed to the NSA. The NSD had restored some semblance of FISA oversight, enough to give the program a patina of legitimacy. But the White House had gotten virtually all it had wanted, only now with a court's blessing.

But the good times didn't last long. The Howard order was valid for only ninety days, and the renewal came before a different judge, Roger Vinson. He was troubled by some aspects of the original ruling, especially by the way it had left the NSA in charge of determining probable cause. A judge did have the power to order the surveillance discontinued, but only on the grounds that the NSA's reasoning was insufficient, and the court had no authority to obtain evidence beyond what the NSA provided. With the NSA in charge of what the court knew, all an agent had to do was come up with a plausible story, and the wiretap would remain in place.

Vinson balked. "The clear purpose of [the FISA laws]," he wrote, "is to ensure that . . . surveillances are supported by judicial determinations of probable cause before they commence." That obviously was not the case here. The Howard ruling undermined Congress's intention "to provide an 'external check' on executive branch decisions to collect surveillance." If the president wanted to proceed that way, he should ask Congress to change the laws governing the FISA Court, rather than embed so sweeping a change in a single order. "Until Congress took legislative action," however, "the Court must apply the statute's procedures." Vinson refused to sign the order, suggesting instead that the NSA go back to Howard for another extension while the problems he had flagged were worked out—preferably by changing the law.

Gonzales later confessed to "disappointment" at Vinson's decision. It "confirmed our concern about going to the [FISA Court]," he told an inspector general. Taking the man out of the White House had evidently not taken the White House out of the man.

But Gonzales could not protect his former bosses from the judge's ruling. In May, Vinson approved a version of the renewal that required more frequent and detailed reports than Howard's had, and FISA judges began to apply what the inspector general later called "a more rigorous standard of review" to the NSA's probable cause claims. Under the judges' scrutiny, the NSA could monitor "only a fraction" of the targets it wanted to, which led the White House to do exactly what Vinson had suggested and what Wainstein and Olsen saw as the most viable option for TSP's future: ask Congress to modify the law.

A complete overhaul of FISA was too complex a task to be undertaken in a short time. So the Bush administration drafted a stopgap measure—the Protect America Act. The PAA addressed Vinson's objections directly but perversely. In its original form, FISA defined the "electronic surveillance" that required a warrant as the interception of communication to or from a person in the United States. According to the PAA, however, "nothing in the definition of electronic surveillance . . . shall be construed to encompass surveillance directed at a person reasonably believed to be located outside the United States." It no longer mattered if the person (or facility) was in the United States, or if the target was a US citizen, or even if there was probable cause to think the target was up to no good. So long as it "reasonably believed" that the communication involved someone in a foreign country (a determination the law left in the NSA's hands), the agency could monitor all the phone calls or emails it wanted to, foreign or domestic. And should the agency run into technical difficulties or want information not available from a single phone or email address, the law gave it the authority to demand the "assistance necessary to accomplish the acquisition" from phone and Internet service providers and then to compel the companies to keep the demand a secret.

The bill went to the Senate on August 1 and to the House of Representatives four days later. Only 28 senators and 183 representatives were disturbed enough by its provisions (or willing enough to

THE CROWN JEWELS   149

oppose a bill claiming to protect America) to vote against it, and the measure passed both houses easily. The ACLU immediately weighed in, arguing that the new law "turned FISA on its head," placing the exact communications it was intended to protect—those of US citizens on US soil—out of the law's reach. The law engendered enough bad press to spur the Department of Justice's public relations arm into action. It sent out a press release titled "Dispelling the Myths," in which it assured the public that the new law did not eliminate civil liberties protections. In place of that "myth," the department offered this "fact":

> The new law simply makes clear—consistent with the intent of the Congress that enacted FISA in 1978—that our intelligence community should not have to get bogged down in a court approval process to gather *foreign* intelligence on targets located in *foreign* countries. It does not change the strong protections FISA provides to Americans in the United States— surveillance directed at people in the United States continues to require court approval as it did before.

The press release did not mention the fact that the new law removed from protection any communication that the NSA decided might end up (or start) in a foreign country, which meant that the agency could engage in "reverse targeting," surveillance that had as its primary target someone in the United States whose overseas communications provided the opportunity to avoid FISA scrutiny. It didn't point out that the NSA was still in charge of determining probable cause and that this assessment was not subject to review, or that its newly granted authority to demand records from the telecommunications industry gave it unprecedented access to the emails and phone calls of virtually everyone. Nor did it make clear what many inside the NSD (and the NSA) likely knew: that a goal of the law was to diminish the role of the FISA Court as a firewall between citizens and the security apparatus. The court, which had never turned down a government surveillance request—and had modified only one—prior to 9/11, might not have been much more than a thorn in the NSA's side, an inconvenience rather than an actual impediment to its surveillance ambitions. But even so, the NSD had sided with the NSA, agreeing that even the paperwork requirements were too onerous, that intelligence agents should be left alone to do their jobs the way they thought best, and that those ambitions should not be thwarted by too absolute a reading of the Fourth Amendment.

In June 2008 the provisions of the PAA were incorporated into the FISA Amendments Act (FAA), a more comprehensive modification of the law. "I thought it was a pretty elegant solution to a difficult problem," Ken Wainstein told me. "How to permit targeting of non-US information but to do so by collecting it within the US." He never thought the law would be used to target Americans directly, but he hadn't counted on the NSA's determination, or on its ability to parse the word *intentionally.*

Fixing the FISA mess was hardly the only major challenge Wainstein faced in his first year. Also in need of immediate attention was the Jose Padilla prosecution. The case had made little progress since Gonzales had announced the charges against Padilla in November 2005. Early in 2007, Padilla's lawyers had asked Judge Marcia Cooke to dismiss the case on the grounds that their client was, in the words of one of their forensic experts, "a broken man" as a result of five years of nearly continuous solitary confinement, not to mention the stress positions, sleep deprivation, and threats of immediate execution to which his lawyers claimed he had been subjected. In addition, according to a psychologist, Padilla was suffering from Stockholm syndrome and was now concerned that if his mistreatment was revealed, it might hinder the government's efforts to extract information from him. His lawyers were claiming that Padilla was unable to assist in his own defense and thus was incompetent to stand trial, and that "through its illegal conduct, the government has forfeited its right to prosecute." Judge Cooke disagreed, ruling that Padilla was a "knowing participant" in his defense and suggesting that the questions about his treatment were a "discussion . . . for another day."

In insisting on letting the trial go forward, Cooke was responding not only to the particulars of Padilla's case but also to the mounting pressures on the federal judiciary to show that it could indeed handle terrorism cases. Even some former prosecutors, including the lawyer who had prosecuted the Blind Sheikh, Omar Abdel Rahman, had expressed their doubts, joining with leading national security figures to advocate for the military commissions as the proper venue for these trials. As it had been in the Moussaoui trial, the burden on the federal court system was immense, the stakes as high as they got.

The government's case against Padilla was relatively weak. The evidence revolved around the data sheet found in Afghanistan with his fingerprints on it, allegedly showing that he had applied to join Al Qaeda. But the government's own witness admitted it was hard to tell who actually had signed the document, or when. Moreover, it turned out that only 7 of the 230 intercepted calls that formed the basis of the conspiracy charges actually had Padilla's voice on them, and in none of these had he plotted violence or other terrorist acts.

The witnesses included a CIA agent who appeared disguised behind a fake beard and under a false name to testify that in 2001 an Afghan man had shown up at an American base outside Kandahar in a Toyota pickup and offered a blue binder to forces there, claiming that he had found it in an office "used by Arabs." The binder, according to the agent, held Padilla's "membership application." Beyond that, however, the prosecution team was hard-pressed to substantiate the connection between Padilla and Al Qaeda. They could not find a witness who had seen Padilla at the al-Farooq terrorist camp, which he allegedly attended, instead calling a defendant from an earlier terrorism case to testify in general terms about the camp. But at every opportunity the prosecution mentioned Osama bin Laden—91 times in its opening statement, and more than 100 in closing. As one defense lawyer put it, it was as if "[t]he government is trying to put al-Qaeda on trial."

The tactic succeeded. On August 16, after just over a day of deliberation, the jury found Padilla guilty on three counts of providing material support to terrorists. In January 2008 Judge Cooke sentenced Padilla to seventeen years—less prison time than John Walker Lindh, Abu Ali, and Zacarias Moussaoui had each received. In handing down her relatively lenient sentence, Judge Cooke noted Padilla's treatment in detention and asserted that "the conditions were so harsh" as to "warrant consideration." (Her reasoning did not pass muster with the appeals court, which in 2014 ruled that the sentence was too lenient and sent the case back for reconsideration. Cooke resentenced Padilla to twenty-one years in prison. At resentencing, Cooke, who refused the prosecutors' request for a thirty-year term, said, "I was then, and am now, dismayed by the harshness of Mr. Padilla's prior confinement.")

The trial showed that prosecutors had a way to use the courts effectively to try suspected terrorists. Despite the various interrogation policies that might make evidence inadmissible, despite weaknesses in the case, and despite the fact that he'd been treated more as a war criminal than as a criminal defendant, Padilla had had a trial. He had been held outside the criminal justice system, interrogated as the government saw fit, and denied access to counsel. He had been shattered by the process. The evidence that he had committed the crimes for which he had been charged (which were different from the crimes for which he had first been arrested) was scant. But the prosecution had a formidable weapon, one that could overcome a case weakened by poor evidence or mistreatment: allege a conspiracy with Al Qaeda, or remind a judge and jury of the mayhem and tragedy that Al Qaeda had unleashed (and was threatening to repeat), or invoke the name of Osama bin Laden, and a prosecutor could make the weakness of the case disappear in a miasma of fear. It was what a *New York Times* legal reporter called "a new prosecutorial model in terrorism cases." And under the new model, civilian prosecution was not so much of a threat to the war on terror as it had once seemed.

The completion of the Padilla trial might have kept the military commissions at bay, but only by changing the rules of the game. Now lawyers could prosecute not only plots, attacks, or tangible acts but associations with terrorists, as in the Padilla case, as well as aspirations to commit a terrorist act, as in Moussaoui's. The hand the prosecutors had been dealt included a trump card, and they were not reluctant to play it.

"That was some of the best lawyering I've ever seen," Kenneth Wainstein told his staff in the early fall of 2007. He was talking about the deal that had brought the Terrorist Surveillance Program in out of the cold, the last in a list of accomplishments he cited in celebrating the first anniversary of the NSD's founding. Standing in front of the statues of justice in the Great Hall of the Justice Department, he congratulated his staff for "not just standing, but standing . . . pretty tall and strong." The division was "fulfilling every mission, meeting every expectation, and doing everything in its power to keep our country safe, free, and secure."

BUT THERE WAS ONE SUBJECT that Wainstein did not bring up: Guantánamo. His lawyers had been working with military commissions lawyers to develop cases against Guantánamo detainees, as the Military Commissions Act had required, but so far only one had been resolved—the case of David Hicks, the Australian detainee who pleaded guilty to charges of providing support to terrorism and was recommended for a sentence of seven years in prison, a term that was whittled down by a plea deal to nine months served in Australia, with the guilty plea ultimately being overturned by a Military Commissions appeals court. And as difficult as the commissions process was proving to be, there was another task that was even trickier: the detainees' lawyers, heartened by the Supreme Court decisions in the Rasul and Hamdi cases, had still not given up trying to gain habeas rights for their clients, and the government had still not given up trying to stop them.

The latest skirmish in the habeas wars was a case brought on behalf of six men of Algerian origin, including Lakhdar Boumediene, for whom the case was named. Boumediene was a Bosnian citizen who had been working for the Red Crescent in Sarajevo when, in late 2001, US intelligence caught wind of a plot to blow up the embassy there. He was rounded up along with five other Algerians and, at the request of the United States, taken into Bosnian custody. In January 2002 the Bosnian Supreme Court determined there was no reason to hold the men and ordered their release. When they left prison, they were immediately captured by US forces and sent to Guantánamo. In 2004 the Center for Constitutional Rights filed a suit on behalf of the six men, challenging their detention and demanding a habeas corpus hearing.

The Algerian Six, as they came to be known, had been among the first Guantánamo prisoners to appear in front of the Combatant Status Review Tribunals (CSRTs) established in order to comply with the Supreme Court's ruling in the Hamdi case. The Court had ruled that "a citizen held in the United States as an enemy combatant [must] be given a meaningful opportunity to contest the factual basis for that detention before a neutral decision maker." At their CSRT hearing, the Algerian men were determined to be enemy combatants, a decision they appealed to the DC District Court, the court designated to hear such cases. In the meantime, however, Congress passed the Detainee Treatment Act, which, along with requiring humane treatment of prisoners, had also instructed the courts to throw out all pending habeas cases, on the grounds that the tribunals were an adequate substitute for a court of law. In 2007 Boumediene, whose case had by then been combined with that of another Guantánamo prisoner, Fawzi al-Odah, appealed that provision to the DC Circuit Court. The circuit court upheld the constitutionality of the law's blanket denial of habeas corpus and ordered all the petitioners to seek their remedy with the CSRTs. The detainees appealed this ruling to the Supreme Court, but in April 2007 the court declined to hear the case. The detainees were ordered to take their case back to the circuit court—a court that had already determined that as they were noncitizens held outside the United States, constitutional rights did not apply to them.

The Supreme Court routinely denies *certiorari,* as requests for judicial review are known, and though the disappointed parties routinely ask the Court to reconsider, the Court nearly always refuses these requests. Nevertheless, the detainees' lawyers petitioned the Supreme Court for a rehearing. And as the appeal made its way onto their schedule, the justices received an affidavit by Stephen Abraham, a former military lawyer who had worked on behalf of the government in the CSRTs. In twenty-four blistering paragraphs, he charged that the CSRTs were "an irremediable sham," a claim he substantiated with evidence from his participation in them. Of the pool of judges, lawyers, and "personal representatives," those assigned to the detainees in lieu of defense attorneys, "[f]ew were trained in either the legal or intelligence fields." Moreover, they were arbitrarily assigned to different roles in the hearings, without regard to their background or skills. The information they worked with was "often outdated, often 'generic,' rarely relating to the individual subjects of the CSRTs." Requests for further information were routinely denied—and not because there was no more material to be had. "I was given no assurances that the information provided for my examination represented a complete compilation," Abraham wrote. "On those occasions when I asked [for] a written statement that there was no exculpatory evidence, the requests were summarily denied," leaving Abraham to " 'infer' that no such information existed." And in the few instances in which a tribunal determined that a prisoner was not an enemy combatant (which they did in less than 10 percent of nearly six hundred hearings), a meeting was called to focus on " 'what went wrong.' " It was as if the only possible cause of a negative finding was a flaw in the tribunal's reasoning.

Abraham recounted a hearing in which he and the other two

tribunal members "found the information presented to lack substance. What were purported to be specific statements of fact
lacked even the most fundamental earmarks of objectively credible
evidence." A request for more information was stonewalled, the personal representative "did not participate in any meaningful way,"
and when the panel determined that there was no evidence that
the prisoner was an enemy combatant, the director of the tribunal
program "immediately questioned our findings" and ordered it to
reconsider. The panel stuck to its original finding, and, wrote Abraham, "I was not assigned to another CSRT panel."

Certiorari deliberations are not public, but as legal scholar and
detainee lawyer Jonathan Hafetz reported, many court watchers
"suspected that Justice Kennedy had been moved by [the] new and
devastating critique" delivered by Abraham. What is known is that
in late June 2007, two months after declining to hear the Boumediene case, the Court reversed itself—the first *certiorari* decision to
be overturned in forty years. It placed the Boumediene case on its
docket for the upcoming term.

In December, Seth Waxman, who had served as solicitor general
under Bill Clinton, told the justices that the CSRTs, despite their legislative origin, were nothing more than an ad hoc procedure set in
place by the executive and were certainly no substitute for habeas
corpus. The hearings, after all, took place as Abraham had detailed—
detainees were left without lawyers or access to all the relevant evidence, subject to the caprice of the tribunal. Just as Neal Katyal
had done in *Hamdan*, Waxman pointed out that the lower court—in
this case the DC Circuit—had merely accepted the evidence presented by the government as "accurate" and "sufficient," taking the
executive branch's assertions at face value even though the very purpose of a habeas petition was to challenge those assertions. A genu-
ine habeas court, Waxman pointed out, would weigh the accuracy
and relevance of the evidence to determine whether continued detention was warranted; without this crucial feature, the tribunal could
not be considered an adequate substitute for a court of law.

Paul Clement once again had the task of convincing the justices that enemy combatants, especially noncitizens held outside the nation's borders, had no rights under the US Constitution. Even if they did, he continued, the CSRTs were an adequate substitute for a habeas court. He pointed out that the rules guiding them were "virtually identical" to the army regulations governing the treatment of prisoners of war, which, in turn, were derived from the Geneva Conventions. "The deviations," he argued, "are ones that, we would submit, enhance the rights of the detainees in this particular circumstance." Clement was being disingenuous; after all, as one expert put it, the right to challenge the CSRTs was "limited to whether the CSRTs followed their own procedures, not the substantive determination of whether someone was an 'enemy combatant' or 'no longer an enemy combatant.'" (Clement didn't bother to mention that had the Bush administration decided in 2001 to treat the detainees as POWs, they would not have had the right to habeas in the first place.)

Justice Stephen Breyer was skeptical and offered a hypothetical situation that was barely hypothetical. Let's say you're a Bosnian held by the United States for six years, he told Clement. You go before a tribunal, and it finds you should remain in custody (although still without charges). Now you go before the DC District Court, which is the court reviewing CSRT decisions, and you concede that the tribunal's "procedures are wonderful, and . . . it reached a perfectly good result." But, Breyer continued, you want to say, "'Judge, I don't care how good those procedures are. I'm from Bosnia. I've been here six years. The Constitution of the United States does not give anyone the right to hold me six years in Guantanamo without either charging me or releasing me.' I don't see anything in this CSRT provision that permits" that argument. "So I am asking you," Breyer said to Clement, "where can you make that argument?"

"I'm not sure he can make that argument," Clement replied.

"Exactly," said Breyer. That had been his whole point: that the CSRTs did not address the central issue of habeas—the right to challenge one's detention. As such, they were not an adequate sub-stitute for the habeas courts, no matter how "wonderful" their pro-cedures might be.

Indefinite detention might have been lawyered into legitimacy, but the Supreme Court was evidently unimpressed by the results. On July 12, 2008, in a 5–4 decision written by Justice Anthony Ken-nedy, the Court ruled in favor of Boumediene. Kennedy's opinion took Congress and the president to task. "Protection for the habeas privilege was one of the few safeguards of liberty specified in a Con-stitution that, at the outset, had no Bill of Rights," he wrote. And the fact that the prisoners were being held in Cuba did not abrogate the government's responsibility to provide this safeguard. The base was not US sovereign territory, and the lease between the US and Cuba stipulated that Cuban law did not apply in Guantánamo; that was one of the reasons the island had been so attractive as a prison loca-tion in the first place. But that didn't mean the base was a land of no laws, and there was no doubt which country was in charge. "The Nation's basic charter cannot be contracted away like this," Ken-nedy wrote. "The Constitution grants Congress and the President the power to acquire, dispose of, and govern territory, not the power to decide when and where its terms apply. To hold that the political branches may switch the Constitution on or off at will would lead to a regime in which they, not this Court, say 'what the law is.'" Guan-tánamo was governed by US law, US law required the president to justify a prisoner's detention or release him, and Congress could not legislate away that burden.

The Boumediene case was returned to the DC District Court, which now had the authority to order the release of the Algerian Six, and after reviewing his file, Judge Richard Leon did exactly that for five of them, including Boumediene. Leon felt he had no choice: "To allow enemy combatancy to rest on so thin a reed would be inconsis-tent with this court's obligation; the court must and will grant their petitions and order their release." He cautioned, however, that "this is a unique case. Nobody should be lulled into a false sense that all

THE CROWN JEWELS   159

of the ... cases will look like this one." But even if the rulings by
both courts did not amount to a get-out-of-jail card for the Guantánamo detainees, taken together they comprised a sharp rebuke to
the president and to Congress. When it came to detention, the courts
were insisting on due process. With the conviction of Jose Padilla
and the release of Yaser Hamdi, no more Americans were being
held as enemy combatants. And the detainees at Guantánamo had
gained the right to challenge their imprisonment. The Bush administration's lawyering might have been good, but it was not good
enough to put an end to the oldest democratic right.

CHAPTER 12

That Dog Will
Not Hunt

The most unusual thing about the case argued in federal court in Providence, Rhode Island, on June 19, 2008, was not that the court convening it, the FISA Court of Review, had met only once before in its thirty-year history. It wasn't the way technicians had swept the room for bugs and cut it off from the Internet, turning Courtroom 3 temporarily into a Sensitive Compartmented Information Facility (SCIF). It wasn't the briefcases full of classified information that the three Justice Department lawyers had physically held on to for the hours-long trip from Washington, or even the intrigue surrounding their journey, which had led at least one of them to lie to his wife about his destination that day. And it certainly wasn't the argument itself, in which a government lawyer once again asserted that the war on terror could not be fought without restricting Fourth Amendment rights, while his opponent countered that to take away civil liberties in the name of national security was to compromise the very principles for which the war on terror was being waged.

No, the strangest thing was that the lawyer worrying over

constitutional rights, Marc Zwillinger, was not from the ACLU or the Center for Constitutional Rights; nor was he representing detainees or tortured prisoners. Instead, he represented a large American corporation: the Internet company Yahoo! The issue at hand was a government order forcing Yahoo! to "assist in warrantless surveillance of certain customers" by turning over records of their communications. Yahoo! had so far failed to comply with this order, a defiance that was about to cost the company $250,000 a day in fines. But Zwillinger's argument in court that day wasn't about the cost or difficulty of supplying the government information about the private communications that passed through its servers in California. And it was only a little bit about the consequences to its bottom line should its customers discover the breach. Mostly Yahoo!'s objection rose above petty corporate interests and invoked the basic principles of American jurisprudence. The government, Zwillinger told the three-judge panel, was compelling his company "to participate in surveillance that we believe violates the Constitution of the United States." It was refusing to supply the data on principle. It was evidently one thing for a corporation to amass huge amounts of data on its customers to sell to other corporations—which was, after all, Yahoo!'s business model—and another for that company to be required to provide its information to intelligence agencies.

The Yahoo! case got on the FISCR docket only after the FISA Court itself ruled that Yahoo! had to comply with the order. The judge in that case, Reggie Walton, was not necessarily a friend to the Bush administration. He was best known for denying bail to Vice President Dick Cheney's chief of staff Scooter Libby pending appeal of his conviction for revealing the identity of CIA agent Valerie Plame. Even so, Walton upheld the government's directives, largely with the same reasoning—straight from John Yoo's infamous memos—that had led Laurence Silberman to order the FISA wall removed: foreign intelligence need not be the "primary purpose" of an investigation in order to qualify for an exception to the Fourth Amendment's requirement for warrants, but only, as the Patriot Act had said, a "significant purpose." Even if the emails of US citizens would inevitably be swept up as part of the Yahoo! order, Walton wrote, the president had the "inherent authority" to "conduct warrantless searches to obtain foreign intelligence information." The limits of that authority, he argued, were at stake in the FISA Court hearing. "There are times when there is an inevitable tension between the interests protected by the Fourth Amendment on the one hand and the federal government's obligation to protect the security of the nation on the other hand." Balance between those interests was "not easily achieved," Walton ruled, but in this case, it was easy to see which one should be given more weight; it was, he ruled, permissible for the government to put its thumb on the scale.

In appealing Walton's decision, Zwillinger argued that there was no balance at all in the surveillance order. He ticked off the problems: the lack of FISA Court (or any judicial) oversight of the NSA's assertions that it had probable cause to conduct a search, the lack of any requirement for the orders to directly and explicitly connect the individual customer to a foreign power, the overall "magnitude of the surveillance," the possibility that a clerical error could result in an American citizen being placed under scrutiny without cause or notice, and the lack of meaningful restriction on what the government could do with the information. Even according to the terms of the Protect America Act—under which, Zwillinger said, it seemed that surveillance was "rampant"—the order (and by extension the PAA itself) failed to meet the "reasonableness" standard for warrantless spying and was therefore unconstitutional. In what might have been an unprecedented move, a major American company had gone to court to protect the rights of American citizens.

The FISCR judges were skeptical, especially about Yahoo!'s claim that the surveillance put its customers, and therefore the company, at risk. "If the order is . . . secret, how can you be hurt?" asked Judge Morris Arnold. "The people don't know that they're being monitored in some way. How can you be harmed by it? What's the damage to your consumer?" Judge Ralph Winter made it personal. "It seems to me it would be highly unlikely there would be any consequences if they got . . . into my email account," he said. "Even if I had something on there that would be even in the remotest interest to anyone else, so what?"

"I don't think the case law suggests that an intrusion into someone's privacy, an invasion of their communications, a ransacking of their private papers is harmless if the government makes no further use of it," Zwillinger replied. "There is . . . harm to individuals when their privacy is intruded upon." But for all his eloquence, Zwillinger was only confirming what the judges were suggesting: that Yahoo! was making an argument on an abstract principle about the right to privacy, one that had at least been weakened, if not abandoned entirely—and one that was not necessarily any of Yahoo!'s business.

Zwillinger conceded as much when, near the end of his argument, he brought up a ruling that the Supreme Court had just issued the previous week. "The Boumediene case," he said, "while about habeas was really about reconciling privacy against security. And the question in Boumediene was, is an executive branch only procedure an effective and reasonable substitute for the Constitutional guarantee of habeas; and the Court said it was not." And the reason for its decision, he continued, was that "you cannot trust constitutional rights of this magnitude to a closed and accusatorial process that is run and determined by an interested party"—the attorney general, who, along with the rest of the executive branch, is neither neutral nor disinterested. As for Boumediene, so too for Yahoo!'s customers, said Zwillinger. "The full panoply of the Fourth Amendment protections . . . are not here. They're not being given," he said, but without specifying that a single customer had been harmed, or that Yahoo! had lost a single dime.

Zwillinger did manage to gain a toehold with at least one judge when he mentioned the possibility that a government armed with an order like the one at hand could be "building a database on millions of people in the United States." This, he suggested, "would be a grave harm."

"Now you're getting close to a real harm," agreed Justice Winter. "I will ask the Solicitor General if that's happening."

It was Judge Bruce Selya who posed the question to Acting Solicitor General Gregory Garre. "Incidental collections from U.S. persons"—communications from someone other than the foreign target, including not only his American correspondent but all the contacts of both parties—are "destroyed and not used or disseminated," he assured the judges. "There is no database that is taken from incidental collections." And who would determine which material was used and which was not? The president, of course. "The presumption is . . . the executive acts constitutionally," he said.

That was exactly the opposite of what Zwillinger was arguing: that the Fourth Amendment's very reason for existing was that you couldn't presume "that the executive will always act in a constitutional manner"—especially, he added, when he is "invading [citizens'] right to be secure in their own homes. . . . We cannot vest that discretion in the executive branch."

But while the court at least listened to the constitutional argument, it wasn't buying it. In August, it upheld Walton's decision. The bar for domestic surveillance might once have been high, but that was before 9/11, the Patriot Act, and the Protect America Act, and, wrote Judge Selya, "that dog will not hunt" any longer. "The interest in national security is of the highest order of magnitude," he explained. So long as the "purpose involves some legitimate objective beyond ordinary crime control," he continued, there is a "foreign intelligence exception to the Fourth Amendment's warrant requirement." Under this reasoning, the president's authorization "at least approaches a classic warrant" and thus preserves enough of the intent of the Fourth Amendment to be considered constitutional.

As to the "parade of horribles trotted out by the petitioner" in support of its claim that the president should not simply be trusted, Selya wrote, "it has presented no evidence of any actual harm, any egregious risk of error, or any broad potential for abuse in the circumstances of the instant case." Indeed, Zwillinger's argument

amounted to "little more than a lament about the risk that government officials will not operate in good faith." There was no reason to
think that "placing discretion entirely in the hands of the Executive
Branch without prior judicial involvement" could lead to abuses. The
executive, he was certain, acted constitutionally.

It would be another five years before Americans—including, presumably, Judge Selya and Solicitor General Garre—were alerted by
Edward Snowden to how misplaced their trust was and to just what
that discretion meant to a president who was at that very moment
assembling the database that Garre had assured the court simply
did not exist.

The day the FISCR ruling was handed down, Attorney General
Michael Mukasey came to the NSD himself to congratulate the
team. The decision was a big win, because the government could
now issue similar orders to Apple, Google, and Facebook, which,
having seen what happened to Yahoo!, would not put up any resistance. It also solidified the government's long-standing assertions
about the president's wartime powers.

The Yahoo! case was not the only victory scored by advocates of
executive power in the summer of 2008. During the month between
the Providence hearing and the FISCR's decision, Congress had been
debating the FISA Amendments Act, the more permanent version
of the Protect America Act, which had expired in February. This
time some Democrats fought the bill. Christopher Dodd (D-CT)
objected to a section that granted telecommunications companies
immunity from the lawsuits their customers were already filing in
response to the discovery that their phone companies were providing their call histories to the government. So long as the corporations could show that the president had assured them the spying was
legal, the FAA provided, the companies could not be sued; the act
thus protected the companies from liability while it also protected
the government from the kind of disclosures required in litigation.
For his part, Senator Russ Feingold (D-WI) was concerned that the
proposed law would threaten civil liberties. "It is possible to defend

this country from terrorists while also protecting the rights and freedoms that define our nation," Feingold said. Most of his colleagues
did not agree, however. He and Dodd filibustered the bill, but only
long enough to delay its passage a few weeks.

When the FAA was signed into law on July 10, it still included
the section protecting telecommunications companies from lawsuits. But of more concern to many was the part of the law known
as Section 702. That section made permanent the PAA's lowered
bar for identifying targets, giving the attorney general and the director of national intelligence authority to order surveillance of anyone they thought was a foreigner in a foreign country. As long as
they weren't "intentionally" targeting an American citizen at home
or abroad, or a noncitizen inside the United States, their requested
surveillance would qualify for the warrant exception built into the
original FISA legislation. They would have to notify the court of
the surveillance and submit a report explaining their reasoning.
But the report would be sealed, to be opened only in the case of a
challenge that occurred within thirty days of its submission to the
court—and if the court overturned the order, the surveillance could
continue for sixty days while the government appealed the decision.
And besides, since the only parties that would know of the order
(besides the attorney general, the director of national intelligence,
and the intelligence agents tasked with its enforcement) would be
the now-immunized telecommunications companies, challenges
would likely be few. (Indeed, until January 2014, no firm had challenged an order, and that company, whose name remains classified,
lost in court.)

The FAA not only codified what the government had been doing
all along—spying on American citizens, without warrants or other
restraint—but also added a particularly Orwellian twist, authorizing the spying even as it forbade it. The proposed law prohibited
the attorney general and the director of national intelligence from
intentionally targeting citizens. So if those officials, both members
of the executive branch, claimed that they did not mean to gather

intelligence about the citizen on the American end of an email, or if they were mistaken in their belief that the target was a noncitizen, still they had the data, and it could be assembled into the database that, the new solicitor general, Gregory Garre, assured the review court, the government was not building. And so long as the attorney general and the director of national intelligence swore to the purity of their intentions in a sealed affidavit that the FISA Court could not read unless the order was challenged within a month (and consider how difficult it would be for anyone to challenge what the attorney general or the director of national intelligence said was inside their heads), it would all, under the FAA, be perfectly legal.

Some legislators had noticed this. Congresswoman Jackie Speier (D-CA), for example, took to the House floor to denounce the bill in terms that would prove prescient. "The proposed FISA law protects no one other than the administration and those within it who may use this new-found power to snoop and spy in areas where they have no business looking," she said. "The truth is, any American will subject their phone and e-mail conversations to the broad government surveillance web simply by calling a son or daughter studying abroad, sending an e-mail to a foreign relative, even calling an American company whose customer service center is located overseas." The ACLU noticed, too. Within hours of Bush's signing, it had filed its complaint challenging the new piece of legislation. The suit—which became known as *Amnesty v. Clapper*—alleged that the FAA "allows the mass acquisition of U.S. citizens' and residents' international communications. In some circumstances, it allows the warrantless acquisition of purely domestic communications as well," because some domestic emails or phone calls pass through servers in foreign countries, at which point they can be considered foreign. Because Amnesty International and other nongovernmental organizations that joined the ACLU suit represent "people the U.S. Government believes or believed to be associated with terrorist organizations," they would have to assume their communications were being intercepted and thus would have to meet with their clients in person or buy expensive encryption programs—burdens that could chill their ability to do their work, regardless of what the president and his men intended. The FAA, according to the complaint, "violates the First and Fourth Amendments to the U.S. Constitution," and by giving so much power to the executive branch, it also violated "the principle of separation of powers." The ACLU asked the Southern District of New York's federal court to strike down the new law.

It was a bold request. For ACLU lawyer Jameel Jaffer, who would argue the case, the concerns raised by the FAA went beyond the obvious surveillance excesses and to the heart of the balance of power problems that had developed in the name of national security. As Jaffer explained to me, "The extent of executive power, and the extent to which it was unsupervised," was once again apparent in "narrowing dramatically the authority of the courts to oversee how that power was going to be used." The FISA Court was now overseeing general procedures rather than ruling on specific cases, just as the courts had either been pushed aside or had reneged on oversight of detention and interrogation issues. The suit would give the federal judges of the Southern District one more chance to reverse that trend. Jaffer hoped that this time they'd take it.

ONE OTHER PROMINENT PUBLIC FIGURE registered his dismay over the FAA. He was a senator from Illinois, and by July 2008 it appeared he would be the Democratic candidate for president. In February, during the first attempt to replace the Protect America Act, Barack Obama had come out against the new law. But now, he said, he had become convinced that "given the legitimate threats we face, providing effective intelligence collection tools with appropriate safeguards is too important to delay." He said he would support the bill, but "with a firm pledge that as President, I will carefully monitor the program" that had evolved from the Terrorist Suveillance Program into what became known as the Section 702 program under the FAA.

This wasn't the only controversial policy Obama would have to monitor after he took office in January 2009. He had to keep an eye on Guantánamo in the aftermath of the *Boumediene* decision, on the lawyers and judges still struggling to sort out how to prosecute terrorists who had been implicated by tortured witnesses and who had sometimes been tortured themselves, and on all the other fallout of the intelligence-first policies that had been put into place after 9/11. And as if that were not enough, the struggle Obama was inheriting had entered a new phase, one that as a former law professor he would have to have noticed: as the rogue policies came out of the shadows, they were making their way into the very institutions in which justice was sought and meted out, and on whose fairness and devotion to the rule of law the society depends.

PART III

THE LONG GAME

CHAPTER 13

A New Beginning

On January 15, 2009, just a few days before Barack Obama was sworn in for his first term, Steven Bradbury, who had headed the DOJ's Office of Legal Counsel for three and a half years, issued a "Memorandum for the Files." Over eleven pages, he repudiated the work of John Yoo and the other assistant attorneys general who had once asserted that the president's wartime powers were absolute and extensive—that, for instance, "Congress may no more regulate the President's ability to detain enemy combatants than it may regulate his ability to direct troop movements on the battlefield." The war on terror might have been urgent and its venues unconventional and diverse, he wrote, but that did not justify recasting detention, imprisonment, adjudication, and surveillance as areas over which Congress and the courts had no jurisdiction.

It's not clear why Bradbury felt the need to write the memo, which was addressed to no one and destined, as its title said, for the file cabinet. Certainly it wasn't to officially withdraw the opinions; the OLC had, as Bradbury pointed out, "already acknowledged the doubtful nature of these propositions" and had not relied on them since 2003. Nor was it to excoriate Yoo and his comrades, whom Bradbury took pains to excuse. They had, after all, been taking up "novel and complex legal questions in a time of great danger and under extraordinary time pressure," and he did not intend to "suggest in any way that [they] did not satisfy all the applicable standards of professional responsibility." Perhaps Bradbury was only trying to leave a message for his successors in case they had missed the stories about the dubious memos, or to inform future historians that the propositions had been isolated incidents of bad legal opinions made under great pressures, or to hope that emphatic candor would head off uncomfortable inquiries or even prosecution.

Whatever his motivation, Bradbury's memo served (and continues to serve) as a comprehensive summary of the slow-motion constitutional crisis that had unfolded in plain view over the past eight years. Taken together with an inquiry launched by Attorney General Michael Mukasey into the CIA's destruction of videotaped torture sessions of Abu Zubaydah and another detainee, it signaled a willingness on the part of the Bush administration to acknowledge in its waning days that something had gone terribly awry. It was too late for the White House to do much about it besides leave memos for posterity or make inquiries that might (although they never did) result in charges of obstruction of justice. The damage had been done. It would be up to the Obama administration to determine its extent—and to decide what, if anything, to do about it.

A WEEK LATER, AND TWO days after his inauguration, President Obama issued an executive order declaring torture illegal and starting a process to close Guantánamo and set up a new detention policy. Henceforth, he said, individuals in US custody in an armed conflict would not be "subjected to violence to life and person (including murder of all kinds, mutilation, cruel treatment, and torture), nor to outrages upon personal dignity (including humiliating and degrading treatment)." He suspended the military commissions adjudicating the detainee cases; no new charges would be lodged, and all pending cases would be paused until the new administration had decided if there was a better way to utilize commissions and, if so, how. And Guantánamo would be closed within the year.

As unambiguous as Obama's rejection of these policies was, he seemed at the outset to be averse to rounding up their perpetrators. Though he didn't "believe that anybody is above the law," he said, when it came to "interrogations, detentions, and so forth," he was not interested in dwelling on the past.

And so if Bradbury was trying to head off legal action against himself or his predecessors, he needn't have worried. The new administration's focus would be on reform rather than redress, and there was certainly plenty to reform. The ship of justice needed to be righted, and the man he hired to take its helm was a man who had plied these waters before, as a prosecutor, a judge, a US attorney, and most recently as a deputy attorney general during Bill Clinton's second term. Eric Holder had been born in the Bronx, raised in Queens, and educated at New York's elite Stuyvesant High School, where he was among the few black students. He cocaptained Stuyvesant's basketball team, which lost twelve of its fourteen games, many by wide margins. His capacity for absorbing pounding opposition had paid off as he made his way up the career ladder, and he soon acquired a reputation as a tough prosecutor, especially when it came to cases of political corruption.

Holder, who had worked in private practice during the Bush years, had not kept his opinion of those years a secret during the Obama campaign. "We have . . . lost our way with respect to [our] commitment to the Constitution and the rule of law," he told the American Constitution Society in June 2008, shortly after the Supreme Court had granted Boumediene his habeas rights. "Our government authorized the use of torture, approved of secret electronic surveillance of American citizens, secretly detained American citizens without due process of law, denied the writ of habeas corpus to hundreds of accused enemy combatants, and authorized the use of procedures that violate both international law and the United States Constitution." For all this abuse of power and contempt for the law, he continued, "the American people are owe[d] a reckoning. . . . We as Americans must stand up and recognize the mistakes that we have made, and we as Americans together must begin the process of correcting those errors as we have in the past."

Comments like this must have heartened those eager for an attorney general who would be willing to break ranks with the president in order to protect the Constitution, including the senators who had to vote to confirm his nomination to the post. They included Senator Chuck Schumer (D-NY), who had previously decried the "rancid politicization" of the attorney general post, especially when it was held by the "blind loyalist" Alberto Gonzales. Arlen Specter (R-PA) echoed Schumer, citing the need for an attorney general who would be "independent . . . and uphold the rule of law." Patrick Leahy (D-VT), chair of the Judiciary Committee, started off the hearing by asking Holder whether waterboarding was torture and therefore illegal.

Holder was unambiguous in his answer. "I agree with you, Mr. Chairman," he said. "Waterboarding is torture."

Leahy also asked whether the president could, by virtue of his role as commander in chief, "immunize acts of torture," a concern echoed by Senator Orrin Hatch (R-UT), who asked about the FISA laws.

"No one is above the law," Holder answered, not even the president, and as "the people's lawyer," the attorney general's job was to keep the president in line with the law. "I am not a part of the president's team in the way that another cabinet office is," he told the senators. "There has to be a distance between me and the president."

But though he gave these assurances, he also hinted that there were limits to how much he would part with the past and how much legal action, if any, he would take against those who had engaged in illegal activities. "The decisions that were made by the prior administration were difficult ones," he told the senators. "It is an easy thing in some ways to look and in hindsight be critical of the decisions that they made." But the nation was at war, he said, and had been at least since the 1998 bombings of the two US embassies in East Africa. The Bush administration was correct to view the Justice Department as a crucial ally in the war on terror, and he vowed to use "every available tactic to defeat our adversaries."

Holder also declined to condemn certain prior policies outright. The FISA Amendments Act was constitutional, he said, and surely would lead to better policies than those the president had implemented without congressional authorization. Torture was illegal, but the people who had carried it out under the guidance of the OLC's opinions were not criminally culpable. Guantánamo had to be closed, but military commissions should continue, he said— although with more due process guarantees in place. And it was possible that detainees who "are too dangerous but nevertheless cannot be tried" might have to continue to be held indefinitely. *Reckoning* apparently meant one thing in a speech to incensed fellow lawyers, and another in testimony to nervous senators. And as the Obama administration unfolded, it would be the latter version that prevailed.

THE SENATE CONFIRMED HOLDER BY a 75–21 vote. His moderate approach had gained bipartisan support, and with it a mandate to address the issues the senators had asked him about at the hearing, including detention of prisoners at Guantánamo, warrantless surveillance under FISA, ongoing terrorism investigations and prosecutions, and the lingering shadow of torture. Most of these reforms would fall to the National Security Division. Holder needed someone to run the NSD who could help provide a forceful yet pragmatic administrative backing for his agenda. For this, he turned to David Kris.

Although he had been a critic of the Bush administration after his departure from the Justice Department, Kris was not a firebrand, choosing instead to express his concerns in the measured tones of law review articles. Neither was he a Fourth Amendment absolutist, preferring to try to safeguard its protections while carving out exceptions in the name of national security. That's exactly what he had intended to accomplish by advocating for the removal of the FISA wall. And, he told senators in his confirmation hearing, he would do more to develop and maximize "the potential synergies between its criminal lawyers and its intelligence lawyers." Interlacing his fingers to illustrate his point, he would later describe how he would make all units of the Justice Department available to discuss strategy and make decisions about arrests and prosecutions. Everyone was responsible in Kris's vision; the whole department had to be able to function as one entity.

Kris sailed through his confirmation and quickly began seeking the synergies he'd described. Some of the work had already been done. Now that the FISA wall was down, for instance, NSD lawyers had open access to the FBI building, something they'd lacked in the past. More substantively, Kris cultivated relationships with leaders at the FBI and the CIA, offered advice and opinions to the general counsels of those agencies (at times supplanting the OLC in these efforts), and inserted his lawyers into ongoing prosecutions. Though he ruffled some feathers, especially among local federal prosecutors who felt the NSD was treading on their turf, he was able to assemble a team and undertake the administrative reforms Holder had in mind.

But as much as Kris was working toward integration, there was discord within the ranks—especially over the transparency that Obama had promised to the American people. Some of the conflict was forced into the open when a judge's order, issued in the waning days of the Bush presidency, came due. According to the ruling, the Justice Department was supposed to release documents on torture to satisfy a Freedom of Information Act (FOIA) request filed by the ACLU. Obama had committed his administration to transparency, and Holder wanted to comply with the judge's order, but some members of the new administration were balking—notably the new director of the CIA, Leon Panetta, who worried that releasing the material would set a dangerous precedent.

Holder won this battle. Jameel Jaffer, one of the ACLU lawyers who had signed the FOIA request nearly six years before, recalls being elated when the first of the documents was released on April 16. They included the Yoo memo that laid out in excruciating detail the particulars of the torture techniques and the legal justifications for them that had later been repudiated by Jack Goldsmith. It was the first time the American public saw exactly what the CIA interrogation program included, and it was also the first time they got to see the memos that had replaced Yoo's. Written by Steven Bradbury in 2005, these papers parsed the differences between "severe" and "serious" pain, and between "torture" and "cruel and inhuman treatment," in the same detached language Yoo had used. They asserted that, for example, shackling a prisoner in a standing position so he could not sleep did not constitute cruel and inhuman treatment because that standard was met only when long-term impairment or injury occurred, which in the case of the shackled prisoner meant edema or blood clots, which could occur only when the prisoner's legs gave out, which the interrogator would immediately know because the prisoner would then "try to support his weight with the shackles suspended from the ceiling," at which point "the application of the technique would be adjusted or terminated," thus allowing the legs "to continue to sustain the detainee's weight and enable him to walk." In 2008 President Bush had vetoed a bill designed to ban further uses of harsh interrogation techniques; they might have been declared off-limits, but they still weren't illegal.

The ACLU was now bringing into public view the full record of the Bush administration's attempt to fashion law that made torture legal. Their continuing efforts, along with the new president's promise to change course, opened the way to bringing to justice those who had broken the laws against torture and violated the Fourth Amendment, the Fifth Amendment, and the Eighth Amendment to the Constitution. These were criminal acts, and the ACLU was hopeful that the new administration would investigate and prosecute them accordingly. Hopes for accountability were bolstered when Holder decided to keep open Mukasey's inquiry into the destruction of the CIA interrogation tapes and to give John Durham, the lawyer running that investigation, the additional task of looking into CIA mistreatment of prisoners, which had allegedly resulted in the deaths of over one hundred detainees.

Holder's enlargement of Durham's portfolio was not popular at the White House, at least not according to press secretary Robert Gibbs, who told the press corps that "a hefty litigation looking backward is not what we believe is in the country's best interest." And Obama would have preferred the focus to be on the reforms suggested by the task force on interrogation policy that he created with his first executive order, which recommended creating a specialized interrogation group at the FBI that would determine the intelligence value of detainees, where they should be detained, and, guided by the Army Field Manual and civilian law (and ultimately by its own practices manual), how to treat them lawfully. The day after the release of the new torture memos, he made clear his preference for the future over the past, and for reform over retribution, announcing that no matter what else happened, the interrogators would be protected from legal sanction. Whatever Holder might have thought, it was left to him to explain his boss's decision that CIA officers "who acted reasonably and relied in good faith on authoritative legal advice from the Justice Department that their conduct was lawful" would not be prosecuted, and the Justice Department would foot the bill for CIA officers facing legal proceedings in the United States or in foreign countries. The torture memos might have been discredited, but they would still provide legal cover for the torturers, and the people who wrote them would not be punished.

Three days after the release of the memos, the president went out of his way—to Langley, Virginia—to make sure CIA employees knew he had their backs. He wanted them to understand that he had released the documents reluctantly and only because of how difficult it would have been "to mount an effective legal defense" to the FOIA order. He told them that he might have tried but for "the fact that so much of the information was public" already, especially after the publication that month of a 2007 report on detainee treatment at the CIA's hands by the International Committee of the Red Cross. He also offered as reassurance his choice of two ex-CIA men—John Brennan, a former analyst and agent, and Robert Gates, a former director of the agency—as his counterterrorism adviser and his secretary of defense, respectively. The CIA would be safe not only from prosecution for past actions, the president seemed to be implying, but also from radical change in the future.

Obama also refused to take a strong lead in another part of the ACLU's FOIA case, this one regarding photographs of prisoner abuse at the hands of the US military at sites other than Abu Ghraib, which a court had ordered be released to the ACLU. In October, with the support of the military as well as Iraqi prime minister Nouri al-Maliki, Congress passed a law, introduced by Senators John McCain, Joe Lieberman, and Lindsey Graham, stating that if the "Secretary of Defense determines that disclosure of [a] photograph would endanger citizens of the United States, or members of the United States Armed Forces, or employees of the United States Government deployed outside the United States," he could keep it out of public view. In December the Supreme Court ruled that the new law required a reconsideration of the ACLU's case and remanded it back to the circuit court for another look in light of the new legislation. For the moment, at least, the military would be spared this scrutiny, and the Obama administration another fight over how deep into the past it should dig, and what to do with whatever it might find there.

Another court ruling also helped the new president to avoid a backward look—or, as the ACLU might have put it, to avoid a legal accounting. In 2007 the ACLU had filed a civil suit against Jeppesen Dataplan, an aviation and marine support company that, the lawsuit alleged, had provided logistical support to the CIA's efforts to fly detainees to the black sites for interrogation. The suit charged that Jeppesen knew that the CIA was torturing prisoners and thus was an accessory to a crime. Testimony was bound to bring even more details of the rendition and torture programs into the public record, but in March 2009 that prospect was quashed by a federal district court, which dismissed the complaint for exactly that reason, citing the state secrets rule, which allows the suppression of evidence that would compromise national security. A three-judge appeals court reversed this ruling, arguing that it "effectively cordon[ed] off all secret government actions from judicial scrutiny, immunizing the CIA and its partners from the demands and limits of the law," and ordered further consideration of which evidence merited state secrets protection. Before that could happen, however, the government appealed to the full Ninth Circuit, which reversed the reversal, thereby affirming the initial dismissal by the district court. According to the appeals court opinion, "Further litigation presents an unacceptable risk of disclosure of state secrets no matter what legal or factual theories Jeppesen would choose to advance during a defense." The Supreme Court declined to review this ruling; whatever details of past abuses the lawsuit might have yielded would remain hidden from public view.

Like his vow of transparency, President Obama's intention to reform detention policy quickly came to look different in practice from how it had sounded on the campaign trail. The DC District Court had issued the Justice Department a deadline of March 13, 2009, to clarify its position with respect to the habeas petitions filed by Guantánamo prisoners in the wake of the *Boumediene* decision. When the Justice Department filed the requested brief, the White House issued a press release announcing a departure from the previous policy. The decision about whom to imprison "does not rely on the President's authority as Commander-in-Chief independent of Congress's specific authorization," it said. People would be detained only when evidence that they "supported al Qaeda or the Taliban . . . was substantial." And, the press release said, the brief "does not employ the phrase 'enemy combatant.'"

But the reality was more complicated, and less of a departure from the past, than the public statement indicated. The brief continued to cite the Authorization for Use of Military Force as grounds for expanding the reach of the war on terror beyond Afghanistan and beyond Al Qaeda and the Taliban. More prisoners would undoubtedly be taken, but the brief readily conceded that the government still had no idea how to define "substantial support" to terrorism when it came to prisoners already in captivity, let alone for those who might be rounded up in the future. The administration had undertaken "a forward-looking multi-agency effort . . . to develop a comprehensive detention policy," but until it completed its work, the question would remain open. In the meantime, no matter what they were called, the detainees would continue to be detained.

That multiagency effort was the result of a pair of executive orders Obama had issued in his second day in office. Each order had spawned its own task force, one to look specifically at Guantánamo and the other to figure out what to do in the future as the war on terror (a term the administration would eventually abandon, even as it continued to fight it) expanded and took more prisoners. The sixty-member committee looking into the fate of the 241 remaining Guantánamo detainees was headed by Matthew Olsen, the lawyer Wainstein had brought in three years earlier to help reform FISA operations at the DOJ. (The Bush administration had reviewed the cases of the detainees and determined that 532 of the original 779 were eligible for release—to their home countries or to a third country willing to take them—as they no longer posed a danger to the United States.) Given Obama's promise to close Guantánamo within a year, and the political and strategic stakes of the possibility that released detainees might turn to terrorism, their job—to determine how to decide who should be released, who should be prosecuted, and who among those who could not be prosecuted was too danger-ous to let go—was daunting. Among other difficulties, they had few materials to work with. The Bush administration had not assembled dossiers on many of the prisoners, so Olsen's task force had to gather data from intelligence and law enforcement agencies at home and abroad before many of the reviews could begin. The task was made even more formidable by Olsen's insistence on getting his task force to come to a unanimous decision about each detainee.

The other task force, the one focusing on the future, had to figure out what to do about the military commissions. Obama's suspension of the trial boards was no great loss: they had managed only three convictions in seven years and in the meantime had sown discontent among the participants. Moreover, there was Stephen Abraham, the disgruntled member of the CSRT who had influenced the Supreme Court to hear the Boumediene case. Several others, including the top official in charge of the commissions, Colonel Morris Davis, had resigned in protest—in Davis's case, over the attempts of his supe-riors to use evidence obtained by torture in the proceedings against the detainees. Even so, it was not yet clear if the program was at an end or only on hiatus. As much as they expressed distaste for the proceedings, Holder had nodded to the possibility of future military commissions in his confirmation hearings, and Obama had men-tioned them as viable options in his presidential campaign.

According to the executive order, the task force was to be run by two people, one from the Justice Department, the other from the Defense Department. Holder appointed Brad Wiegmann, a quiet-spoken career government lawyer with a studious demeanor. A graduate of Harvard Law School, he had a deep familiarity with the legal concerns of government agencies, having worked at the State Department, at the National Security Council, and at Defense. The Pentagon sent a career army lawyer, Colonel Mark Martins, a fast-talking, ambitious Harvard Law graduate who had served as Gen-eral David Petraeus's legal adviser in Iraq. Martins turned out to be instrumental in resuscitating and reforming the military commissions system.

The task force would not release its report until August—but on May 21, Obama gave a speech at the National Archives signaling that the commissions would be revived. The previous administration had made a "series of hasty decisions . . . based on fear rather than foresight," he said, and as a result the country had been led "off course." He intended to set it back on the right path, not only by shifting his military strategy but by "enlist[ing] the power of our most fundamental values," starting with the abolition of torture, then moving toward ending the "misguided experiment" at Guantánamo. To accomplish this goal, he had decided to sort the remaining detainees into five categories. Some would be prosecuted in federal court, some would be released in accordance with court orders already rendered, and some would be transferred to other countries for "detention and rehabilitation." But some would be tried in front of military commissions, and still others, "who cannot be prosecuted for past crimes, in some cases because evidence may be tainted, but who nonetheless pose a threat to the security of the United States," would continue to be detained, indefinitely if necessary.

Obama was at pains to reassure Americans that these changes would not put them at risk. He urged people to resist the inevitable fear-mongering in "30-second commercials," pointing out that the previous administration had released more than five hundred detainees with little difficulty and reminding listeners that no one had ever escaped from an American Supermax prison, where the convicted detainees and those held indefinitely were likely to end up. And he repeatedly assured them, "I am not going to release individuals who endanger the American people."

But Obama also had to reassure the voters who had heard his campaign position as a promise to put an end to these policies completely. He clarified that the justification for indefinite detention was that those prisoners "remain at war with the United States."

They were still outside the protections due to prisoners of war and could be kept until hostilities were over. It was the same conclusion reached by George W. Bush: indefinite detention was a necessity for the safety of the nation. As for restoring the commissions, "some have suggested that this represents a reversal on my part," but, he said, he had been opposed only to the way the legislation establishing them had "failed to establish a legitimate legal framework, with the kind of meaningful due process rights for the accused that could stand up on appeal." Bring the commissions "in line with the rule of law," he said, and the problem would be solved.

To this end, he would propose legislation under which commissions would "no longer permit [as] evidence . . . statements that have been obtained using cruel, inhuman, or degrading interrogation methods." The new Military Commissions Act would, at least according to the Justice Department, provide "a legal framework that will restore military commissions as a legitimate forum for prosecutions." Detainees would have "greater latitude in selecting their own counsel" and would be able to challenge hearsay evidence. But Obama made no promises that counsel for the defense would have access to documents equal to that of the prosecution. Nor would the commissions adopt the federal rules of procedure and evidence, or the transparency of civilian courts—provisions whose absence had spurred the objections to the commissions in the first place. Congress approved the bill in October. Obama had been president for only nine months, but already he was showing a tendency that would come to define his presidency: capitulating to practical and political necessity.

The ACLU had registered its reaction immediately after the National Archives speech, taking out a full-page ad in *The New York Times* that showed Obama's iconic campaign portrait morphing into a photo of George Bush and asking in headline type, "What will it be Mr. President? Change or more of the Same?" But the direction had been set. Change, if it came, would come incrementally and only after long discussion. Those who expected radical action to follow on Obama's election would be disappointed. He was going to be not a decider but a deliberator. His distaste for Guantánamo and all that it represented had turned into ambivalence, and so the detention center would remain open, detentions would remain indefinite, and those who had created the torture policy or participated in its implementation would remain unpunished.

CHAPTER 14

Winning for Losing

The courtroom on the twenty-first floor of the Daniel Patrick Moynihan Federal Courthouse in lower Manhattan filled up slowly the morning of October 12, 2010. All entrants, including the defense attorneys, were required to pass through two metal detectors—one in the lobby and another at the doors to Judge Lewis Kaplan's courtroom. Once visitors were inside, seats were hard to come by—in part because nearly half the seats available to the public were reserved for family members of the 224 Africans and Americans who had been killed in the bombings of the US embassies in Tanzania and Kenya in 1998. Also in attendance were a number of the survivors, some of whom had been among the thousands wounded in the attacks. For some of this audience, it was a second trial: they'd also witnessed the convictions of four of the conspirators in June 2001.

This time around the defendant was Ahmed Ghailani, one of twenty-one individuals (including Osama bin Laden) indicted for the bombings. Ghailani, who had been twenty-four in 1998 and even

now still had the face of a teenager, stood accused of helping to pro-
cure the explosives for the Tanzania attack. Apprehended in 2004
along with twelve other suspected Al Qaeda members in a house in
the northwestern tribal areas of Pakistan, Ghailani had been tortured at black sites, where he was held until being moved to Guantánamo two years later. A devastating act of violence, a defendant
renditioned, evidence obtained through torture: Ghailani presented
the ideal opportunity for Holder to demonstrate what he already felt
confident of—that despite these obstacles, the civilian courts could
successfully prosecute Guantánamo detainees accused of lethal attacks on the United States.

Jury selection had been swift, with the judge often asking the jury
pool questions en masse rather than individually. The resulting jury,
which was kept anonymous, represented a range of professions,
ages, races, and socioeconomic levels. The jurors were instructed
to prepare for a five-month trial—through Thanksgiving, Christmas, even Valentine's Day. Their first glimpse of the defendant
came when he was brought into the courtroom by a US marshal and
flanked by his four attorneys. Wearing a powder blue sweater, he
was standing quietly with his back to the observers when a woman
at the front of the gallery, just behind the wooden rail, called his
name. "Ahmed," she said. "Ahmed, it's me, Dr. Porterfield." Katherine Porterfield was a clinical psychologist who had evaluated
Ghailani at the request of his defense team. The defendant turned
and gave her a wide smile. The woman approached, along with a
pair of uniformed soldiers. The four exchanged hellos and hugs and
stood together until the judge appeared and called the court into
session.

The moment passed quickly, but the jury had seen something
that could not have made the prosecution happy: that the defendant was human, not a monster, and that people—the lawyers who
had represented him before the military commission at Guantánamo, his civilian lawyers now preparing their case, and the psychologist working with them—cared for him, and that he returned

their affection. The potential perils of a trial by jury, at least for the prosecution, were already in evidence.

THE GHAILANI TRIAL WAS NOT the only terrorism prosecution that was making its way through federal court in 2010. Najibullah Zazi, an Afghan American living in Aurora, Colorado, had been under FBI surveillance since shortly after his return in January 2009 from a four-month stay in Pakistan, where he had trained with Al Qaeda. Agents following him and listening in on his phone calls learned that he had bought various explosive agents and was planning, along with others, to detonate suicide bombs on the New York City subway. On September 8 he drove a rented car to New York. On the FBI's request, local police stopped him at the George Washington Bridge for what they described as a random drug search. After they found no contraband in the car (it later turned out that explosives were hidden in a suitcase in the trunk), Zazi was let go. But the search—combined with a phone call that a New York imam had made to Zazi, alerting him to the fact that the authorities were watching—spooked him, and he returned to Colorado without carrying out the plot.

He was arrested on September 19, and in January 2010 he pleaded guilty to conspiracy and providing material support to a terrorist organization. As the Ghailani trial got under way, Zazi was awaiting sentencing in the Metropolitan Detention Center in Brooklyn, just a few miles from the Moynihan building. His two coconspirators, their arrests based in part on Zazi's statements to the FBI, were being held without bail pending a trial. Three more men, including the imam and Zazi's father, were also charged with crimes related to the foiled subway plot.

The month after Zazi's arrest in Colorado, Chicago authorities indicted David Headley, an American conspirator in the 2008 terrorist bombing in Mumbai and in threats against the Danish newspaper that had published cartoons of Muhammad. Born Daood

Sayed Gilani, Headley was a former DEA informant who had been arrested on drug charges and who had begun involving himself with Lashkar-e-Taiba—a Pakistani terrorist group affiliated with Al Qaeda—in 2000, when the DEA sent him to Pakistan on an undercover operation to bust heroin traffickers. In 2002 he trained in a Lashkar camp in Pakistan. In 2005 he adopted his mother's Western-sounding name, and in early 2006 he began working with Pakistani intelligence. He was finally arrested at O'Hare International Airport in October 2009 while on his way back to Pakistan. He pleaded guilty in March 2010 and, like Zazi, was in prison awaiting sentencing at the time of the Ghailani trial.

On Christmas Day 2009, Nigerian-born Umar Farouk Abdulmutallab was apprehended after he attempted to set off a bomb in an airplane as it approached the Detroit airport. Abdulmutallab had boarded the plane in Amsterdam with the device sewn into his underpants. When he ignited it, it did not explode. The fire was quickly extinguished, and Abdulmutallab, who soon became known as the underwear bomber, was subdued by passengers. He was arraigned on federal charges while still in his hospital bed and was in prison awaiting trial as the Ghailani trial got under way.

And in May 2010 the Customs and Border Patrol arrested Faisal Shahzad aboard a Dubai-bound plane at JFK International Airport after he had left a car packed with propane and poised to explode in Times Square. Shahzad was a thirty-year-old Pakistani immigrant who had been naturalized as a US citizen in April 2009. He quit his job as a financial analyst in June 2009 and traveled to Pakistan regularly. In July 2009 he went to Peshawar, where his parents lived, and from there traveled to a terrorist training camp in Waziristan. He had returned from his most recent trip to Pakistan in February 2010. Weeks later he bought an SUV with cash and assembled the car bomb. Shahzad pleaded guilty to all ten charges against him. Just the week before the Ghailani trial started, he was sent to the Supermax prison in Florence, Colorado, for the rest of his life.

These cases were a powerful vindication for Holder's contention that the civilian courts were the proper venue for terrorism cases. They demonstrated that terrorists could be charged, convicted, and sentenced for their crimes. But they did not settle the question of what would happen when defense lawyers began to challenge remote testimony or hearsay or evidence obtained through illegal wiretaps or torture, or when a prosecution's case depended on classified information—all problems that the military commissions were able to sidestep. So the Ghailani case would give Holder's Department of Justice its first real opportunity to showcase its abilities to bring terrorists—even those being held at Guantánamo—to justice in accordance with the principles and guarantees of the Constitution. In short, much was riding on the Ghailani trial.

A year before the trial began, and three weeks after the passage of the new Military Commissions Act, a confident Holder had taken the podium in the briefing room of the Department of Justice. The date was propitious: November 13, 2009, exactly eight years from the date President Bush had issued the military order giving the Pentagon, rather than the Justice Department, oversight of detention and trial for foreign detainees in the war on terror. It was a good time to announce what Holder called the "toughest decision I've had to make as Attorney General." The five most important detainees in US custody—Khalid Shaikh Mohammed; Walid Bin Attash; Ramzi bin al-Shibh; Ali Abdul Aziz Ali, a.k.a. Ammar al-Baluchi; and Mustafa al-Hawsawi, all alleged 9/11 conspirators—were to be tried in federal court in New York. All five of the men had been held and tortured at black sites, but Holder was certain the civilian courts could obtain convictions nonetheless. (In the same press conference, he announced that five other suspects would be tried by military commissions.)

Holder's decision came after a summer and fall in which teams of experts had assessed the viability of holding civilian terrorism trials, taking into account the prospect of challenges made in court over treatment while in detention, the possibility of coerced confessions, the need to consult intelligence agencies about what evidence to produce, and the handling of "outrageous government conduct" motions likely to emerge in response to harsh interrogation practices. After they had reported their recommendations, and after he had talked with some of the victims of the 9/11 attacks, Holder had come to the conclusion that "the venue in which we are most likely to obtain justice for the American people is in federal court." The trial would take place in New York, where, he said, "the Justice Department has a long and a successful history of prosecuting terrorists for their crimes against our nation."

Holder was confident that Ahmed Ghailani's prosecution would be a fitting dry run. Some of his confidence came from the particulars of the Ghailani case. There had already been successful prosecutions for crimes related to the attacks that Ghailani stood accused of perpetrating. The four men who had been convicted by a jury in May 2001 for their participation in the Al Qaeda conspiracy that let to the embassy bombings had been sentenced to life without parole. Some of the same witnesses were available to testify, and some of the forensic evidence from the earlier case was relevant to Ghailani's, too. But the case also offered a new challenge: some of the evidence against Ghailani had been obtained through torture and was thus inadmissible; there was no way to determine how this would affect the outcome. The team of prosecutors was led by Michael Farbiarz, the head of the Counterterrorism and Narcotics Unit at the Manhattan US attorney's office. Farbiarz's team included several assistant US attorneys who had worked with the Obama task force reviewing evidence against Guantánamo prisoners. They were thus familiar with the evidentiary problems created by detainee treatment and could hopefully overcome those hurdles.

The defense was led by Peter Quijano, who cut a distinctive figure with his shock of white wavy hair, his ostrich boots and designer three-piece suits, and his penchant for dramatic gestures and phrasing. At his side was an associate, Anna Sideris, younger and quieter, who remained close by Ghailani throughout the trial. Quijano also brought on board Michael Bachrach, a criminal defense attorney with a specialty in international law as well as experience trying a death penalty case, and Steve Zissou, another prominent criminal defense lawyer. Bachrach and Zissou had worked together success-fully in the past to obtain life imprisonment instead of the death penalty for defendants convicted of capital crimes. At the outset, the defense team indicated its intention of making the fact of Ghai-lani's torture part of the proceedings, including the argument that such treatment meant that the death penalty should be taken off the table. (The government ultimately chose not to pursue the death penalty, though the matter of torture remained an issue through the early stages of the prosecution.)

Ghailani was initially reluctant to attend court. He claimed that the cavity search required each day as he arrived and left the courtroom triggered flashbacks to his torture at American hands. He waived his right to be present at many pretrial hearings but was forced to attend some, including one in which he watched his defense attorneys argue for his right to boycott his own trial. Dr. Katherine Porterfield, the woman Ghailani had greeted on the first day of the trial, took the stand to testify, partially in a closed courtroom due to classification issues, that Ghailani had developed post-traumatic stress disorder as the result of being tortured by the CIA; she explained that stimuli reminiscent of the original trauma can overwhelm people with PTSD. After this hearing, however, Ghailani changed his mind and decided to attend the courtroom ses-sion. Porterfield later told me that his turnabout came when he real-ized for the first time that his defense team was genuinely fighting for him.

Judge Lewis Kaplan, whose specialty was the white-collar crime that makes up much of the caseload in the Southern District of New York, had never presided over a terrorism case. But from the out-set of the proceedings, Kaplan, a judge with a scholarly mien and a tendency to be professorial in the courtroom, showed himself un-afraid, even eager, to confront the murkier aspects of the case, in-cluding the subject of Ghailani's treatment while in detention. That issue surfaced repeatedly, first with a defense motion to dismiss the case because Ghailani had been denied his Sixth Amendment right to a speedy trial. Kaplan denied the motion, on the grounds that Ghailani's extended detention "served compelling interests of national security." The government's decision to detain and question him rather than bring him to trial had been "effective in obtaining useful intelligence," he wrote, adding that his defense had not been impaired by the delay brought about by his time in interrogation.

But Ghailani's treatment raised a much thornier problem. He was the first federal court defendant (and, as of September 2015, the last) who had indisputably been subjected to torture. Kaplan did not avoid that term or the question it forced: Could a legitimate trial could take place in cases where torture had played a role? The issue was inescapable because the prosecution was planning to call a witness from Tanzania, Hussein Abebe, who had, so the defense claimed, been discovered only because of information provided by Ghailani while undergoing torture at a CIA black site in Poland.

This was a confrontation that prosecutors and courts had been avoiding for eight years. In 2002 a plea deal had allowed the government to skirt the issue of John Walker Lindh's abuse while in US custody. The trial judge in the 2005 case of Ahmed Omar Abu Ali, the American citizen detained in Saudi Arabia and then tried in Virginia, determined that he had not been tortured. Khalid Shaikh Mohammed and Ramzi bin al-Shibh, both of whom were tortured, had "testified" in the Moussaoui case only by way of summary statements prepared by others, thus preventing defense lawyers from raising questions about the treatment of witnesses and defendants by the CIA and other government agencies. In both the Moussaoui and the Padilla cases, allegations of abuse had been mostly ignored and never discussed under oath. In the Ghailani case, prosecutors decided early on not to use statements or confessions that he had made while in CIA custody or when questioned, without having been read his Miranda rights, at Guantánamo.

But even if they could do without Ghailani's own words, the

lawyers needed Abebe. Kaplan held a hearing on Abebe's status. Over the course of three days, representatives from the CIA, the FBI, and the Tanzanian national police testified. Occasionally the judge asked the questions himself, sometimes incredulously.

"Here you are asking me to assume for the purposes of deciding the motion that everything Ghailani said from the minute he arrives in CIA custody to the minute he arrives at Guantanamo at least is coerced?" he asked Farbiarz.

"Yes, Judge, yes," replied the prosecutor.

Without any dispute over the facts, the hearing had a pinpoint focus: Kaplan had to decide whether testimony linked to a statement coerced through torture was tainted in the same way as the statement itself. Perhaps this had been the government's strategy all along—to get a decision on the record about circumstances like these, which might affect future cases.

If this was a trial balloon, however, it plummeted quickly. Three weeks after the hearing, Kaplan ruled this pivotal testimony inadmissible. "If the government is going to coerce a detainee to provide information to our intelligence agencies, it may not use that evidence—or fruits of that evidence that are tied as closely related to the coerced statements as Abebe's testimony would be here—to prosecute the detainee for a criminal offense.

"The Court has not reached this conclusion lightly," Kaplan continued. "It is acutely aware of the perilous nature of the world in which we live. But the Constitution is the rock upon which our nation rests. We must follow it not only when it is convenient, but when fear and danger beckon in a different direction. To do less would diminish us and undermine the foundation upon which we stand."

By adhering to constitutional principles, Kaplan did not intend to put an end to terrorism prosecutions. Indeed, by grappling with the issue that judges in cases like Lindh's and Moussaoui's had not, Kaplan was able to suggest a way forward, for the Ghailani case and any other in which torture was at issue. A trial's evidentiary trail would begin when law enforcement was involved and not before. Information gathered by the CIA would be inadmissible, but the fruits of FBI interrogation were fair game. At least in Kaplan's courtroom, there would be a wall between intelligence and law enforcement.

And even if the lack of evidence led to the unthinkable—an acquittal—Kaplan pointed out that Ghailani's "status as an 'enemy combatant' probably would permit his detention as something akin to a prisoner of war until hostilities between the United States and al Qaeda and the Taliban end." As high as the stakes of the trial were, they were in this way low: justice could be done the constitutional way and the integrity of Kaplan's courtroom preserved, and if the government didn't like the outcome, it always had the option of indefinite detention. It was a decision as cynical as it was heroic. Kaplan was defending the integrity of the Constitution and the court system, while at the same time acknowledging a way out. His decision, whatever its other consequences, would not result in Ghailani's release.

THE GHAILANI TRIAL WAS MUCH more orderly than the Moussaoui trial had been. Ghailani never tried to grandstand or wrest control of the proceedings from his lawyers. He remained calm and composed throughout and never provoked the judge. Given the case's high profile, however, Kaplan did take some unusual security precautions. The jury was not only anonymous, as it had been with Moussaoui; it was also transported by bus to a secret entrance to the courthouse. Over the course of the trial, routine measures like metal detectors and a cell phone ban were augmented with other prohibitions. Water bottles, for example, and eventually *The New York Times* and other newspapers became forbidden items, the former because they might contain explosives, the latter because they might contain explosive headlines about the case that could be glimpsed by jurors, who were not supposed to know that Ghailani had been tortured or held at Guantánamo, or that he had worked as Bin Laden's cook and bodyguard.

Stripped of their star witness, prosecutors turned to the evidence before them—the detonator for the bomb found in Ghailani's room, the fragments of explosives among his belongings, and Ghailani's presence at the bomb-making site. Ghailani, they told the jury, had been a part of the plot, had procured the truck and explosives knowing how they would be used, and had fled the country right after the attack, in what they argued could only be understood as a sign of guilt. They alluded to Bin Laden, to Al Qaeda, and to the attacks of 9/11 at every opportunity. The defense didn't dispute the evidence, but it argued that the government had the context all wrong. In "Ahmed's world," Quijano told the jury, brokering deals to buy a truck and some gas cylinders and receiving a commission in return, as Ghailani had done, was just business as usual in Kariakoo, the bustling market section of Dar es Salaam where Ghailani had allegedly arranged the fateful deal. In such a place, "Why would anyone question buying anything?" Quijano asked. "It's not like you're buying a gun. You're buying commercial items in a commercial temple."

The trial yielded at least one pleasant surprise, at least for the jurors: it did not take anywhere near the five months Kaplan had told them to expect. The judge kept the proceedings lean, pushing the lawyers to be efficient in their questioning of the witnesses and helping the pace along with his own questions when the testimony seemed to drag. By November 9, only four weeks into the trial, both sides had rested.

During their deliberations, the jury queried Kaplan about his "ostrich instruction," in which he had explained the legal concept of "conscious avoidance," informing the jury that consciously avoiding knowledge is tantamount to having it—so that if, say, you are asked to buy a truck and some gas cylinders for people you have reason to believe are planning a terrorist attack, then legally speaking, you know what they are up to even if you don't ask and they don't tell. They sent him pointed legal questions whose sophistication he praised. They deadlocked long and hard enough for one juror to send a note to Kaplan saying, "At this point am secure and I have come to my conclusion but it doesn't agreed with the rest of the juror. My conclusion it not going to change. I feel am been attack for my conclusion. Therefore am asking you if there is any way I can be excuse or exchange for an alternate juror." But after five days, the jury signaled that it had reached a verdict.

Within fifteen minutes of the announcement, the courtroom had filled up with reporters, lawyers, and onlookers. At the back of the room was David Raskin, the man expected to be the lead prosecutor in the 9/11 trial should it ever come to federal court. Raskin, his arms folded, had been thinking about how to best empower the federal courts in the post-9/11 era and had not only been part of the Moussaoui prosecution team but had worked with Matt Olsen on the task force that was trying to ferret out those cases suitable for military commissions and those for federal courts. Like most people in the room, he had little reason to doubt what was coming—namely, a conviction for Ghailani. Terrorism cases tried in the federal courts had resulted in convictions at a rate bordering on 91 percent; for those accused of activities resulting in someone's death, the conviction rate was 100 percent.

It was late in the day when the jury filed in, crossed the courtroom, which was lined by US marshals, and took their seats. Ghailani was being tried on 285 charges, and the courtroom deputy could ask about guilt or innocence on each individually. Kaplan warned that no one could enter or leave the room once the proceedings began. The sun was already setting.

Kaplan took a look at the charge sheet, on which the jury checks off guilty or innocent for each charge. He took a second look and passed the paper on to his deputy. "How do you find the defendant on Count One?" the deputy asked the jury.

"Not guilty," came the answer from the jury foreman.

The courtroom was silent. In the hush, the clerk asked, "How do you find the defendant on Count Two?"

"Not guilty."

Suddenly, papers were rustling throughout the viewing gallery. Confusion and disbelief appeared on the faces of the lawyers and the marshals and the FBI agents and the reporters and the witnesses.

Count Three?

Not guilty.

Count Four?

Not guilty.

At the defense table, Quijano's young associate, Anna Sideris, placed her arm over the shoulder of the defendant, who was standing to hear the verdict, dressed again in his blue sweater and tie. David Raskin stood in surprised silence at the back of the room.

Count Five?

Guilty.

Reporters and lawyers scanned their notes. What was Count Five again? A whisper went through the crowd. The *New York Times* reporter, Ben Weiser, often the first to know the details of a case, passed the news down the line: conspiring to destroy US property and buildings—to many ears, the least harmful-sounding of the accusations against the defendant. It seemed possible that the jury had bought the defense's story and believed that Ghailani had neither known nor consciously avoided knowing what his customers had in mind for the items he bought. Raskin felt relief—he had put years of work into terrorism trials, including the early stages of this one.

The clerk then asked for one decision for counts 6 to 285, including the 224 counts for those whose deaths were caused by the bombings.

Not guilty.

The stunned courtroom sat still. How was it possible that a jury sitting just a few blocks from the World Trade Center site, having heard testimony about a crime for which people had already been convicted—in the summer before 9/11—and in a country where two-bit terrorists were convicted as a matter of course and murdering terrorists always were: How was it possible that a jury in such a case could vote for acquittal on 284 out of 285 counts?

The prosecution's prediction that the case was nearly impossible to try successfully without Abebe's testimony might have been correct. Or maybe it was the sudden discovery of the detonator only after Ghailani's room had originally been searched that swayed the jury. Or perhaps Quijano had effectively convinced the jury that Ghailani was only a "kid from Kariakoo" trying to make a buck and unaware of what his customers were up to, or a young innocent trying to please older men whose motives he had no reason to know. Or possibly the jury, despite Kaplan's careful instruction, just didn't accept the concept of conscious avoidance. The jury members' reasoning remained mysterious. They went home without explaining themselves.

What was clear was that the civilian courts, the ones guided by the Constitution and all its guarantees, had done exactly what they were supposed to do: heard evidence and argument, turned the question over to a jury, which deliberated with serious concern for the legal issues, and yielded a verdict reflecting that seriousness. "This case should put to rest any unfounded fears that our federal justice system cannot conduct fair, safe, and effective trials in terrorism cases," said the ACLU's Hina Shamsi. "We should be proud of a system that isn't set up to simply rubberstamp the government's case."

Two months later, when he sentenced Ghailani to life in prison without parole, Kaplan defended the system against a different fear: that it was too lenient. In his sentencing remarks, he tried to counter the notion that the court had gone easy on a terrible man because he had been tortured. "Whatever Mr. Ghailani suffered at the hands of the CIA and others in our government," he said, "and however unpleasant the conditions of his confinement, the impact on him pales in comparison to the suffering and the horror that he and his confederates caused. For every hour of pain and discomfort that he

suffered, he caused a thousand-fold more pain and suffering to entirely innocent people."

Still, Kaplan had done what no judge had yet been willing to
do in the war on terror: confront torture as a legal issue in court
proceedings. A trial in US federal court could not admit evidence
elicited through torture. But the trial *could* take place. Kaplan had
surmounted the hurdles that supporters of the military commissions
had worried about. So, too, had he stood up for the criminal justice system and its judges. Unlike the judges in countless cases since
9/11, he did not defer to the government's claims that national security required changes to the rules of evidence, or to the procedures
for handling classified materials. Instead, he had overseen an efficient, evidence-based trial without compromising the Constitution
and due process, even at the risk of jeopardizing the government's
victory. His rulings stood alone in the annals of justice after 9/11.

But the criminal justice system had succeeded in part by acquit-
ting Ghailani, an accused terrorist, on the vast majority of counts.
This did not bode well for an administration that wished to put torture in the rearview mirror—here was a case that showed that the
issue would not simply disappear. The prosecution had clearly been
hobbled by Kaplan's ruling, and the result—a meager single conviction on a crime against property—was little better than an outright
acquittal, at least from the perspective of politicians and pundits re-
sponsive to a public still smarting from the attacks nearly a decade
earlier. In this respect, the court's victory was also a defeat, for it
gave ammunition to those who believed that the civilian courtroom
might not be the proper venue for a nation to seek its vengeance.

Those politicians and pundits did not lose any time using that ammunition. "This is a tragic wake-up call to the Obama administration to immediately abandon its ill-advised plan to try Guantanamo
terrorists . . . in federal civilian courts," and, as such, demanded an
immediate end to federal prosecutions of Guantánamo detainees,
including Khalid Shaikh Mohammed, Congressman Peter King
(R-NY) said in a statement issued the day after the verdict. King's

colleague Pete Hoekstra (R-MI) agreed. "We must treat them as wartime enemies and try them in military commissions," he argued. "This case was supposed to be the easy one, and the Obama administration failed." And Liz Cheney, chair of Keep America Safe, added her voice, which sounded a lot like her father's, to the chorus: "We urge the president: End this reckless experiment. Reverse course. Use the military commissions at Guantanamo. . . . And, above all, accept the fact that we are at war." Whatever headway Holder had intended to make via the Ghailani trial, his plan had faltered.

CHAPTER 15

Losing Ground

Eric Holder's November 2009 announcement that the government would try Khalid Shaikh Mohammed (KSM) in New York City had sparked an immediate outcry from business and community leaders in lower Manhattan, who worried that the trial would be too disruptive, or even too dangerous, to hold in their neighborhood. They were joined in opposition by their representatives in New York's legislature and then, at the end of January 2010, by Mayor Michael Bloomberg, who had initially backed Holder. Within hours, both of New York's senators had withdrawn their support, and the next day the White House announced that the Moynihan courthouse would not be the venue for the trial.

If he was abandoning the plan of holding the trial in Manhattan, Holder was still determined to try KSM and the four other 9/11 conspirators in civilian court. Yet as he scouted for other possible venues, Congress was debating the National Defense Authorization Act (NDAA), the massive bill it passes every year to fund the armed services. Inserted into its 609 pages were three paragraphs designed to thwart Holder's efforts. One forbade the use of Department of Defense funds to transfer detainees to other countries unless the secretary of defense certified that both the country and the detainee were not agents of terrorism. One prohibited the funding of any modifications to US prisons to accommodate Guantánamo inmates. And the third explicitly prohibited the use of Defense Department money to "transfer, release, or assist in the transfer or release to or within the United States, its territories, or possessions of Khalid Sheikh Mohammed or any other detainee."

Congress had not taken the lesson from the Ghailani trial that Holder had initially intended. In the representatives' eyes, the single conviction and life term didn't vindicate the criminal justice system; rather, the 284 acquittals condemned it. They saw the outcome not as a victory but as a close call that demonstrated the danger of a fair trial—which, of course, can be fair only if there is a possibility that the defendant will be acquitted. In the case of the 9/11 conspirators, this prospect was politically unacceptable, and Congress was using its power over the purse strings to foreclose it. In December, both houses agreed to put an end to any future trials of this sort. The new version of the NDAA passed both houses in December 2011. It strengthened the bans on transfers and specifically forbade the transfer of the central 9/11 defendant, Khalid Shaikh Mohammed, to US shores.

Obama signed the new appropriations bill on January 7, 2011. On April 4, Holder admitted defeat. "I have to deal with the situation as I find it," he announced at a press conference, "and I have reluctantly made the determination that these cases should be brought in a military commission." He was not going quietly, however. He scolded Congress for underestimating the strength of the case— "one of the most well-researched and documented cases I have ever seen," Holder said—and, in the process, "tak[ing] one of the nation's most tested counterterrorism tools off the table," one that would have allowed the government to "prove the defendants' guilt while adhering to the bedrock traditions and values of our laws."

Just a few weeks later the American public witnessed a very different kind of justice. On May 1, Navy SEALs stormed a compound in Abbottabad, Pakistan, and killed Osama bin Laden. President Obama made a triumphant speech announcing the operation from the East Room of the White House. Across the country, people celebrated in the streets. But as much as Bin Laden had been identified as the enemy in the war on terror, his death did not signal that the mission had been accomplished. The military was not going to stand down, and neither were the civilians in Congress or the White House—at least not to judge from what happened when certain provisions of the Patriot Act came up for renewal later that month.

Early indications were that the law was in some trouble. The new Republican majority in the House included a knot of libertarian-leaning freshmen representatives. In February they had joined with Democrats to thwart an attempt to extend the Patriot Act until the end of the year, renewing it instead only for three months. Meanwhile in the Senate, Patrick Leahy, chair of the Judiciary Committee, was proposing a bill that would dilute the government's data-collection power and impose new oversight. In the ensuing debate, members of Congress from both chambers invoked the Bin Laden assassination—not as a reason to support initiatives like Leahy's but as a reason to leave the Patriot Act intact. "The raid that killed Osama bin Laden also yielded an enormous amount of new information that has spurred dozens of investigations yielding new leads every day," said Senate Majority Leader Harry Reid (D-NV). "Without the Patriot Act, investigators would not have the tools they need to follow these new leads and disrupt terrorist plots, needlessly putting our national security at risk."

Reid's Republican counterpart, Mitch McConnell (R-KY), agreed. If Bin Laden's death has any impact on the law's fate, "I hope ... it'll be in the direction of extending the current law," he said. "Most of us believe it's been an effective tool in the war on terror." And Holder endorsed the emerging consensus. "Now more than ever," he said, "we need access to the crucial authorities in the

Patriot Act." The bill cleared both houses by strong majorities. What had started as emergency measures taken to pursue an urgent mission were on their way to becoming permanent.

THE SUPREME COURT'S EFFORTS TO return to pre-9/11 justice were also foundering. In the year and a half since the Court's ruling that Guantánamo prisoners were entitled to habeas corpus hearings, lawyers working on behalf of thirty-four detainees had argued to the Washington, DC, District Court, the sole court authorized to hear the cases, that the government's evidence did not justify their clients' continued detention. In twenty cases, the court had agreed and ordered the prisoners released. Some were repatriated, and others found new homes in countries around the world, including Switzerland, Bermuda, and Palau. Lakhdar Boumediene, for whom the Supreme Court case was named, was resettled in France.

Five of the district court's decisions, all denials, were appealed to the circuit court. By February 2010 only one had been decided by the circuit, and the denial had been upheld. But then the circuit judges heard the case of Mohammed Al-Adahi. A Yemeni security guard, Al-Adahi had left his job and home country in the summer of 2001 to take his sister to Afghanistan, where she was to be wed to a man described as a "close associate" of Osama bin Laden's. After the wedding, which Bin Laden hosted, Al-Adahi stayed in Afghanistan, shuttling back and forth between Kabul, Khost, and Kandahar. He spent a week at al-Farooq, an Al Qaeda training camp, and met twice with Bin Laden.

About six weeks after the American invasion of Afghanistan on October 7, the US military took Al-Adahi off a bus loaded with wounded Arabs that had been stopped near the Afghani-Pakistani border. He claimed that his broken arm and other injuries were the result of a motorcycle accident, that he was on vacation in Afghanistan, that the visit to Bin Laden was purely social, and that he didn't know that the others on the bus were fighters. He was sent to Guantánamo, where a hearing by a Combatant Status Review Tribunal determined that he was an Al Qaeda member. On June 23, 2009, his lawyers presented his case to the district court, which found "no reliable evidence in the record that Petitioner was a member of al-Qaeda" and, on August 21, ordered him released. In February 2010, the government asked the appeals court to reverse that decision. On July 13 the court obliged, reversing a Guantánamo habeas order outright for the first time.

In its opinion, the appeals court was unstinting in its criticism of the lower court. Citing, in addition to the usual precedents and law books, two books on "mathematical illiteracy" and another called *Historians' Fallacies*, Circuit Judge A. Raymond Randolph took the court to task for requiring "each piece of the government's evidence to bear weight without regard to all (or indeed any) other evidence in the case." This "fundamental mistake"—a "failure to appreciate conditional probability analysis," Randolph called it—had "infected the court's entire analysis," leading it to conclude that because the government couldn't prove its individual charges—for instance, that Al-Adahi had been trained at al-Farooq rather than simply visiting, or that his Casio watch was Al Qaeda issue rather than something he happened to buy—it had not demonstrated by a preponderance of the evidence that Al-Adahi was an enemy combatant.

"Having tossed aside the government's evidence, one piece at a time," Randolph continued, "the court came to the manifestly incorrect—indeed, startling—conclusion": that Al-Adahi should go free. It had judged each tree on its own merits and concluded that there was no forest. Randolph proceeded to reconstruct the evidence in the way he thought made more sense: as a mosaic rather than as a collection of unrelated facts. He concluded that "Al-Adahi was—at the very least—more likely than not a part of al-Qaeda." That was enough to satisfy the law. Mohammed Al-Adahi was going to stay at Guantánamo.

The appeals court's rebuke went well beyond the Al-Adahi case.

The *Boumediene* decision had left open the question of just how the district court should decide habeas petitions, and at least in Randolph's opinion, the approach that was emerging was unsatisfactory. The district court had failed to make "any findings about whether Al-Adahi was generally a credible witness." It had taken his story at face value, while expressing deep doubt about the government's. Though the government had the burden of proving that the detainee should continue to be held, in this case, the district court had gotten the balance wrong—especially given that Al Qaeda's "instructions to detainees are to make up a story and lie." The appeals court was disagreeing with the lower court not about points of law but about the facts themselves, about which evidence the district court should have considered and how it should have analyzed it. Appellate courts rarely revisit the factual findings of a case, instead giving deference to the factual determinations of the lower courts. In this case, in addition to telling the lower court it had gotten its facts wrong, the circuit judges seemed to be telling their district brethren that they should give the government the benefit of the doubt, if not take its word outright, in these cases.

If that was the intended message, it appeared to pay off almost immediately. Prior to the *Al-Adahi* decision, the district court had granted nearly 60 percent of the habeas petitions it heard. Of the twelve cases that came before it in the two years after the *Al-Adahi* decision, it denied eleven. An analysis of those cases by a group of legal scholars led by Seton Hall's Mark Denbeaux and Jonathan Hafetz attributed this reversal not to some fundamental difference between the earlier and later cases but to an increase in "judicial deference to the government." The court was accepting the government's narrative far more often than it had in the past. In Denbeaux and Hafetz's view, now that the court had been ordered to give extra weight to the government's case, "meaningful review is out." The Supreme Court might have ordered habeas hearings for Guantánamo prisoners, but at least according to the circuit court of appeals, that didn't mean judges had to take the explanations offered by the detainees as seriously as they took those offered by the government. Meanwhile, of the four cases pending in the circuit court before the *Al-Adahi* decision, two were remanded for reconsideration, and two more were reversed.

IF THERE WAS ANY DOUBT that the appeals court meant to clip the lower court's wings (and with them the prisoners'), the twelfth case, the sole petition the district court granted after the *Al-Adahi* decision, put an end to it. Like Al-Adahi, Adnan Farhan Abdul Latif was a Yemeni taken into custody near the border between Afghanistan and Pakistan at the end of 2001. He'd been sent to Guantánamo in early 2002. He was twenty-seven years old. According to the government, he'd been recruited in Yemen for jihad by a man named Ibrahim al-Alawi in the summer of 2001. After a circuitous journey, he'd wound up with al-Alawi in a training center near Kabul, then fighting for the Taliban against the Northern Alliance in the US-led war before fleeing to Pakistan. But Latif told the judges of the district court a different story. He claimed he'd gone to Pakistan to meet Ibrahim, who was supposed to help him get treatment for a head injury sustained in a car crash. But Ibrahim, who had arranged for the trip as part of his job working for a charitable organization, had left for a religious institute near Kabul. Latif went to Kabul and took up residence at the religious center, but after several weeks Ibrahim had still not taken him to the doctor, and when Latif heard the US forces were closing in on Kabul, he fled back to Pakistan, where he was apprehended.

According to the government, Latif had already confessed to being a jihadist; this new story, prosecutors argued, had been fabricated to win his habeas hearing. For his part, Latif claimed that he had been the victim of a botched translation compounded by clerical errors that had turned his attempt to get medical treatment into a confession. At the hearing, prosecutors were unable to produce notes or transcripts for the interviews at which Latif had allegedly confessed, so it was impossible to tell if indeed he was the victim of a translator's mistakes. "There is serious question as to whether the [report] accurately reflects Latif's words, the incriminating facts in the [report] are not corroborated, and Latif has presented a plausible alternative story to explain his travel," the district court ruled, granting his habeas petition.

By a 2-to-1 vote, the circuit court of appeals reversed the decision, and it did so scathingly. "The district court's analysis suffers from the same omission" as its *Al-Adahi* decision—the failure to consider the credibility of the prisoner and his tale. In this case, the appeals court ruled, it wasn't the "intrinsic implausibility" of that story but, rather, its peculiar correspondence with the prosecution's account that made it "so hard to swallow." Latif had taken the same facts and woven them into a different story, one that the court felt had cleverly made use of the raw materials out of which the government had constructed its case. But "what series of innocent statements could possibly have been so badly corrupted?" asked Judge Janice Brown in her majority opinion. To accept this version of events, as the district court had, one would have to believe that "an elaborate game of telephone between Latif, a translator, a note-taker, and a report-writer" had twisted his story beyond recognition. "But as most children would tell you," the judge wrote, "any good game of telephone requires more than four participants to produce a result dramatically different from the starting phrase." The lower court, in other words, didn't have even a child's common sense.

"A body of judge-made law is not born fully-formed," Brown continued. "This case finally forces the issue." The district court, with its innumerate logic and foolish credulity, was bumbling the job the Supreme Court had handed it in the *Boumediene* decision: to form the law regarding how to conduct habeas reviews. It was time for the grown-ups to step in and settle the problem once and for all.

According to Brown, the issue forced by the Latif case was the *presumption of regularity*, a common-law concept by which courts must presume that government officials have done their jobs properly unless there is evidence to the contrary. If an official's job is to generate documents, then the court must presume that the documents are valid. So if, say, a marriage certificate from any state in the country is offered as evidence that a person is married, then in the absence of a superceding document such as a divorce decree or evidence of malfeasance or incompetence on the part of the officials who executed and recorded the document, a court is bound to presume that the document is valid and that the person in question is thus ineligible to be married for a second time. Brown's way of forcing the issue was to extend this presumption to "intelligence reports like the one at issue here." The interviews might have taken place in a war zone, the prisoners might have been tortured, the translations might have been less than stellar, but even so the court was not to question their accuracy any more than it would question a birth certificate or a marriage license, at least not unless the defendant offered it a compelling reason to. According to the appeals court, Latif had not done that, and so it returned the case to district court, with instructions to "evaluate Latif's credibility as needed in light of the totality of the evidence." Here as in the Guantánamo habeas cases overall, it was the defendant, and not the government, who had the burden of proof.

For Latif, the opinion's consequences proved too much to handle. On June 11, 2012, the Supreme Court refused to hear the appeal in the case. Three months later Latif was dead. An inquiry by navy investigators determined that he had taken an intentional overdose of an unspecified psychiatric medication. They were unable to explain how Latif had gotten hold of enough pills to kill himself; nonetheless the death was officially ruled to be suicide.

The *Latif* ruling was a devastating setback for Guantánamo detainees and the lawyers who represented them. In his dissent, Judge David Tatel called the decision an "assault on *Boumediene*" that amounted to "moving the goal posts and then call[ing] the game in the government's favor." Brown had not hidden her disdain for the Supreme Court ruling in that case. "As the dissenters warned and as the amount of ink spilled in this single case attests," she wrote, citing the *Boumediene* dissents of Justices John Roberts and Antonin Scalia, "*Boumediene*'s airy suppositions have caused great difficulty for the Executive and the courts." The Supreme Court had over-reached by issuing a ruling that "fundamentally altered the calcu-lus of war, guaranteeing that the benefit of intelligence that might be gained—even from high-value detainees—is outweighed by the systemic cost of defending detention decisions." She concluded on a sarcastic note. "*Boumediene*'s logic is compelling," she wrote. "Take no prisoners." Brown's argument recalled John Yoo's: the president should be free to conduct a war as he sees fit, and the judiciary, including the Supreme Court, should not impinge on that authority. To Brown, the Latif case was an opportunity not only to instruct the lower court on how to implement the decision but also to let the higher court know how wrong that decision had been to begin with and even to contravene it.

According to Steven Vladeck, an expert on national security law after 9/11, Brown's rebuke was unusual. "Bad enough to try to avoid the consequences of a Supreme Court ruling," he told me. "But to do so with such open and brazen contempt seems especially atypical." By 2013 one of the appeals court judges would wonder whether deci-sions like these were rendering the habeas proceedings "function-ally useless." But he posed that question in the course of upholding the denial of a petition (the only denial among the nineteen appeals), and the body of law was soon formed: habeas hearings would be granted, just as the Supreme Court had ordered, but the government would have a much louder voice than the prisoners, denying them their rights at the same time that it avoided what Jonathan Hafetz referred to as "calling the jailer to account." The *Boumediene* ruling, which once promised to restore the rule of law to the war on terror, had effectively been vacated.

CHAPTER 16

Further
Consequences

When Judge Janice Brown wrote that the logic of the *Boumediene* decision compelled the government to take no prisoners, she was probably being facetious. But even as she was contemplating the fate of Adnan Latif, the government was developing a plan to kill at least one enemy outright rather than capture him. On September 30, 2011—just two weeks before the *Latif* decision was handed down—that plan was carried out. A Predator drone operated by the CIA fired Hellfire missiles at a car in Yemen, killing the five men inside. The dead included Samir Khan and Anwar al-Awlaki, both American citizens.

Khan, twenty-five years old, was the editor in chief of *Inspire*, an Al Qaeda in the Arabian Peninsula magazine that ran articles so slick and topical—Osama bin Laden's ruminations about global warming, for instance, and a how-to on making explosives in your mother's kitchen—that some thought it was an elaborate hoax. Al-Awlaki was believed to be the mastermind behind the magazine and other Al Qaeda propaganda efforts online; one Saudi news outlet called him the "bin Laden of the Internet." His work was not only online, however. Charismatic, articulate, and persuasive, he'd been a source of information about the Muslim world for the news media in the days following 9/11, he'd led prayers for the Congressional Muslim Staffers Association, and he'd been the inspiration for many high-profile terrorists, including Ramzi bin al-Shibh, Nidal Hassan (the Fort Hood doctor who opened fire on his own comrades and killed thirteen of them), Umar Farouk Abdulmutallab (the Christmas Day underwear bomber), and Faisal Shahzad (the would-be Times Square bomber). Al-Awlaki had also issued fatwas, including one announced in *Inspire* for a Seattle cartoonist who helped organize Everybody Draw Mohammed Day in May 2010. And sometime that same year, the Obama administration issued its own version of a kill order, placing him on a list of terrorists it wanted to kill. Khan was not on the list; he just had the bad luck to be in the car, although it is hard to imagine his death was mourned by anyone in the US government. But he had something else in common with al-Awlaki: both men were US citizens, the first known to be assassinated by drone by their own government in the war on terror.

Death comes to most as a surprise, arguably at no time more so than when it comes by way of a Hellfire missile fired from an unseen aircraft. But al-Awlaki couldn't have been shocked. The fact that he was in the government's sights had been an open secret since at least April 2010, when news outlets confirmed a report, which had first surfaced in the *Los Angeles Times* in January, that the United States was planning to send a drone after him. This plan was complicated by al-Awlaki's US citizenship, and it came only after lawyers in the Justice Department had determined that it would be legal to kill him—rather than to indict and capture him and bring him to the trial to which American citizens are generally entitled. The opinion came from Obama's Office of Legal Counsel, the same office in which John Yoo had worked under Bush, and while its argument did not sink to Yoo's level of ideological casuistry, still it declared legal an unprecedented exercise of executive power—in this case, the power to execute an American citizen without due process.

The memo, authored by David Barron, assisted by fellow OLC lawyer Marty Lederman, was submitted in July 2010. It started exactly where Yoo's memos had—with the Authorization for Use of Military Force enacted by Congress in 2001, which gave the president the power to "use all necessary and appropriate force" to prosecute the war on terror. So far the AUMF had not been used to justify killing American citizens overseas, but, Barron reasoned, "just as the AUMF authorizes the military detention of a U.S. citizen captured abroad who is part of an armed force . . . it also authorizes the use of 'necessary and appropriate' lethal force against a U.S. citizen who has joined such an armed force." Because the country was at war, and national security at stake, the government could use its "public authority justification"—the doctrine that allows a fire truck to run red lights or police officers to use deadly force—to break its own laws against murder. And because the war was not between nation-states but rather a "non-international armed conflict between the United States and al-Qaida," the United States could take the battle anywhere the terrorists happened to be. So long as killing al-Awlaki (who was the explicit subject of the memo) was an act of the authorized war, it was not against either US or international law.

But was al-Awlaki one of those US citizens who had taken up arms against his own country? How much was his inspiration of others tied to operational directives and advice? How much of a danger was he? According to the memo and a white paper that the Justice Department subsequently issued on the subject, even if he was not killed on a battlefield or while actively plotting to blow up a building, an Al Qaeda leader was a legitimate target so long as three conditions were satisfied: that "capture is infeasible," that the target had been determined by "an informed, high-level official" to "pose an imminent threat of violent attack against the United States," and that the operation was carried out in accordance with the laws of war. The first criterion was a matter of judgment, while the third was governed by rules already established. But the middle criterion, the one about imminence, was troublesome. Barron and Lederman cited no evidence that al-Awlaki was planning a specific attack against the United States, either himself or by proxy, or that his role was anything other than the one for which he had already established an extensive reputation: propagandist, American Al Qaeda member, religious leader.

The white paper is more frank about the nature of the threat posed by al-Awlaki. It argues from the outset that "the condition that an operational leader present an 'imminent' threat of violent attack against the United States does not require the United States to have clear evidence that a specific attack on US persons and interests will take place in the immediate future." Indeed, given the way Al Qaeda operates, to wait for a threat to become imminent, in the everyday sense of that word, before carrying out a drone strike "would create an unacceptably high risk that the action would fail and that American casualties would result." The war on terror, the white paper concludes, "demands a broader concept of imminence," which the white paper spells out this way:

> Thus, a decision maker . . . must take into account that certain members of al Qa'ida (including any potential target of lethal force) are continually plotting attacks against the United States; that al-Qa'ida would engage in such attacks regularly to the extent it were able to do so; that the U.S. government may not be aware of all al-Qa'ida plots as they are developing and thus cannot be confident that none is about to occur; and that, in light of these predicates, the nation may have a limited window of opportunity within which to strike in a manner that both has a high likelihood of success and reduces the probability of American casualties.

In the same way that it is in the nature of a scorpion to sting, it was apparently in the nature of a certain Al Qaeda leader to continuously plot against the United States; he is therefore always an imminent threat.

By conflating *continuous* with *imminent,* the opinion broadens the latter concept almost beyond recognition, in such a way as to make not just al-Awlaki but anyone affiliated with Al Qaeda a potential target of lawful killing—and not only according to US law. By Barron and Lederman's reasoning, the killing of al-Awlaki also complied with international law, or at least with Article 3 of the Geneva Conventions, by which warring parties must protect people not actively engaged in hostilities. When it came to Al Qaeda leaders, everyone was by definition continuously engaged in active hostilities. So long as the bombing was selective and didn't cause too much collateral damage, al-Awlaki was fair game.

As Yoo's memos did for the Bush White House, so the Barron memo did for the Obama administration. The lawyers had their marching orders—in Yoo's case, to justify torture and warrantless surveillance, and in Barron's, to justify killing al-Awlaki. In both cases, the argument was that national security justifies extraordinary measures and an expansive reading of the law. But only in the more recent case did that justification come after the fact. The CIA did not begin its full-fledged enhanced interrogation program until after getting Yoo's green light on August 1, 2002. But we do know that on Christmas Eve 2009, seven months before Barron issued his opinion, a drone attack destroyed a home in Yemen's Shabwa Province, reportedly killing at least thirty people. The house belonged to the al-Awlaki family; according to the Yemeni embassy in Washington, Anwar al-Awlaki was "presumed" to be meeting there with other Al Qaeda members. The order to fire, according to *Newsweek* reporter Daniel Klaidman, was given by President Obama. There was as yet no legal authorization for killing an American citizen with a drone strike. At least in this case, Obama's executive power grab resembled something Bush might have done. And in some ways, Obama seemed to be going even further than his predecessor.

Anwar al-Awlaki may have been the first US citizen executed in the war on terror by a presidential order, but he was neither the first nor the last person Obama ordered to be killed by drone. In weekly meetings, the president's security team examined the dossiers of suspected terrorists, discussed the merits of their cases, and forwarded to Obama nominations for a "kill list." On a less frequent basis, the president, collaborating with his national security adviser, John Brennan, and other top officials, went over the names and decided who should actually be placed on the list. Obama had more latitude with these targets than with al-Awlaki, as they were not US citizens, but the logic of the decision was similar. The country's highest-ranking official was deciding whom to kill, and membership in Al Qaeda seemed to be sufficient qualification for a person to make the list. The policy was loose enough to stir objections within Obama's inner circle. "One guy gets knocked off, and the guy's driver, who's No. 21, becomes 20?" William Daley, Obama's onetime chief of staff, told *The New York Times*. "At what point are you just filling the bucket with numbers?"

And it was a big bucket. Between the presidential inauguration in January 2009 and the spring of 2011, the Obama administration had launched more than two hundred drone strikes, resulting in well over one thousand deaths, and had taken into custody only one suspected terrorist abroad. Many observers on both sides of the political divide suspected that the policy reflected Obama's wish not to add to his problems with closing Guantánamo, and the other complexities of detaining and prosecuting prisoners, by capturing more Al Qaeda operatives. "Their policy is to take out high-value targets, versus capturing high-value targets," Senator Saxby Chambliss (R-GA) told *The New York Times*. Obama seemed to be fulfilling the take-no-prisoners mandate Judge Brown had seen lurking in the *Boumediene* decision.

Whether this was his intention, and whether he was as determined as Bush and his team had been to expand presidential power, the only check on Obama's war policies came from within the executive branch. Indeed, at least one attempt to limit the president from out-side resulted in a judicial endorsement of broad executive authority.

The occasion arose when the ACLU tried to use the courts to challenge the president's right to put an American on a kill list. (It also sent Obama a letter pointing out that it was illegal to execute an American without due process; the president did not write back.) The organization then sent two staff lawyers, Jameel Jaffer and Ben Wizner, to Yemen, where they met with al-Awlaki's father, Nasar al-Awlaki. While the lawyers were preparing a lawsuit on Nasar's behalf, seeking to prohibit the United States from killing Nasar al-Awlaki's son, Anwar was placed on another list, created by the Bush administration, called the Specially Designated Global Terror-ists List. Anwar's placement on it meant, among other things, that Nasar's lawyers had to get a license from the Office of Foreign As-sets Control before they could represent their client. Several months later the ACLU, along with the Center for Constitutional Rights, finally filed their motion.

In December 2010 Judge John D. Bates of the DC District Court dismissed the ACLU suit on the grounds that al-Awlaki's father did not have standing to sue. He could have stopped there, without ad-dressing the merits of the case. Instead he issued an eighty-three-page opinion asserting that "there are circumstances in which the Executive's unilateral decision to kill a US citizen overseas is 'consti-tutionally committed to the political branches' and judicially unre-viewable. . . . This case squarely presents such a circumstance." The lawsuit raised the same fundamental questions of separation of pow-ers that had haunted the courts since 9/11. But, Bates ruled, even if the detention of a US citizen without access to courts was unconsti-tutional, the killing of a US citizen, at least one whom the president had determined posed an imminent threat, was not. Congress had given the president the power to prosecute a war on terror, and it was not for the courts to tell him whom he could and could not kill.

The ACLU did not appeal Bates's decision, but it did pursue two other lawsuits related to the killing of al-Awlaki, one demanding the release of government documents authorizing the strike, the other charging Secretary of Defense Leon Panetta, CIA director David Petraeus, and two high-ranking military officers with violating the Fourth and Fifth Amendments and the constitutional prohibition of bills of attainder, in which the government declares a person guilty and punishes him without due process. This time it was Judge Rosemary Collyer of the DC Circuit Court who determined that the question was beyond the scope of the judiciary. Government officials, she reasoned, "must be trusted and expected to act in accordance with the U.S. Constitution when they intentionally target a U.S. citizen abroad at the direction of the President and with the concurrence of Congress." It was a stinging defeat for the ACLU—and for its client. "For a long time, I had faith that an American court would decide whether the killings of at least these American citizens violated the U.S. Constitution's guarantee of due process," Nasar al-Awlaki wrote, explaining his decision not to appeal the case further. The killing, and the subsequent court opinion, "shattered" that faith, he continued. "This isn't justice."

BARACK OBAMA MIGHT HAVE COME into office on promises to restore the balance between national security and civil liberties and to dial back the claims made for executive power by the Bush administration. But by the time he started gearing up for his reelection campaign, he seemed to be reconsidering. He'd ordered Guantánamo closed, but he had yet to engage in the political battle it would take to enforce the order. He'd ended torture but allowed targeted killing. Indeed, he had ordered it, at least according to one of his national security advisers, who told *The New York Times* that he insisted on final approval of drone targets—on the grounds, the adviser said, "that he's responsible for the position of the United States in the world." Whether that was his motive, and whether his sense of responsibility was more admirable than it was chilling, the targeted killing program could not help but increase the power of the presidency to override civil liberties in favor of national security. And the courts were supporting Obama, not only by dismissing cases like the ACLU's but also by issuing rulings that diluted and sometimes seemed to defy the Supreme Court's strongest attempt to trim the executive branch's sails—the *Boumediene* decision.

Obama's apparent, and perhaps unexpected, taste for presidential power found further expression in his administration's penchant for secrecy. Some of this came in the form of continuing policies from the Bush years—in particular, reliance on a set of tactics referred to by critics as "secret law." As the name implied, this secrecy went beyond a particular piece of evidence in a criminal prosecution, or the identity of an individual target of surveillance, to the very nature of the law itself. Justice Department memos marked as classified, FISA Court proceedings, and legal reasoning made public in one form but kept secret in their full legal detail: these tactics had been familiar since Bush declared that the country was at war with Al Qaeda and that keeping vital information out of the hands of an enemy without borders or uniforms required unprecedented levels of secrecy. And as the confirmation hearing of Lisa Monaco, the Justice Department lawyer designated to replace David Kris as head of the National Security Division, demonstrated, the new administration, whatever its commitment to transparency and rule of law, was not going to take a vastly different approach from its predecessor.

Toward the end of the hearing, Senator Ron Wyden (D-OR) reminded Monaco of a discussion they had had previously, about his objections to such overarching secrecy. Of course, he said, intelligence requires secrecy, which means that "the public won't always know the details, obviously, about what intelligence agencies are doing." However, he added, "they also ought to be able to look at the law and figure out what actions are permitted and what actions are prohibited." The public was entitled to know how the Justice Department viewed the laws it was charged with enforcing, which was impossible when interpretation of the law—the kind that sanctioned torture and warrantless wiretapping—was kept from it. "I don't think our government ought to be able to write secret law," he concluded. "Do you disagree with that judgment?"

"I understand the Committee's interest and importance of your knowing how we're exercising those functions, because you stand in the shoes of the public in exercising your oversight responsibility," she answered. "So in short, I think the points you made in the correspondence that we discussed are quite valid."

Wyden tried again. "Do you agree that the government's official interpretation of the law should be public?" he asked. "That is to me a yes or no answer."

"Well, respectfully, Senator . . . sometimes the manner in which we're applying the [FISA laws] and the facts surrounding them have to necessarily be kept secret from our adversaries so that those tools can't be used against us. I certainly agree that we need to make as much public as possible and to be as transparent as possible in how we're using the authorities that the Congress has given us."

"I still don't get a sense of urgency or conviction that this issue of secret law is of any real concern," Wyden said. Monaco was not going to answer the question directly; nor would she promise to renounce the privilege of secret law, or consent in advance to limits on it. Intelligence concerns, and the legal secrecy the administration claimed they demanded, would continue to dominate the work of the Justice Department and its national security hub. As Monaco would tell a group of Washington lawyers a year after she took office, "Law enforcement's approach to terrorism has become intelligence-led and threat-driven."

This deference applied not only to ongoing operations—for which, as Monaco put it, the NSD would serve as "a traffic light, rather than a stop sign"—but also to those from the past. In the two years following Monaco's confirmation, the Justice Department greatly reduced the number of cases it routed through criminal court. Prosecutions of terrorists in federal court fell by more than 50 percent, continuing a trend that had started during David Kris's tenure. The Ghailani verdicts and the political resistance to holding the Khalid

Shaikh Mohammed trial in New York seemed to have cooled the Obama administration's ardor for civilian trials, with all their transparency and the public glare they invited.

But nowhere was the White House's sudden publicity shyness more evident than in its decisions about internal affairs. In the summer of 2012 Holder announced that John Durham's investigation into two deaths of detainees undergoing enhanced interrogation had come to an end. Durham's inquiry was the only remnant of the Justice Department's look at the torture policy, an investigation Holder had called off in August 2012. There would be no prosecutions against anyone involved in carrying out the policy, not even when death was the result. Coupled with his 2010 decision not to seek criminal charges in the destruction of Abu Zubaydah's videotaped torture session, Holder's announcement seemed to put an end to the prospects not only for bringing policy makers and torturers to account, but also for the airing of information about the particulars of the program that a trial would inevitably bring. The past would remain in the past, the secrets buried, the perpetrators unpunished—and not only unpunished but free to go on *60 Minutes*, as CIA agent Jose Rodriguez did in April 2012, to explain his decision to destroy the best evidence a lawyer could have of criminal wrongdoing. "This program wasn't about hurting anyone," he told viewers. It was done, he explained, "to protect American lives." The enhanced interrogations, he asserted, had been lawful and effective, and he had destroyed the tapes to prevent terrorists from identifying and targeting the interrogators.

Two weeks later the FBI's Ali Soufan responded to Rodriguez's assertions in an interview with *The New Yorker*'s Amy Davidson. He repeated his firsthand account, in which Zubaydah provided valuable information *before*, not after, he was waterboarded. And he speculated that Rodriguez destroyed the tapes because "if [they] ever got into [the] public domain . . . they would make us look terrible." Of course, there was more at stake than reputation: a full accounting would have exposed to prosecution the architects of the policy and the interrogators who, unlike Soufan, carried it out. With reporters doing the cross-examination and the case tried only in the court of public opinion, however, the vital questions remained unanswered.

JUST BEFORE THE ELECTION, THERE was one more opportunity for the ACLU to reduce the scope of the security state, this time in the matter of surveillance. In 2011 the Second Circuit Court of Appeals had overturned a lower court ruling in *Amnesty v. Clapper*, the suit the ACLU and other organizations had filed on the very day the FISA Amendments Act passed in 2008. The plaintiffs claimed that Section 702 of the FAA, which granted the government increased power to spy on citizens and to compel telecommunications providers to share their records, not only compromised their ability to provide confidentiality to their clients but was unconstitutional. The case had been making its way through the courts for nearly four years, but no judge had yet ruled on its merits. Instead, the litigation had been limited to the question of whether the ACLU had standing to bring the suit. The district court had ruled that it did not, but the appeals court had reversed that ruling. The Supreme Court had now agreed to hear the government's appeal of that decision.

It was a momentous day for the ACLU, which had been trying to bring the surveillance policies into the courtroom for nearly a decade. Even as the morning approached, the goalpost seemed to be moving. Argument was scheduled for October 29, 2012, just as Hurricane Sandy was making a beeline for the New Jersey coast. Federal buildings all over Washington were closed, but the Supreme Court was open for business.

Though the argument was over standing, the question of who was affected by Section 702 could not help but take the case into the substance of the law. The ACLU's position, after all, hinged on the claim that the FAA, as Jaffer told the justices, signaled a return to the days when the government had been able to sweep up information like a "vacuum-cleaner," as one Church Committee witness put it. The ACLU had standing, in other words, because Section 702 had nullified the government's obligations under FISA to specify its targets, to make sure they were agents of a foreign power, to guarantee that foreign intelligence was a significant purpose of the surveillance, and to minimize the impact on US citizens. Anyone could be a target, intentional or incidental, and so the ACLU, which might represent anyone, had standing to challenge the law.

The government's position, argued by Solicitor General Donald Verrilli, was diametrically opposed: the fact that the targets of surveillance were secret meant that the ACLU couldn't possibly claim that its clients were targets. The case was thus built on "a cascade of speculation," and it was dangerous to boot, as the discovery that would ensue if the ACLU were given standing might serve as a "mechanism for . . . foreign terrorists who think they may be under surveillance, to find out whether they are or not." The ACLU was apparently too naïvely focused on civil liberties to understand that it was at risk of aiding and abetting the enemy.

The Kafkaesque nature of this argument did not escape the notice of Justice Sonia Sotomayor. "General, is there anybody who has standing?" she asked. Or would the secrecy nearly always prevent a challenge to the law? "As I read your brief, standing would only arise at the moment the Government decided to use the information against someone in a pending case." This meant, she pointed out, "that if there was a constitutional violation in the interception . . . no one could ever stop it until they were charged with a crime." In other words, how could anyone ever have the facts necessary to bring a suit?

Verrilli replied that the justice was correct. The FISA law required the government to notify a person when information gained through surveillance was going to be used in court. "If an aggrieved person, someone who is a party to a communication, gets notice that the government intends to introduce information in a proceeding against them," he said, "they have standing."

Verrilli's explanations satisfied the Court, or at least five of the justices on it. In an opinion written by Justice Samuel Alito and delivered on February 26, 2013, the Court ruled that the ACLU did not have standing. There was no concrete evidence of injury, wrote Alito, and no "objectively reasonable likelihood that their communications with their foreign contacts will be intercepted." Alito relied in part on Verrilli's assurances about notifying targets of surveillance: "Additionally, if the Government intends to use or disclose information obtained or derived from a [702] acquisition in judicial or administrative proceedings," he wrote, "it must provide advance notice of its intent, and the affected person may challenge the lawfulness of the acquisition."

In a dissenting opinion, Justice Breyer declared that there was "a high likelihood" that the government, under the FAA, "will intercept at least some of the communications" described by the plaintiffs. It had both "the motive and the capacity to listen" to communications of US citizens. Believing that a government as motivated as the United States was to prevent terrorist attacks would not use that capacity was as foolish as believing that "despite pouring rain, the streets will remain dry."

But what none of the justices knew as they deliberated was that Verrilli's statement about notification was not true. Verrilli himself did not even know it—because the Justice Department lawyers who reviewed his briefs and prepped him for his argument did not tell him that the Department of Justice had never notified a defendant that warrantless surveillance had been used to make the case against him and had no plans to do so in the future. Six months later, when Verrilli learned about the lack of notifications from an article in *The New York Times,* he was reported to be furious. He realized he had been misled and had in turn misled the Court. He demanded that the Justice Department reform the practice and start to provide the required notifications. In January 2013 it finally began to do so. But the decision stood. The Obama administration had taken up the battle that began under Bush, protecting its power to put Americans under surveillance without their knowledge. It had won on technical grounds abetted by a lie, without ever bringing the program itself into public view. The scope of warrantless wiretapping and other surveillance would remain a secret.

The argument between Verrilli and his colleagues at Justice remained behind closed doors, and with it the truth about the uses of the PRISM program enabled by Section 702.

But there was one man who had been watching from afar for years as the DOJ succeeded in portraying the ACLU and others concerned with the excesses of the security state as meddlesome purveyors of paranoid fantasies. He was a twenty-nine-year-old computer analyst who had been working for the NSA from his home in Hawaii. He had the proof that the ACLU's worries were not misplaced, that the government was lying, and that Americans—all Americans—were under surveillance. And he was ready to act.

CHAPTER 17

The Snowden Effect

"Do you have standing now?"

It was one of the first questions Edward Snowden asked ACLU lawyer Ben Wizner when they finally "met" in early July 2013. Over an encrypted chat, Snowden, at that moment the world's most famous fugitive, his passport revoked and his prospects dim for ever leaving the transit area of Moscow's Sheremetyevo International Airport, was asking for Wizner's help. But he was also offering something vital to the ACLU's interests. The documents he had downloaded and handed over to journalists validated the organization's long-standing allegations about warrantless wiretapping, confirming that the Patriot Act and the FISA Amendments Act had indeed become a license for the NSA to put every American with a phone or an Internet connection under surveillance.

Snowden had also given the ACLU something its lawyers had been seeking for over seven years: a ticket to the federal courts, which had repeatedly refused to grant the ACLU entry on the grounds that it could not prove it was suffering damages as a result of the government actions it was alleging. As the first document re-leased from Snowden's cache showed—and as Snowden, who had been following the ACLU's efforts closely, knew—one of the com-panies that had been commanded to provide its records to the NSA "every day and for the duration of this order" was Verizon Business, and Verizon Business just happened to be the ACLU's telephone provider. Its records had been turned over to the government; its standing was no longer in question. "We've been banging our head against this wall for nine years, and now the wall's not there," Wiz-ner said. The government had been hoist on its own petard.

Wizner had known about Snowden months before he knew his name. Laura Poitras, an award-winning documentary filmmaker, had come to him in January 2013, seeking advice about encrypted emails she had been receiving from someone going by the name Citizenfour. The mysterious correspondent claimed to be work-ing as a senior officer in the intelligence community, where he had come into possession of classified documents about a massive do-mestic surveillance program. Poitras wanted Wizner's advice about Citizenfour's credibility. Should she take this seriously? Wizner, whose work with the ACLU had made him an attractive target for people spinning elaborate paranoid fantasies in long, convoluted emails, read over some of the correspondence. Citizenfour seemed rational, his tone measured and sober, missing the telltale exaggera-tions of the crank. Wizner advised Poitras to stay in touch with the man. Within months, Poitras and lawyer-turned-journalist Glenn Greenwald had engineered the release of the documents in Ameri-can and British newspapers, and the full extent of the surveillance program had become public.

Congresswoman Jackie Speier (D-CA), who had warned her col-leagues years before that the FISA Amendments Act on which they were about to vote "will subject [any American's] phone and e-mail conversations to the broad government surveillance web," had been duly suspicious. Since well before the law was passed, the NSA had been amassing data on every American's telecommunications through a variety of projects with fanciful names: MonsterMind, X-Keyscore, Dropmire, Boundless Informant, Bullrun, MYSTIC, TUMULT and TURMOIL, and PRISM, a program that targeted, according to a PowerPoint slide leaked by Snowden, "E-mail, Chat-video, voice; videos, photos, stored data, VoIP, File transfers, video conferencing . . . logins, etc; online social networking details; and Special Requests." Under these programs, which it claimed were authorized by Section 215 of the Patriot Act, the NSA was tracking the numbers, time, and length of phone calls made in the United States. In addition, the agency was monitoring the content of emails, a collection that it maintained was allowed under Section 702 of the FISA Amendments Act.

Equipped with its readings of these laws, the NSA had developed a secret playbook, one that guided intrusions even more egregious than those the ACLU had originally gone to court to question. The NSA wasn't collecting data on Americans only as a by-product of foreign surveillance; nor was it sufficiently minimizing its acquisition or storage of that data. Instead, it seemed, it was able to collect and retain vast quantities of information about US citizens, including those who were not suspected of crimes, and thanks to the weakened FISA courts and the compliant federal courts, it had been free to carry out its intention without any real check from the judiciary. This was executive-ordered dragnet surveillance plain and simple—and, now that the Snowden documents were public, undeniable.

The ACLU did not waste any time. Six days after the news of the Section 215 program broke, it filed another suit against NSA director James Clapper, this one in the Southern District of New York. It had been over seven years since Michigan Judge Anna Diggs Taylor's decision granting the organization standing to challenge the Patriot Act had been overturned. This time around the ACLU had not only its newfound claim to standing but also fresh and convincing evidence, evidence taken right from the government's files, to bolster its allegation that the spying was "akin to snatching every American's address book," as the ACLU complaint asserted. The government had interpreted the Patriot Act in such a way that it now had "a comprehensive record of our associations and public movements, revealing a wealth of detail about our familial, political, professional, religious, and intimate associations."

The decision to file *ACLU v. Clapper* was easy, or at least straight-forward. The decision to represent Snowden was more complicated. When he was finally charged, on June 14, he was not accused of garden-variety crimes but, rather, of theft of government property, unauthorized communication of national defense information, and giving classified information to an unauthorized person.

In his twelve years as ACLU executive director, Anthony Romero had taken on a number of cases, such as the surveillance suits, that the ACLU knew it was likely to lose but that it hoped might still provide an opportunity to subject the government to public pressure. And now he had to decide whether to take on another possibly lost cause, to put the organization's reputation, and the faith of its half million members, on the line for someone accused of leaking government secrets, and called a traitor, even accused of espionage, by leading government officials. "There were those who thought we should choose only projects aimed at legislative reform or litigation," Ben Wizner told me, "and not step right into the conflict zone."

By the time the question came up, whatever expectations Romero might have had that the new administration would reverse the excesses of the previous one had long ago been dashed. The disappointment had set in by May 2009, when he had placed the ad in *The New York Times* in which Obama's photo morphed into a picture of Bush. It had been strengthened by the Justice Department's continued reliance on challenges to the ACLU's standing and on the state secrets doctrine to frustrate its attempts to get a hearing on the merits of the surveillance cases. It had been deepened by Eric Holder's appointment of Patrick Fitzgerald to investigate whether the ACLU had compromised the identity of CIA agents at Guantánamo—a three-year investigation that Romero characterized as retaliation "for our activism on behalf of detainee rights," which wasn't dropped until January 2012. And it had been solidified by the killing of al-Awlaki and Khan. By the time Snowden got in touch with the ACLU, Romero had virtually abandoned his once cordial relationship with his fellow Princeton alumnus Robert Mueller, refusing the FBI director's request to address the annual meeting of the ACLU, as he had in 2003, and he'd nearly given up on the rest of the Obama administration. A complex criminal case might not have been in the ACLU's wheelhouse, but Romero wasn't going to let this latest government excess pass. He gave Ben Wizner the go-ahead to represent Edward Snowden.

IN JUNE 2013, AMERICANS WERE evenly divided on the question of whether Snowden was a hero or a villain. By the end of the summer, one poll showed that a majority of Americans considered him a whistleblower rather than a traitor. With public outcry growing over the incontrovertible evidence of mass collection of both metadata and content, the government scrambled into action. Congress held four hearings on the Snowden documents between the first revelations and the end of July. Obama administration officials defended both spying programs, arguing that they were necessary, legal, authorized by statute, conducted in a limited way, and subject to internal and external oversight. Meanwhile, the Department of Justice began extradition proceedings with Russia, which, having granted Snowden asylum, seemed unlikely to comply, even after Holder promised that "Mr. Snowden will not be tortured" or subjected to the death penalty should he return to face charges.

Obama himself addressed the matter on August 9. "Repeated leaks of classified information have initiated the debate in a very passionate, but not always fully informed way," he said, without mentioning Edward Snowden by name. Here was another instance of friction between "counterterrorism and our values," he said, and the American people were right to be skeptical. "If you are the ordinary person and you start seeing a bunch of headlines saying . . . Big

Brother [is] looking down on you, collecting telephone records, et cetera," he said, "well, understandably, people would be concerned. I would be, too, if I wasn't inside the government."

Actually, Obama had been concerned even when he'd been inside the government, when, as a senator, he "expressed a healthy skepticism about these programs." But now, apparently even better informed than when he was in the Senate, he was confident that the programs were crucial and that the data collection could be conducted in a way that upheld civil liberties. Still, he acknowledged, "it's not enough for me, as President, to have confidence in these programs. The American people need to have confidence in them as well," and he announced the specific steps that he was taking to provide it. He would seek reform of Section 215 of the Patriot Act, the section that was used to compel phone companies to provide records to the government. He left vague exactly what those reforms would be, but he did have a specific recommendation for fixing the FISA courts: to give "civil liberties concerns . . . an independent voice . . . by ensuring that the government's position is challenged by an adversary." He would also end secret law by "mak[ing] public the legal rationale for the government's collection activities under Section 215," appoint a "full-time civil liberties and privacy officer," and order the "intelligence community" to make more efforts to "give Americans . . . the ability to learn more about what . . . [it] does and what it doesn't do, how it carries out its mission, and why it does so," including a "website that will serve as a hub for further transparency." And finally, he was appointing "a high-level group of outside experts" to review the surveillance apparatus and to "consider how we can maintain the trust of the people." It was reminiscent of the 2009 National Archives speech on Guantánamo. An expert panel, a nod to practicality, a red line against secrecy, and a stated respect for constitutional guarantees.

Obama tapped five outside experts for what became known as the Review Group on Intelligence and Communication, among them Clinton counterterrorism adviser Richard Clarke. Obama did not include former assistant attorney general David Kris, who by then was working in private industry, but that didn't stop Kris from weighing in on the subject with his own analysis. Kris also flagged the confidence problem, but he saw its roots in Stellar Wind, which at that time was the subject of an investigation by the Department of Justice's inspector general, a draft of which Kris, like Obama, had seen. The Bush administration had indeed far exceeded the surveillance allowed by law as the public understood it, especially by targeting along the lines of broad rather than narrow relevance.

For Kris, as for Obama, the problem was one of balancing secrecy and transparency. "Secrecy can best be preserved only when credibility is truly maintained," he wrote, quoting Justice Potter Stewart and suggesting that a new calibration might be in the works along the lines that the president had suggested when he first publicly mentioned his intention to appoint a President's Review Board to assess the current controversial surveillance policies. "How will the United States recalibrate the tension between secrecy and transparency, and what will follow from that recalibration?" he asked.

To the President's Review Board, however, it wouldn't be enough to bolster the nation's confidence with platitudes about the natural tension between civil liberties and national security or reassurances that the president's heart was in the right place, then get on with business. "It is tempting to suggest," the board wrote, "that the underlying goal is to achieve the right 'balance' between the two forms of security. . . . But some safeguards are not subject to balancing at all." Sometimes, in other words, the government must simply be stopped.

When the board issued its report in December, it made sweeping recommendations for reform—forty-five in all. Just as the ACLU had been arguing all along, suspicion should be individualized, not generalized, the board wrote, and orders under Section 215 made specific. The government bore the burden of proving that there was "reasonable ground to believe" that the information sought was relevant to an authorized investigation that was demonstrably intended to protect "international terrorism or clandestine intelligence activities" and that this order was limited in its "focus, scope and breadth." And the collection of metadata, regardless of whether it was legal under Section 215, should be "terminated as soon as reasonably practicable."

As for the surveillance authorized by the FAA's Section 702, which allowed for the collection of content—and for spying on Americans so long as it could be somehow related to foreign communications—the board conceded that it had "served an important function in helping the United States to uncover and prevent terrorist attacks" but noted that it had been intended for foreigners, not for US persons. Because communications of citizens could be swept up in a program like this one, the board recommended three measures to limit the incursions into privacy. First, data about citizens should be purged "unless it has foreign intelligence value or is necessary to prevent serious harm to others"; second, even if it had such value, the government should be unable to use it to prosecute the citizen; and finally, the content of communications should be searched only if it is necessary to "prevent a threat of death or serious bodily harm or unless the government obtains a warrant on probable cause" that the citizen is "planning or is engaged in acts of international terrorism."

IN AT LEAST ONE WAY, Eric Holder beat the review board to the punch. During the fall of 2013, the Justice Department had started to do what Donald Verrilli had told the Supreme Court it had been doing all along, and what the law required it to do: inform defendants that information obtained under surveillance authorized by Section 702 had been used in their cases. Between October 2013 and February 2014, three defendants were notified of evidence gathered under that provision.

But the high-stakes game was being played in the district court for the Southern District of New York. That's where, on November 22, the ACLU, armed with the Snowden-verified claim to standing, squared off with the government once again over surveillance. "Nothing in the text or legislative history of [the Patriot Act] remotely suggests that Congress intended to empower the government to collect information on a daily basis, indefinitely, about every American's phone calls," Jameel Jaffer told Judge William H. Pauley III. "This kind of dragnet surveillance is precisely what the Fourth Amendment was meant to prohibit," he later summed up for the press.

ACLU lawyer Alex Abdo told the judge that now that his group's standing was undeniable, it was time to move on to the substance of its claim and the two questions it raised: Was the spying carried out under the authority of Section 215 really lawful? And did the law itself violate the First and Fourth Amendments?

Abdo argued that the privacy and "associational rights" of the entire nation, not just the ACLU, had been violated by Section 215—and not only by having their phone calls tracked. Congress had passed the law without a full account from the intelligence agencies of what they were up to and of the legal analysis they were relying on, which meant that the people had not enjoyed the representation to which the Constitution entitled them. And then there was the biggest issue of all. Citizens expected their government to leave them alone, to honor their right to privacy outside specific and grounded suspicions of criminal activity. Snowden's revelations showed that the government had betrayed this expectation of privacy, which in turn led to a crisis of confidence. This expectation was also, not coincidentally, what FISA had been enacted to uphold: the government's ability to conduct its secret business while still maintaining its credibility. At stake, then, was not only the confidentiality of the ACLU's phone records but the always fragile relationship between a government, for which secrecy is sometimes a necessity, and its citizens, who rightly fear it as a tool of an authoritarian state.

Stuart Delery, the Justice Department's lawyer, was not ready to abandon the strategy that had brought the government so much success. He again urged the judges to deny the ACLU standing, arguing this time that there was no proof of a "chilling effect" on its speech or that of its clients. He added another technical argument that might forestall the judges' ability to grapple with the substantive issues: that the proper venue for this case was not the district court but, rather, a FISA court. On the issue of representation, Delery claimed that the "government has repeatedly and faithfully kept Congress informed about the Section 215 bulk telephony-metadata program." And because national security demanded this kind of activity, he argued, the section did not violate the Fourth Amendment, which "bars only unreasonable searches and seizures."

As for the charge that the NSA was virtually knocking on every door, Delery argued that not only had the vast majority of the information swept up in the dragnet "never been reviewed by any person," but even if it had been, there was "no reasonable expectation of privacy" when it came to metadata. After all, people knew the phone company made a record of their phone calls; it showed up on their bills every month. And, he reasoned, it was also well known that police could obtain those records. Indeed, this very question had been answered by the Supreme Court in 1979, when it ruled that phone call records were fair game for criminal prosecutors, and what was true of phone numbers was true of electronic metadata—to seize that information was not to violate the Fourth or Fifth Amendment. And since the metadata collection didn't target content, he argued, it couldn't violate the First Amendment, either.

ACLU v. Clapper wasn't the only case in the federal courts challenging the surveillance programs. The same week the ACLU filed its suit, Larry Klayman, the founder of the conservative activist organization Freedom Watch, had sued the NSA, the Justice Department, and government officials on behalf of his organization and "all other similarly situated consumers, users, and U.S. citizens who are subscribers, users, customers, and otherwise avail themselves to Facebook, Yahoo, Google, Microsoft, YouTube, AOL, PalTalk, Skype, Sprint, AT&T, and/or Apple." The lawsuit accused

the officials of violating the right of freedom of association by making them and others wary and fearful of contacting people "via cell
phone out of fear of the misuse of government power." Klayman addressed the violation of privacy directly. "Generalized surveillance
of this kind has historically been associated with totalitarian and
authoritarian regimes," he wrote in his motion to the court, "not
with Constitutional democracies." On December 16, DC District
Court Judge Richard Leon granted Klayman standing.

Leon didn't issue a final ruling on the merits of the case, but it
was apparent that his sympathies lay with the plaintiff. He thought
Klayman's Fourth Amendment claim had a "substantial likelihood
of success," in part because the 1979 precedent no longer applied.
"It's one thing to say that people expect phone companies to occasionally provide information to law enforcement," he wrote in his
decision. "It is quite another to suggest that our citizens expect all
phone companies to operate what is effectively a joint intelligence-
gathering operation with the Government." The "almost-Orwellian
technology" that allows this kind of operation was "unlike anything that could have been conceived in 1979." A new world needed
new law.

The Klayman case wasn't going to make for new law anytime
soon; the government was appealing Leon's decision. And eleven
days after the decision was announced, the judge in the ACLU case
in New York's district court, William Pauley, released an opinion
that was diametrically opposed to Leon's. He bracketed his opinion
with a discussion of the 9/11 attacks. "While Americans depended
on technology for the conveniences of modernity," he wrote, "al-
Qaeda plotted in a seventh-century milieu to use that technology
against us. It was a bold jujitsu. And it succeeded because conventional intelligence gathering could not detect diffuse filaments connecting al-Qaeda." The program to which the ACLU was objecting
was an attempt to use modern technology *for* us by allowing the
government to detect those filaments before they could converge in
another attack, and Pauley was not going to prevent the government

from doing so. The ACLU's motion was denied on December 27. The ACLU appealed later that day.

AS 2014 BEGAN, BOTH LEGAL cases were in limbo, awaiting appeal, and the opposite conclusions to which the two district court judges had come only underscored how unsettled the legal question remained. In at least one arena, however, a consensus was emerging.

The President's Review Board wasn't the only commission looking into the surveillance programs. The nation also heard from the Privacy and Civil Liberties Oversight Board (PCLOB), a committee established, at the suggestion of the 9/11 Commission, to "look across the government at the actions we are taking to protect ourselves to ensure that liberty concerns are appropriately considered." It had been disbanded in 2007, in accordance with Patriot Act implementation guidelines, but Obama had revived it, and it reopened for business on May 27, 2013, nine days before Snowden went public.

The new PCLOB's first report, issued on January 23, 2014, was even more critical of the metadata-collection program than the review board's. "Section 215 does not provide an adequate legal basis to support the program," it said. The law was originally designed "to enable the FBI to acquire records that a business has in its possession . . . when those records are relevant to the investigation." But by its very nature, a bulk collection "cannot be regarded as 'relevant' to any FBI investigation . . . without redefining the word 'relevant' in a manner that is circular, unlimited in scope, and out of step with the case law." Not only that, but the statute had authorized only the FBI to make these inquiries: "It does not authorize the NSA to collect anything."

As if it weren't bad enough that the NSA was engaged in illegal activity, the oversight board wrote, its actions were also raising "concerns under both the First and Fourth Amendments." Reasoning, as Judge Leon had in the Klayman case, that the constitutionality of this kind of surveillance had not been determined, the board noted that the government now has "capabilities to collect, store, and analyze data not available when existing Supreme Court doctrine was developed."

"Any government program that entails such costs requires a strong showing of efficacy," the commission wrote. And perhaps if the surveillance had paid off, the PCLOB would have been less critical. But "based on the information provided to the Board, including classified briefings and documentation, we have not identified a single instance involving a threat to the United States in which the program made a concrete difference in the outcome." Nor had it "directly contributed to the discovery of a previously unknown terrorist plot or the disruption of a terrorist attack." It had, on a single occasion, helped identify a previously unknown terrorism suspect, but "even in that case, the suspect was not involved in planning a terrorist attack, and there is reason to believe that the FBI may have discovered him without the contribution of the NSA's program."

The program was both illegal and ineffective, and it raised the risk of government abuse—and, "given historical abuse of personal information by the government during the twentieth century, the risk is more than merely theoretical." There was only one remedy: "The government should end its Section 215 bulk telephone records program."

The PCLOB report came out on January 23, but President Obama had reportedly known about its conclusions when he gave a speech at the Department of Justice the week before. Certainly he knew that the group he had appointed after the Snowden disclosures had recommended the discontinuation of the bulk collection program. And he no doubt knew that one district court judge, in an opinion that could have remained silent on the issue, had all but declared the program unconstitutional, while another, this one friendlier to Obama's agenda, had nonetheless characterized it as a "blunt instrument" whose scope was "breathtaking." The attorney general had begun to notify defendants in October 2103 that material swept up in the government's other mass surveillance program, the content collection authorized by Section 702, was being used against them. To a president who professed to lead from behind, it was clear in what direction the herd was moving. So it was no surprise when Obama told his audience at the Justice Department that the government would stop the Section 215 bulk collection of metadata as it currently existed.

The announcement came about a half hour into a forty-five-minute speech during which Obama addressed the continuing fallout from Snowden's disclosures. Once again he described himself as maintaining a "healthy skepticism toward our surveillance programs"—not only, as he had said previously, as a senator but "after I became President." He described the steps he had taken to counter the "danger of government overreach," such as increases in oversight and new rules for surveillance. "What I did not do is to stop these programs wholesale," he acknowledged, explaining that they "made us more secure," and in addition, he said that nothing he had discovered "indicated that our intelligence community had sought to violate the law or is cavalier about the civil liberties of their fellow citizens." But, he acknowledged, the purity of intentions among analysts and policy makers, even the ones gathered for his speech, was not a reliable safeguard. "Given the unique power of the state," he told them, "it is not enough for leaders to say: Trust us, we won't abuse the data we collect."

Of course, it had been enough for leaders to say exactly that (at least to themselves and each other) until citizens knew just how much information about them was being collected. The president was promising numerous reforms—less secret law, more transparency, requirements that investigators specify the reason for a surveillance request based on metadata collection and that they limit their inquiries to phone numbers called from targeted numbers (rather than allowing a "third hop"), and tightened rules on foreign electronic spying. But whether these reforms would actually limit the power of the state remained to be seen. Nor was it yet clear whether the Klayman and ACLU cases now making their way toward the appeals court would take some of the cards out of the president's hand, or what would happen when Congress began to debate a new surveillance law. But one thing was certain: Edward Snowden had made it impossible for the government to continue to operate in the manner to which it had become accustomed since 9/11. Incontrovertible evidence had shown just how far into Americans' private lives it had reached. All the clever lawyering in the world was not going to allow it to hold on to the immense prerogatives it had claimed—at least not without a fight.

CHAPTER 18

The Ever-Elusive
Pendulum Swing

On September 25, 2014, President Obama announced the resignation of Attorney General Eric Holder, pending the confirmation of his yet-to-be-named replacement. Both men gave the kind of anodyne speeches expected at such events. The president lauded Holder's accomplishments in his nearly six years in office. Each made warm reference to the other's family, expressed gratitude for his hard work, and offered best wishes for the future. Holder just barely brushed against the problem that had dogged him from his first day in office: the ongoing failure to bring the 9/11 conspirators to justice. "We have kept faith with our belief in the power of the greatest judicial system the world has ever known to fairly and effectively adjudicate any cases that are brought before it," he said, "including those that involve the security of the nation that we both love so dearly."

A year earlier, however, he had been less reticent about the gap between his belief in that power and his ability to exercise it. It was the fourth anniversary of the announcement of his ill-fated decision to try Khalid Shaikh Mohammed and his codefendants in civilian court, and a reporter asked Holder to comment on the occasion. "I was right," Holder said. "I think that the facts and events that occurred since that date demonstrate that." Politicians, with their dire warnings of $200 million trials and disruptions in lower Manhattan, had prevented him from going forward with a case he was sure he could win. It was, Holder said, an "example of what happens when politics gets into matters that ought to simply be decided by lawyers and by national security experts." Had they been left in charge, he declared, "the defendants would be on death row as we speak."

Whether his confidence was justified, Holder's negative view of the military commissions was indisputable. While five defendants had pleaded guilty during the Obama years, not a single trial had been brought to completion since he had taken office. In fact, no trial had even begun. Questions about hearsay and evidence elicited through torture, obscured by the fog of war, or otherwise tainted by activity of intelligence agents continued to dog attempts to move beyond pretrial maneuvering, sometimes in unexpected ways. The FBI was caught trying to turn a defense security officer into an informant. Ramzi bin al-Shibh complained to his judge that the interpreter he'd been assigned "was working at the black site" where he'd been held, so he was reluctant to trust him. And in perhaps the most bizarre twist, a white-noise generator used at the judge's discretion to mask argument that might include classified material mysteriously turned on during one of the countless pretrial hearings for the 9/11 conspirators, leaving spectators unable to hear. The judge in the case was rankled when he discovered that the CIA, which was monitoring the proceedings, had installed its own switch, which it could flip on if agents thought testimony was straying into dangerous territory.

If progress was slow to the point of being imperceptible, an October 2012 decision by the DC Circuit Court threatened to bring it entirely to a standstill. The ruling came in the case of Salim Hamdan, the same detainee whose case had led the Supreme Court to invalidate the military commissions in 2006. Congress had responded to this decision with a new Military Commissions Act, and Hamdan had been the first defendant tried under the new law. He was convicted on the charge of providing material support to terrorism, sentenced to five and a half years, and upon completing the sentence in 2008 had been returned to Yemen. But his lawyers continued to challenge his conviction even after his release. Only war crimes could come before a military commission, they argued, and material support hadn't been a war crime until the 2006 MCA had made it one. Since Hamdan's support for Al Qaeda had come long before 2006, he had committed the wrong kind of crime for a military tribunal to charge or try him for, and thus, they argued, his conviction should be overturned.

The DC Circuit Court had not proved a friendly venue for Guantánamo prisoners, commonly rejecting habeas appeals, but it agreed with Hamdan and threw out his conviction. Immediately, other defense attorneys began to file motions to overturn the material support convictions of their Guantánamo clients. So, too, did they begin to challenge the conspiracy charge. Michel Paradis, the lawyer for one defendant, Ali al Bahlul, alleged to be an Al Qaeda public relations director, argued successfully that the conspiracy for which his client had been convicted had also not been a war crime when he committed it. By the summer of 2015, four of the eight convictions had been overturned. The military commissions were not only failing to make forward progress; they appeared to be on the verge of moving backward.

IN THE FEDERAL COURT SYSTEM, however, momentum seemed to be gathering. In March 2014 Bin Laden's son-in-law Sulaiman Abu Ghaith had been convicted in the Southern District of New York on charges of conspiracy and material support and sentenced to life in prison. Two months later, after a long extradition battle, Mostafa Kamel Mostafa, also known as Abu Hamza al-Masri, was tried, convicted of terrorism charges, and sentenced to life without parole.

These were legacy cases, long-delayed trials for crimes related to
9/11. But more recent cases were also coming into the criminal justice system under the direction of the National Security Division,
now headed by John Carlin. Carlin was one of an emerging group
of professionals working at the intersection of law enforcement, national security, and intelligence. He was a protégé of his predecessor
at the NSD, Lisa Monaco, who was now directing counterterrorism efforts at the White House, and his roommate at Harvard Law
School had been Rajesh De, now the general counsel of the NSA.

Under Carlin's leadership, the new cases, long in the works, proceeded with little drama and much efficiency but with Washington
in more control of cases than in pre-9/11 times. The three men who
had plotted to explode bombs in the New York subway were already
serving their prison sentences. And two foreigners captured overseas and tied to terrorist groups, who in the past might have been
brought to Guantánamo, had instead been taken into civilian custody. Ahmed Abdulkadir Warsame, a Somali national accused of
being a military commander for the terrorist group Al Shabab, was
captured by Americans en route from Yemen to Somalia in April
2011. Over objections from members of Congress, he was given his
Miranda warning and indicted by a grand jury, and in December he
pleaded guilty in the Southern District of New York. His plea agreement was sealed but was widely reported to have included a promise
of cooperation with authorities. To date, there has been no public
notice of any sentencing. Ahmed Abu Khattala, a Libyan member
of the terrorist group Ansar al-Shariah, was captured by US Special Forces in June 2014 and indicted in October 2014 in the DC
District Court. As of November 2015, he was awaiting trial at the
Alexandria Detention Center.

Civilian authorities had arrested and prosecuted both men for
criminal actions, but that didn't mean the military and intelligence
agencies lost their opportunity to question them. Prior to entering the custody of law enforcement officials, Warsame and Khattala were questioned by the High-Value Interrogation Team (HIG),

formed at the recommendation of a task force appointed by Obama to examine policies about treatment of captives. The interrogation, carried out aboard US naval vessels, was extensive; in Warsame's case, it lasted for two months, in Khattala's two weeks. Once the intelligence team was finished with them, the prisoners were read their rights, then questioned anew by the FBI, which turned over the results to the grand jury that then indicted the men.

The men were not held indefinitely, they were not tortured, and the intelligence and criminal interrogations remained separate. At least in this case, old-fashioned justice seemed to be working even in an age of terror, just as it did when the United States took into custody a twenty-nine-year-old US citizen, Mohanad Mahmoud Al Farekh. His name had once been on the "kill list," but in the last days of his tenure at the DOJ, according to Mark Mazzetti and Eric Schmitt of *The New York Times,* Holder and other Justice Department lawyers had persuaded the president to capture and try him rather than kill him by drone strike. In May 2015 material support charges were filed against Al Farekh in federal court in Brooklyn; as of September 2015, he awaits a trial date.

No crime has demonstrated the ability of the federal courts to handle terrorism cases as convincingly as the one committed by Dzhokhar and Tamerlan Tsarnaev, American citizens who in April 2013 set off bombs at the finish line of the Boston Marathon, killing three people and wounding 264 more, many of them grievously. Tamerlan was killed in the manhunt that followed, but Dzhokhar was captured and taken into custody. He was held in federal prison, tried, and sentenced to death just two years after he committed his crime. Neither abuse in custody nor illegal interrogation practices nor undisclosed surveillance techniques had hampered the trial. Prosecutors, defense attorneys, the jury, and the judge were able to stay focused on the facts of the case and the applicable laws. The brisk efficiency of the Tsarnaev trial stood out mostly for its contrast with the horror of the crimes—and for its vindication of the criminal justice system as a venue for terrorism trials. Even as the prosecution of Mohammed and his codefendants remained stuck in the military commissions labyrinth, the worst terrorist attack in the United States since 9/11 was prosecuted in civilian court and went off without a hitch.

ALTHOUGH THE OBAMA ADMINISTRATION TENTATIVELY turned toward the courts to handle terrorism cases, it continued some of the rogue policies of the past. Notably, the White House abandoned its early pledge to restore transparency to the conduct of the war on terror. It did release documents related to Bush-era torture, but its own policies often remained shrouded, and it made great efforts to keep them that way. FOIA requests, such as those filed by the ACLU for information on surveillance and targeted killings, were routinely denied, and the photos of torture that the ACLU had sought for years had still not been released. Moreover, leakers were ferreted out and punished without hesitation. Between 2010 and 2015, seven people were indicted for leaking government secrets, six of whom were tried, convicted, and sentenced in civilian courts—to terms as long as three and a half years. Edward Snowden is the seventh. An eighth leaker—army private Chelsea Manning—was convicted by court-martial and sentenced to thirty-five years in military prison.

Prior to 2010, there had been only three such convictions in the nation's history. One, a 1984 conviction of a naval intelligence civilian analyst who had provided classified information to the press, resulted in a twenty-four-month sentence that was overturned years later by President Clinton. Another, a leaker convicted during the Bush years, led to a sentence of ten months at a halfway house and community service. In perhaps the most high-profile such case, the prosecution of Daniel Ellsberg for releasing the Pentagon Papers, the charges had been dropped. In this respect, Obama once again seemed unashamed of his excesses.

But the president did not have full control over the release of information about the war on terror. At the end of 2014, the Senate

Select Committee on Intelligence released the results of a five-year investigation into the enhanced interrogation program. Neither the White House nor the CIA was keen on releasing the report; they had held it up for eight months and insisted on redactions that in some places made the public version (a six-hundred-page executive summary of a six-thousand-page report) nearly unintelligible. It also spawned ferocious battles between the committee—especially its chair, Dianne Feinstein—and the CIA, with each side lodging charges of spying and theft against the other.

When it finally came out, in December 2014, the report was unstinting in its depiction of the CIA's practices. From Senator Feinstein's introductory remark that "it is my personal conclusion that, under any common meaning of the term, CIA detainees were tortured" in the CIA's "enhanced interrogation" program to its conclusion that the program "was not an effective means of acquiring intelligence or gaining cooperation from detainees," the report was comprehensive and devastating. Issued as the *Committee Study of the Central Intelligence Agency's Detention and Interrogation Program*, it rapidly became known as the Senate torture report. Based on millions of documents, including email exchanges that detailed the role of various officials and government agencies in the program, the report introduced terms like "rectal feeding" and "mock execution" to the American public. It provided details about the treatment of specific detainees in CIA custody that had theretofore been unknown, including a cable suggesting that whatever was inflicted upon Abu Zubaydah, "we need to get reasonable assurances that [he] will remain in isolation and incommunicado for the remainder of his life." The report left no doubt that the CIA had systematically lied to both the president and Congress about its actions. And it made clear that the Bush administration had told its own lies, and spun its own version of the truth, in order to mislead the American people about the depth and depravity of the program, which had been "brutal and far worse" than the CIA had previously admitted.

The Senate torture report also left no doubt that whatever intelligence torture might have produced could have been (and often was) elicited in other ways and with much greater accuracy, since people being tortured will often say whatever they think their interrogators want to hear. Even the CIA knew this, although it was reluctant to acknowledge or act on it. According to Senator Feinstein, "Sometimes, the CIA knew detainees were lying. Other times, the CIA acted on false information, diverting resources and leading officers or contractors to falsely believe they were acquiring unique or actionable intelligence and that its interrogations were working when they were not." But, at least according to the Senate torture report, at all times the CIA acted to avoid oversight. The program it worked so hard to preserve, the report concluded, had "damaged the United States' standing in the world" and was a "stain in our history that must never be allowed to happen again."

What the torture report failed to do was name names. Countries that hosted black sites and individuals who participated in the torture were given pseudonyms in the full version, but the White House and CIA balked at releasing the executive summary with those fictitious names intact. In the final version, the countries' aliases are preserved, but the torturers' are redacted. The White House claimed this was to prevent anyone from figuring out the real names of the participants, but with all names blacked out, as Andrea Prasow of Human Rights Watch put it, "You don't know if the same person who got memos saying this isn't working later said everything's fine, this guy's talking and then decided to up the severity of the abuse." But it wasn't just narrative coherence that suffered from the redactions. As Josh Gerstein wrote in *Politico*, "the result is a report that states what happened but defies many attempts to establish a chain of responsibility." Which might have been exactly the point: an administration that had been from its first days eager to leave the past behind, that had never sought to prosecute interrogators who tortured prisoners or lawyers who tortured the law, wasn't about to allow the release of a public document that might identify those who could be held accountable.

FOUR MONTHS AFTER THE RELEASE of the Senate torture report, another extensive document about government wrongdoing came into public view, this one conducted inside the executive branch rather than Congress. In April 2015 the Department of Justice made public the *Report on the President's Surveillance Program*, which had been compiled by the inspectors general of five agencies, including the CIA, the NSA, and the Department of Justice. A thirty-eight-page version of the report, released in 2009, had already alerted citizens to the existence of Stellar Wind and the surveillance programs launched under it, and, of course, the Snowden disclosures had filled in the details of domestic spying in the two years prior to the release of the full report. But the full 407-page DOJ part of the report was filled with new revelations, not the least of which was the conclusion that the surveillance programs, like torture, were largely ineffective at preventing terrorist attacks. One FBI official, responding to NSA complaints that they weren't hearing enough about the results of the information they were passing along, explained to the inspectors that he was receiving "little feedback from field offices other than, 'You're sending us garbage.'"

The DOJ inspector general's report, like the Senate report, also detailed the efforts made to evade and subvert the law in order to carry out the program. And it identified people in the government, such as Jack Goldsmith and James Comey, who had noted the program's illegality and objected to it. But as the report detailed, much of this dissent was squelched, sometimes openly, as James Baker had discovered when he was still the head of the Office of Intelligence and Policy Review. As he was reviewing a request for a FISA warrant, he began to wonder if the information leading to the request had come from a FISA-authorized wiretap, as it should have. The only way to answer his question was to let him in on the secret Stellar Wind program and the John Yoo memo that had declared it legal. Baker disagreed with Yoo's reasoning and pressed the Justice Department to inform the FISA Court of the program and the memo. Attorney General Ashcroft not only refused; he forbade Baker, in writing, to inform them himself.

According to the report, Baker made at least one other attempt to interfere with a process that he sensed was operating outside the rules. He went to the Justice Department's Professional Responsibility Advisory Office (PRAO) to get an opinion on the ethics of the situation. The head of PRAO agreed with Baker that it was his duty to inform the FISA Court about Stellar Wind, that indeed he should not sign the pending FISA application unless the FISA Court knew the whole story. At the White House, Addington declared that Baker should be "fired for insubordination," ordered Baker off the job, and directed his fellow Justice Department lawyer Daniel Levin to sign the application and present it to the FISA Court judge. Levin complied, but not before Baker called the judge to tell him what was going on. The judge approved the application anyway. Baker remained head of the OIPR, but eventually his department and its portfolio disappeared into the newly formed National Security Division. Baker might or might not have intended to speak over the inspectors general's heads and to history. Either way, their report surely vindicated him. It is impossible to read the report and not conclude that the surveillance programs skirted the law and damaged the relationship between citizens and their government—and for no discernible benefit.

NEITHER THE SENATE'S TORTURE REPORT nor the inspectors general's report on Stellar Wind called for prosecution or other sanctions. Most of those who designed and implemented the policies continue to thrive in their professional lives. But the reports did shift the momentum within the institutions of government, especially in the courts, where the legacy of the expansive security state was bound to have an impact. It has been left to organizations like the ACLU and the Center for Constitutional Rights (CCR) to seek accountability—if in no other way than to make sure that information illegally obtained or withheld cannot be used to convict terrorists.

But in early 2014 it was a federal prosecutor, and not lawyers from the ACLU or CCR, who informed the Eastern District of New York court of government misconduct "that has changed the landscape" of a terrorism case. As Loretta Lynch, who a year later would be appointed attorney general, told Judge John Gleeson, the government's charges against Albanian architect Agron Hasbajrami, who had pleaded guilty to one count of material support in April 2012, had depended in part on information acquired through surveillance authorized by Section 702 of the FISA Amendments Act—a fact of which Hasbajrami hadn't been informed until two years after his guilty plea. Hasbajrami's was one of the cases that were being revisited in the wake of Verrilli's discovery that defendants who were discovered via 702 intercepts had not actually been informed of that fact.

Here was an opportunity for the ACLU to make the government pay a price for violating its own laws. And Hasbajrami seemed determined to seek the maximum redress. He didn't want only to challenge the use of the 702 materials. He wanted to withdraw his plea and start all over again with the prospect, in his mind, of a dismissal or even an acquittal. His lawyers advised against this. When he announced the sentence in 2012, Judge Gleeson had complained bitterly. "If I were the prosecutor, I wouldn't have given you this deal," he said, making it clear that he would have preferred to mete out a more severe punishment than the fifteen years he'd given Hasbajrami. And as Hasbajrami's lawyers pointed out to him, the original charges carried potential sentences totaling sixty years.

Still, their client wanted to take the gamble. The ACLU was following the case with interest. It had long wanted an opportunity to challenge the constitutionality of the surveillance laws in court. It had come close in its case against the NSA, receiving standing in the district court, only to have it overturned by the circuit court. "We were looking for any door or window" into the Fourth Amendment questions, Ben Wizner once told me, and the Hasbajrami case seemed to provide one.

Hasbajrami already had a crack team of defense lawyers, all experienced at terrorism cases, and ambitious enough to want to argue any Supreme Court case that might result from the retrial. But the ACLU had the expertise on the Fourth Amendment issue. It entered the case with an amicus brief and a promise that its lawyers would participate in arguing the constitutional question in court.

That question came up almost immediately. Gleeson granted Hasbajrami's plea withdrawal motion in October, noting that the failure of the prosecution to notify the defendant of the source of the evidence against him had resulted in "the overwhelming—and false—impression that no FAA-obtained information figured in the government's case." In January 2015 he heard arguments about the Section 702 evidence. Hasbajrami's lawyers wanted the evidence excluded on the grounds that it was not collected in accordance with 702, and even if it had been collected in accordance with Section 702, it still was not lawful because Section 702 authorized surveillance "without a determination of probable cause," without "any particularity regarding the place, time, person or thing that can be searched," and with minimal FISA Court oversight, and was therefore unconstitutional. So the evidence was "the fruit of the poisonous tree," said lead lawyer Michael Bachrach. Also, like evidence derived from torture, he argued, it should be considered the product of "outrageous government conduct" and thus ruled ineligible as evidence.

At the end of his argument, Bachrach drew on the film *American Sniper*, which had just opened, for a striking metaphor about the true nature of Section 702: "Instead of using a sniper's rifle, [the FAA] uses a machine gun. Instead of using a scope, it puts on a blindfold.

And instead of targeting foreign persons abroad, it turns around with the machine gun and just sprays across at anything it can hit on U.S. soil. That is not constitutional, Your Honor." Even if he'd seen the movie, Gleeson was not persuaded. He denied the defense's motion seeking suppression of the 702 materials. He gave no reason for his ruling, promising a written opinion—which, as of November 2015, he still had not presented. But when Hasbajrami ultimately decided to plead guilty again, Gleeson consented and added one year to the sentence. Both parties agreed that the appeal would be limited to the issue of the 702 materials and the sentence itself.

The Hasbajrami appeal wasn't the ACLU's only active challenge to the FAA. In March 2015 it filed a complaint on behalf of the Wikimedia Foundation. The subject was new—UPSTREAM, a program exposed by Snowden that intercepts text-based communications while in transit. The argument was by now familiar: FAA-authorized mass surveillance—which allows the NSA to read the content as well as gather the metadata of communications of any conversation involving a foreign address (or just a switch or server in a foreign country), even those with an American participant—would chill expression, in this case, the debates for which the foundation's flagship project, Wikipedia, was famous and on which it thrived. It thus violated the First and Fourth Amendments.

As that case began its journey through the courts, another ACLU case reached a crucial milepost. On May 7, 2015, the Second Circuit Court of Appeals announced its decision in *ACLU v. Clapper,* the case built on the organization's relationship with Verizon. The decision was a bombshell, one that marked a turning point in the fourteen-year conflict between security and justice. In an opinion written by Judge Gerard Lynch, it ruled that the bulk collection of telephone records exceeded the intent of Congress when it enacted Section 215 of the Patriot Act—in other words, the program was illegal.

At issue, in particular, was the government's definition of the term *relevance.* As Lynch explained, the creation of "a vast trove of records . . . to be held in reserve in a data bank, to be searched if and when at some hypothetical future time the records might become relevant," relied on a definition of *relevant* bounded by neither "the facts of the investigation or by a finite time limitation." That definition only works if "there is only one enormous 'anti-terrorism' investigation, and that any records that might ever be of use in developing any aspect of that investigation are relevant to the overall counterterrorism effort." And surely if Congress intended to make the "momentous decision" to define relevance in a way that would result in "an unprecedented contraction of the privacy expectations of all Americans," Lynch wrote, "we would expect such a momentous decision to be preceded by substantial debate and expressed in unmistakable language."

But Congress had held no such debate and had written no such language into the law; indeed, as Lynch pointed out, even though the data collection had been going on since at lest 2006, most representatives and senators didn't even know about it at the time they passed the Patriot Act, so they couldn't have debated, let alone "ratified a program of which [they] were not aware." Congress had meant to authorize the collection of specific data related to specific investigations; the NSA had clearly exceeded its authority.

The circuit court judges did not rule on the Fourth Amendment question; under the doctrine of constitutional avoidance, once it finds a violation of the law, a court is not supposed to go on to address larger constitutional issues. But Section 215 surely raised Fourth Amendment questions. Because "the seriousness of the constitutional concerns . . . has some bearing on what we hold today, and on the consequences of that holding," Lynch did not shy away from those concerns—or from suggesting a way to resolve them. "Congress is better positioned than the courts to understand and balance the intricacies and competing concerns involved in protecting our national security," he wrote, "and to pass judgment on the value of the telephone metadata program." Such a judgment "would carry weight" with the courts, and so, Lynch suggested, Congress should take up the question directly and decide just how far the expectation of privacy should be contracted in the fight against terror.

Congress, as Lynch noted, would have the opportunity to do that very soon. The Patriot Act was set to expire in just a few weeks, and there was already a replacement bill pending, the USA Freedom Act (like the Patriot Act, a bulky acronym, standing for "Uniting and Strengthening America by Fulfilling Rights and Ending Eavesdropping, Dragnet-collection and Online Monitoring Act"). Perhaps Congress would vote to explicitly allow a program like the one under discussion, at which point "there will be time to address appellants' constitutional issues." Or perhaps it would vote to end dragnet collection. Either way, with the decision so close at hand, the appeals court was not going to grant an injunction against metadata collection but, rather, would leave that ruling to the district court, which would have a different legal landscape in which to make its decision.

In the meantime, the monitoring of every phone call, every day, indefinitely would continue at least for a few weeks. But on June 1 the Patriot Act would expire, and unless Congress voted to extend or replace it, metadata collection would end. Throughout May, Justice Department officials, including James Comey and the recently confirmed Loretta Lynch, urged lawmakers to find a way to extend the program, lest the government suffer "a serious lapse in our ability to protect the American people." But members of Congress also heard from another voice within the DOJ: the FBI's inspector general, who had been investigating Section 215 surveillance. The report reiterated the conclusions that the President's Review Board and the PCLOB had each made more than a year earlier. According to the FBI IG's report, issued in May 2015, FBI officials had been "unable to identify any major case developments that resulted from use of the records obtained through use of Section 215 orders." Information obtained through 215 surveillance had been useful to corroborate facts and discover new leads, but not to develop existing leads or prevent attacks.

By the end of May, it was clear that Congress was prepared to let the Patriot Act's Section 215 die by passing the Freedom Act, which it did on June 2. The new law put an end to the bulk collection of metadata collection, at least by the government. Telecommunications companies would still have to hold on to data for eighteen months, which the Federal Communications Commission already required, and the government would need to get an individualized warrant to search that data. Information about citizens' calling and emailing and browsing would still be amassed, but by corporations, which could use it to annoy them with advertisements, in contrast to the government, which could arrest them. The Freedom Act also enacted other reforms, notably that the FISA Court would have to publish its significant decisions and that a "special advocate" would participate in FISA Court proceedings, representing (without their knowing it, of course) the proposed targets of surveillance.

The ACLU opposed the new law on the grounds that it did not force investigators to be specific enough about their targets, and it asked for an injunction against a short-term continuation of the Section 215 program that Congress had allowed. But still, the outcome, first in the courts and then in Congress, was encouraging. It had taken persistence, the slow turning of public opinion, the work of Congress in its oversight capacity, and the actions of one renegade NSA contractor, but after fourteen years of battling, and mostly losing, the organization standing for the country's allegiance to the constitution could finally claim a victory.

It was possible that the tide was turning, that the wave of fear that had swamped civil liberties was finally beginning to recede.

EPILOGUE

Whether the momentum will continue, whether the attempt to preserve America will also preserve Americans' values and their rights under the Constitution, remains to be seen. As Barack Obama's presidency draws to a close, the flames of the counter-terrorism frenzy that were ignited fifteen years ago have begun to die down. Neither civil liberties nor the rule of law was consumed. Instead, what lie in the ashes are the most egregious violations of them: torture, mass surveillance, indefinite detention, extrajudicial trials, and indiscriminate drone killings, all of which, after bruising battles, have been reined in, if not abolished.

This might not have been the case had the handful of officials who first objected to these policies at the end of George Bush's first term not worked hard and tried, quietly and without fanfare, to change them. Nor would it have happened if the Obama administration had not been determined to return to the federal courts the jurisdiction that military tribunals and secret law had taken away, and to commission and make public reports, like the inspectors general's account of Stellar Wind, that detailed the scope of government surveillance. And, of course, it could not have occurred without the lawyers and activists at organizations like the ACLU, or the defense attorneys drafted into the war on terror, or, finally, Edward Snowden. Their efforts might have accomplished less than they hoped, but they have at least succeeded in pulling off the veil. They have, in other words, made possible what is essential to any democracy: open debate. And they have at least partially repudiated Alberto Gonzales's view that in a time of terror, constitutional guarantees are "quaint" and "obsolete."

Still, the struggle to restore rights—and the courts that embody and adjudicate those rights—to their transcendent status in American law and policy is not over. President Obama might have ended torture, declaring it once again to be illegal; he might yet succeed in closing Guantánamo, and his use of drones might have come under some restraints. But some detainees will most likely be moved to federal prisons and kept there indefinitely, and the Obama administration continues to put names, potentially including those of Americans, on kill lists.

Above all, Obama has refused to punish those who designed, justified, carried out, and covered up torture. Without accountability, there is little to deter a future John Yoo from fashioning opinions to suit the exigent needs of a future president. Some of those who had a part in building these programs have confessed to me their remorse, the way their participation keeps them up at night, but this sorrow remains as secret as the programs once were. And all of them, remorseful or not, are free to pursue their careers and, if called upon, to comment, as Dick Cheney and John Yoo still sometimes are, to defend torture as a useful weapon in the war on terror.

It is in this uncertain climate, in which we are struggling to square recent threats to social order and safety with old ideals about freedom and privacy, that terrorism has taken on a new face: ISIS, a global gang that thrives on a vast social media outreach to discontented youths. It has set its sights on fulfilling Osama bin Laden's dream of a caliphate, a Muslim homeland extending across the globe. ISIS is reckless and ruthless, openly determined to wreak havoc wherever and whenever it can. And it will likely sometimes succeed. Terror attacks are as sure to happen as a devastating earthquake on the West Coast or a hurricane on the East, as a pandemic of SARS or Ebola or influenza, or as the failure of a vital piece of our deteriorating infrastructure. They are, in other words, a condition of our current existence.

That isn't to say we are helpless to mitigate the threat but, rather, that fear should not be our primary guide, as it was in the aftermath of 9/11. Terrorism in its twenty-first-century form, and particularly as it arises in ISIS, is borderless and faceless, relying on an outside community to spread its word. It attracts loners, outcasts, the alienated, and the bullied, and in this respect it is symptomatic of a world that is faster paced, less local, and more global, harder to find one's way in, and less static than ever before. The challenge is immense, but the challenge is bigger than ISIS; the challenge arises from the flaws that have always lurked in modernity and that have surfaced from time to time in events that are disruptive, sometimes shockingly so.

After World War I, Europe faced one of these ruptures. The war featured advances made possible by new technologies—in flight, in weaponry, and in communications. Information moved faster than ever before, people moved faster than ever before, and it was easier than ever before to inflict death on a massive scale. Even after the horror of the war subsided, these rapid changes overwhelmed governments. The younger generation, which might have adapted to the pace of the new age, had largely been killed off in the war, leaving decisions largely to the old men of the nineteenth century. Gripped with fear and confusion, unable to grasp the depth of the changes— or to come to terms with them—they did their best, and failed, even with such technology at their disposal, to bring either peace or prosperity to Europe, descending into fascism carried out by totalitarian governments that, among other excesses, considered rights and the rule of law an impediment to order and national honor.

America is facing a parallel challenge. In the decade after 9/11, this country came perilously close to losing the protections of the Bill of Rights—to undermining the country's foundation on the rights to freedom of speech and religion, to freedom from capricious searches and seizures, to due process and fair treatment, and to protections from cruel and unusual punishment. These rights come as close to the credo of a national religion as we have. That they were so easily abrogated, and with the help of the people to whom we entrusted them, should give us pause and lead us to think hard before once again tossing them aside in the face of terror.

Living with impermanence and instability, the hallmark conditions of our age, requires courage and steadfastness. Rather than distract ourselves with futile efforts to create a kind of safety that can't be achieved, it might be a good idea to teach our children—not to mention our policy makers—to keep a firm footing no matter how much terrifying information comes their way each day. We should urge those in whom we have entrusted the future of the country to focus not on symptoms of the time so much as on what underlies them—in the case of the events described in this book, all the pathologies that give rise to movements like Al Qaeda and ISIS. We should force them to take responsibility for and action against those conditions for which we bear responsibility and which, unlike terrorism itself, can be controlled through careful action. And above all, we should insist that they hew to the rule of law and the constitutional principles that it embodies. We have seen what happens when fear leads to the abandonment of those principles. What remains to be seen is whether we can face down terror even as we uphold those principles, whether we can have the courage to believe that what we cherish can see us through.

ACKNOWLEDGMENTS

Gratitude for the making of this book extends far and wide. The roster of colleagues, friends, family—and strangers—who took the time and energy to contribute to this book would require its own chapter. I conducted hundreds of interviews, witnessed dozens of hearings and trials, and was encouraged and schooled by numerous lawyers, experts, and journalists—many more than I will be able to name here, but all of whom have my thanks.

The Center on National Security at Fordham Law fueled much of the thinking that went into this book. Sheila Foster made it her cause to bring me and my work to Fordham Law School, laying the foundation for the Center and in so doing providing a productive home for this book. Dean Mike Martin's enthusiasm is greatly appreciated as well. Dean Matthew Diller added his support in the final stages. Susan Quatrone, who leads the research on terrorism trials for CNS, and who has a hand in so much of what the Center does, has provided not only painstaking research on terrorism cases but thoughtful guidance through many drafts of the book. Kevin

Garnett was an indispensable research assistant for much of the book. Jacqueline Barkett's research and magnificent chart launched the book's formative stages. Andrew Dalack's help made all the difference in the final stages of research. Thanks to Josh Brandman and Rachel Landry as well. Conor Walsh, Seth Weiner, Justin Pitts, Lara Bernstein, Benjamin Haas, Stephen Calabria, Jonathan Masters, Rachel Landry, and Carolyn O'Hara helped keep the Center running and pitched in where they could.

For legal advice and direction, I sought input from many quarters, and many perspectives. No one was more generous than Joshua Dratel, whose knowledge of terrorism cases is a national treasure and whose kindness toward me was unwavering. David Raskin has for years given me painstaking tutorials in the art and skill of terrorism prosecutions. Ali Soufan was always available as a fount of knowledge and a moral compass. Ken Wainstein kindly walked me through the players, the issues, and the context of the early days of the National Security Division. Donna Newman, Andrew Patel, and Ed MacMahon were generous with their time and thoughts. Don Borelli provided his always candid, clear-eyed view of events. Robert McFadden graciously offered his expertise. Jameel Jaffer's patience and guidance over the years has been immensely helpful. Ben Wizner shared his insights throughout.

David Kelley, Neil McBride, Todd Hinnen, Jamil Jaffer, Matt Olsen, Dan Jones, and numerous officials and former officials shared their memories, their views, and their work—as did so many lawyers, including Anthony Romero, Michael Bachrach, Donna Newman, Andrew Patel, Michel Paradis, Tom Durkin, Gabor Rona, Jonathan Hafetz, Scott Horton, Hina Shamsi, Alex Abdo, Joshua Larocca.

When it came to the theory of law, my teachers were unsurpassed. David Kris and Jack Goldsmith held my hand through repeated conversations about the intricacies of the Patriot Act and subsequent national security reforms. Steve Vladeck, Marty Lederman, and Stephen Holmes pitched in, ever helpful in clarifying the law as it evolved from year to year.

Journalists helped guide me through the rules of the trade as I fell deeper and deeper into the complexities of the war on terror. Peter Bergen, Benjamin Weiser, Phil Hirschkorn, Tom Engelhardt, Bob Windrem, Adam Goldman, Paul Cruickshank, Dina Temple-Raston, Joe Conason, and Tara McKelvey encouraged me at various stages along the way. Larry Wright was a welcome beacon at many junctures throughout. David McCraw offered his gentle encouragement.

The support of colleagues was essential to this book. Michael Sheehan, longtime friend and partner in various projects, along with Vinnie Viola, whose trust and thoughtfulness has inspired me for years. Tony Manganiello and Tim Strabbing, from the Madison Policy Forum, reassured me time and time again.

I am likewise indebted to those who shared their stories with me: Janis Karpinski, Coleen Rowley, Frank Lindh, and the many federal judges, lawyers, and policy makers who met with me to discuss the ins and outs of these issues and their personal journeys through post-9/11 legal tangles. Burton Wides generously gave of his time, his memories, and his impressions over many decades.

Thanks go to my editor, Rachel Klayman at Crown, whose clarity of mind guided the work throughout, and to my agent, Gillian MacKenzie, whose vision was the initial impetus for this book. John Berger, now as always, guided me with the longtime friendship that has touched each of my books.

The manuscript, as it reached maturity, received support from colleagues and friends. Karma Kreizenbeck, along with Maeve and Caleb, cleared the space more than once for me to gather my thoughts. Karma read and commented on draft chapters, always engaged, always insightful, always kind. Alexandra Starr helped me put pen to paper before the idea of this book was fully formulated, and continued to encourage me at crucial junctures along the way. Sam Douglas provided vital editorial suggestions at a crucial stage of writing. Jeff Grossman carefully commented on the early premises of the argument. Beth Elon gave me love and support throughout, even from afar. Elliott Millenson brought not only friendship but the reality of policy making into greater focus. Carol Dysinger infused the filmmaker's eye into the emerging narrative. Pat Bernard provided a constant sounding board for the many hurdles that had to be overcome to put this story together. Jiana Paladino and Nick Lacey offered to help always and in any way.

My dad, Larry, read early chapters and made careful edits, while Jo Larsen cheered me on. My mother, Ruth, was a source of encouragement. My sister-in-law, Susan—ever strong, ever poetic, ever supportive, ever wise—swept in at numerous times to remind me of the light at the end of the tunnel. My brother Rich was a constant companion. His ideas, expertise, and judgment calls were invaluable at every stage of the way.

My children—Adam and Katie—were supportive and confident cheerleaders from beginning to end. Adam's political savvy and unique insights into our changing world and Katie's talent for intellectual precision, the importance of character, and the art of narrative flow—and their joint appreciation for the importance of this story—made for the kindest and most thought-inspiring companions a writer could ever hope for. My grandson, Addison, breathed life into the book as into my life in general, and along with his sister, Jacqueline, gently nudged me to the finish line. My daughter-in-law, Jessica, sympathetically shared the pleasures and perils of book writing.

Danny Goldberg was there day and night, welcoming this at times unruly guest like one of the family. His patience, love, commentary, and willingness to help nurture various iterations provided safe haven on two coasts, amid whatever turmoil the universe offered up. I am forever grateful.

Without my brother Gary, this would have been a different book. Born on my second birthday, and the yin to my yang for nearly sixty years now, his braver, wiser, more experienced eye helped infuse this book with the magic and candor that only an almost twin can inspire. He has made me feel like the luckiest person on earth.

NOTES

INTRODUCTION

3 **"have to work the dark side"**: Jane Mayer, *The Dark Side: The Inside Story of How the War on Terror Turned into a War on American Ideals* (New York: Anchor, 2009), 9–10. Also see Dick Cheney's appearance on *Meet the Press*, NBC, September 16, 2001, https://www.youtube.com/watch?v=KQBsCIaxMuM.

CHAPTER 1: JUSTICE AT WAR

11 **"From that moment forward"**: John Ashcroft, *Never Again: Securing America and Restoring Justice* (New York: Center Press, 2006), 130.

12 **"we should nail them"**: "John Ashcroft Discusses His New Job as Attorney General," *Larry King Live*, CNN, February 7, 2001, http://www.cnn.com/TRANSCRIPTS/0102/07/lkl.00.html.

13 **"the major threat"**: *Confirmation Hearing on the Nomination of Robert S. Mueller III to Be Director of the Federal Bureau of Investigation*, July 30–31, 2001, http://www.gpo.gov/fdsys/pkg/CHRG-107shrg80335/html/CHRG-107shrg80335.htm.

13 **"what is the bureau doing today"**: "FBI Director Robert Mueller Describes Agency's Post-9/11 Transformation," *The Harbus*, October 16,

2012, http://www.harbus.org/2012/fbi-director-robert-mueller-describes-agencys-post-911-transformation/.

13 **"a total breakdown"**: John Ashcroft, Testimony Before the Senate Committee on the Judiciary, 107th Cong., September 25, 2001, http://www.gpo.gov/fdsys/pkg/CHRG-107shrg81140/html/CHRG-107shrg81140.htm.

13 **"human error"**: "Statement of Attorney General Ashcroft Regarding the Inspector General's Report on the FBI's Handling of McVeigh Documents," Department of Justice, March 19, 2002, http://www.justice.gov/archive/opa/pr/2002/March/02_ag_158.htm.

14 **no networked computer system:** "FBI Failure to Create a Modern Computer Network," Center for Public Integrity, December 10, 2008, http://www.publicintegrity.org/2008/12/10/6291/fbi-failure-create-modern-computer-network.

14 **cripplingly short on able translators:** Robert Worth, "Agents Wanted. Should Speak Pashto," *New York Times*, October 1, 2001.

14 **"deeply and fundamentally flawed"**: *Attorney General's Review Team on the Handling of the Los Alamos National Laboratory Investigation* (the Bellows Report), May 2000, 3, http://fas.org/irp/ops/ci/bellows/chap1.html.

15 **"can do the job"**: *The 9/11 Commission Report*, 424, http://www.911commission.gov/report/911Report.pdf.

16 **"antique weapons"**: Ashcroft testimony to Judiciary Committee.

17 **"our fight against terrorism"**: Ibid.

18 **"you won't believe this"**: Michael Chertoff, interview by author, August 27, 2013.

18 **"This is a guy who could fly"**: Coleen Rowley, interview by Paul Jay, Realnews.com, October 23, 2009, http://therealnews.com/t2/index.php?option=com_content&task=view&id=31&Itemid=74&jumival=12367.

18 **"I am nothing!"**: "Flight Instructor Gets $5 Million for Catching Terror Suspect," CNN, February 25, 2008.

20 **"allegations of substantial, even massive wrong-doing"**: *Church Committee Report, Book I: Introduction* (1976), 1, http://www.aarclibrary.org/publib/church/reports/book1/pdf/ChurchB1_1_Introduction.pdf.

21 **the Church Committee reported:** *Final Report of the Select Committee to Study Governmental Operations with Respect to Intelligence Activities, United States Senate: Together with Additional, Supplemental, and Separate Views* (1976), https://archive.org/stream/finalreportofselo1unit/finalreportofselo1unit_djvu.txt.

22 **Janet Reno turned a strict interpretation:** Barbara A. Grewe, "Legal Barriers to Information Sharing: The Erection of a Wall Between Law Enforcement and Intelligence Investigations, Commission on Terror Attacks

Upon the United States," staff monograph, https://fas.org/irp/eprint/wall
.pdf.

22 **the "FISA wall":** Cedric Logan, "The FISA Wall and Federal Investigations," *NYU Journal of Law and Liberty,* vol. 4, 209 (2009). See also David
Kris, *The Rise and Fall of the FISA Wall, Stanford Law and Policy Review,*
vol. 17, 487 (2006).

22 **"being used sub rosa":** *In re All Matters Submitted to Foreign Intelligence
Surveillance Court,* 218 F.Supp.2d 611, 620 (FISA Ct. 2002) *Abrogated by
In re Sealed Case,* 310 F.3d 717 (FISA Ct. Rev. 2002), http://fas.org/irp/
agency/doj/fisa/fisc051702.html.

22 **"alarming number":** Ibid., at 620.

23 **"this statement could easily come back":** Coleen Rowley to FBI director
Robert Mueller, May 21, 2002, http://www.rense.com/general25/facts
.htm.

CHAPTER 2: THE PROBLEM

28 **"passion rather than reason":** David Kris, "Certification in the Criminal
Law," *Journal of Legislation* 19, no. 1 (1993): 1.

28 **Kris was particularly concerned:** Good summaries of Kris's thoughts were
made in testimony before Congress. See "Statement of Associate Deputy
Attorney General David Kris," September 10, 2002, http://fas.org/irp/
congress/2002_hr/091002kris.html. See also David Kris, Testimony Before the House Subcommittee on Crime, Terrorism, and Homeland Security,
"Implementation of the USA Patriot Act: Section 218—Foreign Intelligence
Information ('The Wall')," 109th Cong., April 28, 2005, http://commdocs
.house.gov/committees/judiciary/hju20877.000/hju20877_0f.htm

28 **"From lawyer access":** Kris Testimony Before House Subcommittee,
2005.

29 **"is *mandatory* and is to be":** Larry Thompson to Criminal Division,
OIPR, and FBI on Information Sharing, August 6, 2001, http://fas.org/
irp/agency/doj/fisa/dag080601.html.

29 **"too timid, too cautious":** Larry Thompson, interviews by author,
April 27, 2013, and September 14, 2015.

29 **Four days later:** For a chronology of legal decrees immediately following
9/11, see, for example, Marcy Wheeler, "The Precedent for Using Presidential National Emergency Proclamations to Expand Surveillance,"
emptywheel.net, April 3, 2015.

29 **"two guys unilaterally":** Thompson interview, September 14, 2015.

30 **Yoo, a thirty-four-year-old lawyer:** John Choon Yoo faculty profile, University of California, Berkeley Law School, https://www.law.berkeley
.edu/php-programs/faculty/facultyProfile.php?facID=235.

32 **"the government's interest against"**: John Yoo to David Kris, "RE: Constitutionality of Amending Foreign Intelligence Surveillance Act to Change the 'Purpose' Standard for Searches," U.S. Department of Justice, Office of Legal Counsel, September 25, 2001, 3, http://nsarchive .gwu.edu/torturingdemocracy/documents/20010925.pdf.

32 **his undergraduate thesis**: Paras D. Bhayani, "Ex–Bush Official's Thesis Reflects Current Views," *Harvard Crimson*, February 13, 2006.

33 **"criminal investigation constitutes"**: Yoo to Kris, September 25, 2001.

34 **"A warrantless search"**: Yoo was quoting from the Supreme Court decision in *Griffin v. Wisconsin*, 483 U.S. 868, 873 (1987) (internal quotations omitted).

36 **"measures that would . . . lead"**: Laura W. Murphy and Gregory T. Nojeim, "Letter to the Senate Urging Rejection on the Final Version of the USA Patriot Act," October 23, 2001, https://www.aclu.org/letter/letter -senate-urging-rejection-final-version-usa-patriot-act.

36 **speech delivered in Cleveland**: Anthony Romero, "In Defense of Liberty at a Time of National Emergency," City Club of Cleveland, OH, copy in author's possession.

37 **"allows FISA to be used *primarily*"**: John Ashcroft to FBI Director, Criminal Division Assistant Attorney General, Counsel for Intelligence Policy, and United States Attorneys, "Intelligence Sharing Procedures for Foreign Intelligence and Foreign Counterintelligence Investigations Conducted by the FBI," U.S. Department of Justice, Office of the Attorney General, March 6, 2002, http://fas.org/irp/agency/doj/fisa/ag030602.html.

38 **John Yoo was writing another memo**: John C. Yoo, "Memorandum for the Attorney General," November 2, 2001, http://www.justice.gov/sites/ default/files/olc/legacy/2011/03/25/johnyoo-memo-for-ag.pdf.

38 **top secret edict**: "A Review of the Department of Justice's Involvement with the President's Surveillance Program," Office of the Inspector General, U.S. Department of Justice, July 2009, 1, https://oig.justice.gov/ special/s0907.pdf.

39 **Hayden's reservations**: Ibid., 14.

CHAPTER 3: A PAWN IN THEIR GAME

43 **Frank received an email**: Frank Lindh, interview by author, July 13, 2015.

44 **"an obligation to assist"**: "Prepared Statement of John Walker Lindh to the Court," October 4, 2002, US District Court, Eastern District of Virginia, Alexandria, VA, http://news.findlaw.com/hdocs/docs/lindh/ lindh100402statment.html.

44 **"All I want to do is talk to you"**: Colon Soloway, " 'He's Got to Decide If He Wants to Live or Die Here,' " NBCNews, December 6, 2001.

45 **"malnourished and in extremely poor"**: Government Discovery Letter #2, cited in "Proffer of Facts in Support of Defendant's Suppression Motions," *USA v. John Phillip Walker Lindh*, 13.

45 **"simple training camp"**: John Walker interview, CNN, December 2, 2001.

47 **"You've got to be kidding me"**: Jess Bravin, *Terror Courts: Rough Justice at Guantanamo Bay* (New Haven: Yale University Press, 2013), 41.

47 **He was enraged**: Jane Mayer, *The Dark Side: The Inside Story of How the War on Terror Turned into a War on American Ideals* (New York: Anchor, 2009), 82–83.

49 **"He was sleep-deprived, malnourished, hungry and in pain"**: Motion to Suppress at 2, *U.S. v. Lindh*, No. 02-37A (E.D. Va. June 13, 2002), 2.

50 **"wasn't going anywhere"**: David Kelley, interview by author, December 23, 2014.

50 **bound to elicit sympathy**: See, for example, comments from *Los Angeles Times* readers to "Ascribing Intelligence to John Walker Lindh," *Los Angeles Times*, June 19, 2002, http://articles.latimes.com/2002/jun/10/opinion/le-bec10-1.

52 **"I plead guilty"**: Bob Franken and John King, "'I Plead Guilty,' American Taliban Says," CNN, July 17, 2002. See also "Lindh Has Fulfilled Plea Deal, U.S. Says," *Los Angeles Times*, September 28, 2002.

52 **"I have never supported terrorism"**: "Prepared Statement of John Walker Lindh to the Court," October 4, 2002, http://news.findlaw.com/cnn/docs/terrorism/lindh100402statment.html.

52 **"almost miraculous"**: Frank Lindh interview.

CHAPTER 4: TEARING DOWN THE WALL

55 **David Kris had argued**: *In re All Matters Submitted to Foreign Intelligence Surveillance Court*, 218 F.Supp.2d 611, 620 (FISA Ct. 2002), *Abrogated by In re Sealed Case*, 310 F.3d 717 (FISA Ct. Rev. 2002), http://fas.org/irp/agency/doj/fisa/fisc051702.html.

56 **"the Court is not persuaded"**: Ibid., 623.

56 **"potential matter of life or death"**: "Hearing," *In re All Matters*, U.S. Foreign Intelligence Surveillance Court of Review, September 9, 2002, http://fas.org/irp/agency/doj/fisa/hrng090902.htm.

57 **"October Surprise"**: Gary Sick, *October Surprise: America's Hostages in Iran and the Election of Ronald Reagan* (New York: Three Rivers Press/Times Books, 1992). See also "Bush Appoints Iran-Contra Figure to Head up Iraq 'Intelligence' Probe," *Democracy Now!*, February 12, 2004; "Ex-judge on Iraq Inquiry 'Involved in Cover-up,'" *Guardian*, February 9, 2004; "The Partisan 'Mastermind' in Charge of Bush's Intel Probe,"

Salon, February 10, 2004. See also Barbara Hoenegger, "October Surprise," *Chicago Tribune*, August 18, 1989, and "The 'Surprise' That Must Be Probed," *Baltimore Sun*, June 26, 1991.

57   **efforts to impeach Bill Clinton:** "The Partisan 'Mastermind' in Charge of Bush's Intel Probe," *Salon*, February 10, 2004. See also David Brock, *Blinded by the Right* (New York: Crown, 2002).

57   **voting to reverse:** For the *North* decision, see *U.S. v. Oliver North*, 910 F.2d 843 (D.C. Cir. 1990).

57   **involved in the Federalist Society:** For a good overview of the history of the Federalist Society, see Steven M. Teles, *The Rise of the Conservative Legal Movement* (Princeton, NJ: Princeton University Press, 2008).

58   **"audacious reinterpretation of FISA":** Brief for the ACLU as Amicus Curiae, *In re Sealed Case*, 310 F.3d 717 (FISC Ct. Rev. 2002), http://fas.org/irp/agency/doj/fisa/091902FISCRbrief.pdf; Brief for the NACDL [National Association of Criminal Defense Lawyers] as Amicus Curiae, ibid.

58   **Ashcroft . . . testimony to Congress:** John Ashcroft, Testimony Before the House Committee on the Judiciary, 107th Cong., September 24, 2001, http://www.justice.gov/archive/ag/testimony/2001/agcrisisremarks9_24 .htm.

58   **"accomplish the vital and central purpose":** Theodore Olson, Oral Argument, *In re Sealed Case*, 310 F.3d 717 (FISC Ct. Rev. 2002) (No. 02-001), http://fas.org/irp/agency/doj/fisa/hrng090902.htm.

59   **"dreadful box":** Ibid.

59   **Leahy . . . had written a letter:** Senators Patrick Leahy, Charles Grassley, and Arlen Specter to Judge Colleen Kollar-Kotelly, Senate Judiciary Committee, July 31, 2002, http://fas.org/irp/agency/doj/fisa/leahy073102.html.

59   **"The public needs to know more":** "Dishonesty in the Hunt for Terrorists," *New York Times*, August 26, 2008.

59   **"to fundamentally change FISA":** *The USA PATRIOT Act in Practice: Shedding Light on the FISA Process*, Hearing Before the Committee on the Judiciary in the U.S. Senate, 107th Cong., September 10, 2002, http://fas.org/irp/congress/2002_hr/091002transcript.html. Leahy was particularly incensed over the fact that Kris's brief had cited the senator himself as thinking there was no longer a need for a distinction between "using FISA for a criminal prosecution and using it to collect foreign intelligence." "They are wrong. It is not my belief. When they cite me, they ought to talk to me first."

60   **"What is at stake here really":** Ibid.

61   **register their dismay:** Later in the hearing, Senator Leahy underscored his concern that the changes could erase the safeguards FISA had originally introduced. "I don't want to go back to the days in the past," he said, "when we started going into these investigations because we didn't like

somebody's political views or religious views, because that is a sword that can cut too many ways." Ibid.

61   **forceful opinion:** See *In re: Sealed Case*, 310 F.3d 717 (FISC Ct. Rev. 2002), http://news.findlaw.com/hdocs/docs/terrorism/fisa1118020pn.pdf.

61   **"Legally, the wall came down":** David Kris, interview by author, February 14, 2013.

61   **Supreme Court turned down:** The ACLU and the National Association of Criminal Defense Lawyers filed a petition of *certiorari* to the Supreme Court asking for a review of the FISCR decision but were denied a hearing without comment.

CHAPTER 5: THE TWILIGHT ZONE

64   **"Your client is no longer here":** Donna Newman, interview by author, May 12, 2014.

64   **Ashcroft news conference:** Attorney General John Ashcroft Regarding the Transfer of Abdullah Al Muhajir (Born Jose Padilla) to the Department of Defense as an Enemy Combatant, June 10, 2002, http://www.justice.gov/archive/ag/speeches/2002/061002agtranscripts.htm.

65   **In January 2002 Yoo had advised the president:** Jay Bybee to John Ashcroft and William Haynes, memo regarding "Application of Treaties and Laws to al Qaeda and Taliban Detainees," January 22, 2002, 6.

65   **"Twilight Zone":** Newman interview.

65   **Nazi saboteurs:** "George John Dasch and the Nazi Saboteurs," FBI Famous Cases and Criminals, http://www.fbi.gov/about-us/history/famous-cases/nazi-saboteurs. See also Andrew Kent, "Judicial Review for Enemy Fighters: The Court's Fateful Turn in *Ex parte Quirin*, the Nazi Saboteur Case," *Vanderbilt Law Review* 66, no. 1 (2013): 153–253, http://www.vanderbiltlawreview.org/content/articles/2013/01/Kent_66_Vand_L_Rev_153.pdf.

66   **"This is the model we all fear":** Adam Liptak, Neil A. Lewis, and Benjamin Weiser, "After Sept. 11, a Legal Battle on the Limits of Civil Liberty," *New York Times*, August 4, 2002.

67   **"falsely able to avoid the consequences":** Gabor Rona to author, September 13, 2015.

68   **Among the interrogators was FBI special agent Ali Soufan:** Ali Soufan, *The Black Banners: The Inside Story of 9/11 and the War Against al-Qaeda* (New York: W. W. Norton, 2011), 376–87.

68   **"do something new":** Ibid., 394

68   **Soufan asked the psychologist:** Ibid., 395–96.

69   **refusing to "stand by":** Ibid., 421.

69   **"a brain transplant away":** Ibid., 408.

69 **"who met up with him in Chicago"**: Ibid., 407.

70 **death threat**: Philip Shenon and Benjamin Weiser, "A Washington Outsider with Many Sides," *New York Times*, September 18, 2007.

73 **"no conditions could be set"**: *Padilla v. Rumsfeld*, 352 F.3d 695, 702 (2d Cir. 2003), *rev'd* 542 U.S. 426 (2004).

73 **he ought to retract it**: Barton Gellman and Jo Becker, "Pushing the Envelope on Presidential Power," *Washington Post*, June 25, 2007.

73 **"There is no possibility"**: Phil Hirschkorn, "Government to Fight Padilla Access to Counsel," CNN.com, March 26, 2003.

74 **conditions that were known to cause hallucinations**: "What Does Solitary Confinement Do to Your Mind," *Frontline*, April 22, 2014; Atul Gawande, "HellHole," *New Yorker*, March 30, 2009.

74 **"Never before in this nation's history"**: Transcript of Oral Argument at 41–42, *Padilla v. Rumsfeld*, Nos. 03-2235(L) & 03-2438(con) (2d Cir. 2003), http://www.asser.nl/upload/documents/DomCLIC/Docs/NLP/US/Padilla_2ndDistrict_OralArguments_17-11-2003.pdf.

CHAPTER 6: DEFANGING THE COURTS

78 **Chertoff favored Virginia**: Although he was intent on bringing things closer to DC, Chertoff took care not to lose the expertise of New York's federal prosecutors and decided to appoint a joint New York–Virginia team to the case. In a symbolic way, the joint team was the physical form of the demise of the FISA wall; the hard-core prosecutors from New York, talented in evidence and knowledge of terrorism prosecutions of Al Qaeda, were joining forces with the prosecutors whose involvement with the intelligence agencies was part of their customary business.

79 **"If we will not try Zacarias"**: Charles M. Madigan and Naftali Bendavid, "Objections Arise in Terror Case," *Chicago Tribune*, December 13, 2001.

79 **"specter of the military commissions"**: David Raskin, interview by author, November 22, 2013.

79 **"a horde of blood sucker[s]"**: Siobhan Rath, "Frank Dunham's Odyssey," *Legal Times*, July 22, 2002, http://www.nationallawjournal.com/id=900005372854/Frank-Dunhams-Odyssey.

80 **"Burn in the USA"**: Neil A. Lewis, "Logic Turns Upside-Down During Moussaoui Trial," *New York Times*, April 17, 2006.

80 **"any case on record"**: Joshua Dratel, interview by author, May 19, 2015.

81 **Chertoff was at a meeting**: John Rizzo, *Company Man: Thirty Years of Controversy and Crisis in the CIA* (New York: Simon & Schuster, 2014), 192.

81 **to attend a Sheryl Crow concert**: Ibid.

82 **"many significant problems"**: Phil Hirschkorn, "Moussaoui Judge: Death Penalty Still on Table," CNN, March 15, 2006.

82 **"the public's interest in a fair trial"**: *United States v. Moussaoui*, 333 F.3d 509, 513 (4th Cir. 2003).

82 **reviewed the classified evidence**: Federal judges are granted security clearances when they arrive on the bench.

82 **"undermine the Government's contention"**: *United States v. Moussaoui*, 282 F.Supp.2d 480, 486 (E.D. Va. 2003), *rev'd in part, aff'd in part* 382 F.3d 453 (4th Cir. 2004).

84 **"would simply be unfair"**: Ibid., 487.

84 **"we would like to get" Bin al-Shibh**: Transcript of Oral Argument at 12, *United States v. Moussaoui*, 382 F.3d 453 (4th Cir. 2004) (No. 03-4792).

85 **"purpose of our courts"**: Ibid.

86 **"architect of the defense"**: Ibid., 64–66.

86 **would have to settle for summaries**: The "substitutions" for deposition testimony that were ultimately used at trial were jointly prepared based on the summaries by both the prosecution and the defense. David Raskin to author.

CHAPTER 7: THE JUSTICES WEIGH IN

89 **just plain unlawful**: Transcript of Oral Argument at 56, *Hamdi v. Rumsfeld*, 542 U.S. 507 (2004) (No. 03-6696), http://www.supremecourt.gov/oral_arguments/argument_transcripts/03-6696.pdf.

92 **"torture somebody"**: Ibid., 50.

94 **"the Founders wanted to place limits"**: Transcript of Oral Argument at 56, *Rumsfeld v. Padilla*, 542 U.S. 426 (2004) (No. 03-1027), http://www.supremecourt.gov/oral_arguments/argument_transcripts/03-1027.pdf.

95 **pictures from Abu Ghraib prison**: "Introduction: The Abu Ghraib Files," *Salon*, March 14, 2006; Rebecca Leung, "Abuse of Iraqi POWs by GIs Probed," CBS, April 27, 2004, http://www.cbsnews.com/news/abuse-of-iraqi-pows-by-gis-probed/.

95 **"the audacity to stand up"**: Donna Newman, interview by author, January 12, 2015.

96 **"state of war is not a blank check"**: *Hamdi v. Rumsfeld*, 542 U.S. 507, 536 (2004).

96 **"a trap on the Executive"**: *Rasul v. Bush*, 542 U.S. 466, 497 (2004) (Scalia, J., dissenting).

CHAPTER 8: LEGAL COVER—UNCOVERED

101 **"improbable choice"**: Jack Goldsmith, *The Terror Presidency: Law and Judgement Inside the Bush Administration* (New York: W. W. Norton, 2007), 19.

102   "War Council": Ibid., 23.

102   Yoo was "not competent": Ibid., 25.

102   "keeping the Attorney General": Ibid., 338.

102   of his loyalty: Jack Goldsmith, interview by *Frontline*, PBS, August 22, 2007, http://www.pbs.org/wgbh/pages/frontline/cheney/interviews/goldsmith.html.

103   "question his decision": Goldsmith, *Terror Presidency*, 41.

103   "even if harm may result": Ibid., 148.

103   "to its limits": Ibid., 142.

103   "deeply flawed": Ibid., 10.

104   "the one guy": John Rizzo, *Company Man: Thirty Years of Controversy and Crisis in the CIA* (New York: Simon & Schuster, 2014), 186.

104   "an increased pressure phase": Senate Select Committee on Intelligence, *Committee Study of the Central Intelligence Agency's Detention and Interrogation Program*, available at http://www.feinstein.senate.gov/public/index.cfm/files/serve?File_id=7c85429a-ec38-4bb5-968f-289799bf6d0e&SK=D500C4EBC500E1D256BA519211895909.

104   "lost our senses": John Rizzo, interview by author, January 16, 2015.

104   "provided the 'no way' was put in writing": Rizzo, *Company Man*, 190.

105   "graphic detail": Rizzo interview.

105   Yoo's memo to Rizzo: Jay S. Bybee (attributed to John Yoo), memorandum to John Rizzo, "Interrogation of al Qaeda Operative," Office of Legal Counsel, US Department of Justice, August 1, 2002, http://www.justice.gov/sites/default/files/olc/legacy/2010/08/05/memo-bybee2002.pdf.

105   "a technique called 'the waterboard' ": Ibid., 3–4.

106   "harmless insect": Ibid., 3.

106   Congress had defined torture: Ibid., 9.

106   none of the techniques causes pain: Ibid., 10

106   "Discomfort" and "muscle fatigue": Ibid. 10.

106   "the slap is delivered": Ibid., 11.

106   "Zubaydah remains quite flexible": Ibid, 10.

106   mental harm: Ibid., 11–12.

107   "adverse mental health reaction": Ibid., 5.

107   "surprise at some of the techniques": John Rizzo, interview by author, January 16, 2015.

107   in total isolation for forty-seven days: Senate Select Committee on Intelligence, *Committee Study of the Central Intelligence Agency's Detention and Interrogation Program*, December 3, 2014, 31 http://www.nytimes.com/interactive/2014/12/09/world/cia-torture-report-document.html.

108   authorizing twenty-four techniques: John Yoo to William Haynes II, "Re: Military Interrogation of Alien Unlawful Combatants Held Outside the United States," Office of Legal Counsel, US Department of Jus-

tice, March 14, 2003, https://www.aclu.org/files/pdfs/safefree/yoo_army
_torture_memo.pdf.

108 **"on the President's ultimate authority"**: Jay S. Bybee, memorandum to
Attorney General Alberto Gonzales, "Re. Standards of Conduct for Interrogation under 18 U.S.C. §§ 2340-2340A," Office of Legal Counsel,
US Department of Justice, August 1, 2002, http://academics.smcvt.edu/
jhughes/Bybee%20Memo.htm.

109 **"careful and sober legal advice"**: Goldsmith, *Terror Presidency*, 148.

109 **Goldsmith's view**: Ibid., 149–51.

110 **"elaborate safeguards"**: Ibid.,151.

110 **authorized were actually legal**: Ibid., 155–56.

111 **"Every day the OLC failed"**: Ibid., 158.

111 **"withdrawn so many legal opinions"**: Ibid., 161.

112 **alerted to the program**: "A Review of the Department of Justice's Involvement with the President's Surveillance Program," Office of the Inspector General, US Department of Justice, July 2009, https://archive.org/
stream/Report-President-Surveillance-Program-2009/Report-President
-Surveillance-Program-2009_djvu.txt [hereafter OIG DOJ Report], 191.

112 **an opinion also authored by John Yoo**: John C. Yoo, "Memorandum for
the Attorney General," November 2, 2001, 9, http://www.justice.gov/
sites/default/files/olc/legacy/2011/03/25/johnyoo-memo-for-ag.pdf.

112 **"mind to be blown"**: OIG DOJ Report, 110.

112 **"at war with terrorists"**: Goldsmith, *Terror Presidency*, 180–81.

112 **"one bomb away"**: Ibid., 181.

112 **Yoo had cherry-picked**: OIG DOJ Report, 104.

113 **"the presumption of legality flipped"**: Ibid., 125.

113 **"Just fix it"**: Ibid., 120.

113 **surveillance programs carried out**: Stellar Wind had three programs:
Section 215, which covered telephone metadata; the pen register trap and
trace, which authorized the collection of Internet metadata; and TSP,
which covered the content of phone and Internet communications.

113 **authorization . . . would expire**: OIG DOJ Report, 120.

114 **by the head of Ashcroft's bed**: Ibid., 134–39.

114 **"Ashcroft then stunned me"**: James Comey, Senate testmony, in John
Conyers, *Reining in the Imperial Presidency: Lessons and Recommendations
Relating to the Presidency of George W. Bush* (New York: Skyhorse, 2009), 153.

114 **"He lifted his head"**: OIG DOJ Report, 138.

115 **"I decide what the law is"**: Barton Gellman, *Angler: The Cheney Vice
Presidency* (New York: Penguin, 2008), 318.

115 **"Here I stand, I can do no other"**: Ibid.; OIG DOJ Report, 155.

115 **officials prepared to resign**: OIG DOJ Report, 155–56.

115 **"do what Justice thinks needs to be done"**: Gellman, *Angler*, 320.

115   **"by far the hardest challenge"**: Goldsmith, *Terror Presidency*, 182.

116   **"an unconstitutional infringement"**: OIG DOJ Report, 183.

117   **A memo written collectively**: Gellman, *Angler*, 314–15.

117   **Fuck-You Memo**: Ibid., 320–21.

117   **"based on a misunderstanding of the President's expectations"**: OIG DOJ Report, 33.

117   **"the whole ordeal could have been avoided"**: Goldsmith, *Terror Presidency*, 182.

CHAPTER 9: GLIMMERS OF LIGHT

120   **"excruciating and agonizing"**: Daniel Levin to Deputy Attorney General James B. Comey, "Re: Legal Standards Applicable Under 18 U.S.C. §§ 2340–2340A," Office of Legal Counsel, US Department of Justice, December 30, 2004, 8, https://www.aclu.org/files/torturefoia/released/082409/olcremand/2004olc96.pdf.

120   **a series of memos**: Steven G. Bradbury to John A. Rizzo, "Application of 18 U.S.C. §§ 2340-2340A to Certain Techniques That May Be Used in the Interrogation of a High Value al Qaeda Detainee," Office of Legal Counsel, US Department of Justice, May 10, 2005, http://fas.org/irp/agency/doj/olc/techniques.pdf; Steven G. Bradbury to John A. Rizzo, "Application of U.S. Obligations Under Article 16 of the Convention Against Torture to Certain Techniques That May Be Used in the Interrogation of High Value al Qaeda Detainees," Office of Legal Counsel, US Department of Justice, May 30, 2005, http://fas.org/irp/agency/doj/olc/article16.pdf.

121   **"shock and drama"**: Bradbury to Rizzo, May 10, 2005, 8.

121   **"prevent physical pain or suffering or mental harm to a detainee"**: Ibid., 15.

123   **"Only when the government was threatened"**: Spencer Ackerman, "Suspect Policy," *New Republic*, March 14, 2005.

124   **Gonzales called a news conference**: "Prepared Remarks of Attorney General Alberto R. Gonzales at the Press Conference Regarding the Indictment of Jose Padilla," US Department of Justice, November 22, 2005, http://www.justice.gov/archive/ag/speeches/2005/ag_speech_051122.html.

124   **"asking for our client to be charged"**: Donna Newman to author, August 20, 2015.

125   **"took up arms on behalf"**: *Padilla v. Hanft*, 423 F.3d 386 (4th Cir. 2005), http://www.ca4.uscourts.gov/opinions/published/056396.p.pdf.

126   **two terrorism defendants**: Vanessa Blum, "Pair in Terror Case Maintain Innocence," *Sun-Sentinel* (Florida), January 19, 2008.

126   **traveling to a training camp:** Deborah Sontag, "In Padilla Wiretaps, Murky View of 'Jihad' Case," *New York Times,* January 4, 2007.

126   **to withdraw the decision:** Phil Hirschkorn, "Court Rejects Government Request to Move 'Enemy Combatant,'" CNN, December 22, 2005.

126   **"surpassing importance":** *Padilla v Hanft,* 432 F.3d 582 (4th Cir. 2005), http://www.washingtonpost.com/wp-srv/nation/documents/padilla_v _hanft_122105.pdf.

127   **"be held militarily":** Ibid.

127   **"the most conservative judge":** Jess Bravin and J. Lynn Lunsford, "Breakdown of Trust Led Judge Luttig to Clash with Bush," *Wall Street Journal,* May 11, 2006.

127   **"legally irrelevant":** "Attorney General Gonzales Holds Briefing on the Indictment of Jose Padilla," *Washington Post,* November 22, 2005.

CHAPTER 10: EVERYTHING IS BROKEN

129   **"black sites":** Dana Priest, "CIA Holds Terror Suspects in Secret Prisons," *Washington Post,* November 2, 2005.

129   **"a lot of third-country dungeons":** "U.S.: Abu Ghraib 'Only the Tip of the Iceberg,'" Human Rights Watch, April 27, 2005.

130   **eavesdropping on Americans:** James Risen and Eric Lichtblau, "Bush Lets U.S. Spy on Callers Without Courts," *New York Times,* December 16, 2005.

130   **"the constitutional responsibility":** Transcript, "President Bush's News Conference," *New York Times,* December 19, 2005.

131   **"an early warning detection system":** William E. Moschella to Pat Roberts et al., Office of Legal Affairs, US Department of Justice, December 22, 2005, https://nsarchive.gwu.edu/NSAEBB/NSAEBB178/surv34 .pdf.

131   **released a white paper:** "Legal Authorities Supporting the Activities of the National Security Agency Described by the President," US Department of Justice, January 19, 2006, https://epic.org/privacy/terrorism/fisa/ doj11906wp.pdf.

131   **along with a letter:** Attorney General R. Alberto Gonzales to William H. Frist, January 19, 2006, https://www.epic.org/privacy/terrorism/fisa/ doj11906ltr.pdf.

132   **"prohibits the kind of electronic":** David Kris, FISA Discussion, n.d., http://balkin.blogspot.com/kris.fisa.pdf.

134   **"Critical evidence is not available":** Oral Argument, Transcript of Hearing, *ACLU v. NSA,* June 12, 2006, E.D. Mich., 26.

134   **"wide swath of communications":** Ibid.

134   **"Because of the very secrecy":** *ACLU v. NSA,* 438 F. Supp. 2d (E.D. Mich.

2006) http://www.washingtonpost.com/wp-srv/nation/documents/wiretap _ruling.pdf.

135   **government presented its now familiar case:** Phil Hirschkorn, "U.S. Rests in Moussaoui Sentencing Trial," *CNN*, March 23, 2006.

135   **"Moussaoui managed to annoy everyone":** "Substitution for the Testimony of Riduan Isamuddin ('Hambali')," *United States v. Moussaoui* (E.D. Va., May 3, 2006) (No. 01-455-A), http://www.vaed.uscourts.gov/notable -cases/Moussaoui/exhibits/defense/946.pdf.

135   **"a problem from the start":** "Substitution for the Testimony of Khalid Sheikh Mohammed," Defendant's Exhibit 941, *United States v. Moussaoui* (2006), http://law2.umkc.edu/faculty/projects/ftrials/Moussaoui/ sheikhstmt.pdf.

135   **"undone more than four years of work":** Phil Hirschkorn, "Moussaoui: White House Was My 9/11 Target," CNN, March 27, 2006.

136   **"We can go on and on":** Phil Hirschkorn, "Moussaoui: 'No Remorse' for 9/11," CNN, April 13, 2006.

136   **six consecutive life sentences:** Verdict Form, *United States v. Moussaoui* (2006), http://law2.umkc.edu/faculty/projects/ftrials/Moussaoui/ juryverdict.pdf.

136   **"America, you lost":** Neil A. Lewis, "Moussaoui Given Life Term by Jury over Link to 9/11," *New York Times*, May 4, 2006.

136   **"classification issues":** "Moussaoui's Trial Won't Open Doors, Legal Experts Say," Associated Press, May 7, 2006.

136   **"some alternative form of military trial":** "Sins of Commissions," editorial, *Washington Post*, March 27, 2006.

137   **Neal Katyal:** Nina Totenberg, "Law Professor Beats the Odds in Detainee Case," NPR, September 5, 2006.

138   **"too vague":** Transcript of Oral Argument at 22, *Hamdan v. Rumsfeld*, 548 U.S. 557 (2006) (No. 05-184).

139   **"magic words":** Ibid., at 59.

139   **the president had operated outside the law:** Ibid., at 3.

139   **"We can do nothing":** U.S. House Majority Leader John Boehner (R-OH), Statement on Terrorist Tribunals, September 26, 2006, http:// www.speaker.gov/speech/boehner-floor-statement-terrorist-tribunals.

140   **differed in significant ways:** Jennifer K. Elsea, *The Military Commissions Act of 2006, Analysis of Procedural Rules and Comparison with Previous DOD Rules and the Uniform Code of Military Justice,* Congressional Research Service Report, September 27, 2007, http://oai.dtic.mil/oai/oai?verb =getRecord&metadataPrefix=html&identifier=ADA472664.

140   **torture or cruel, unusual, or inhumane treatment:** a reference to the prohibition on "cruel, unusual or inhumane" treatment as set out in the Fifth, Eighth, and Fourteenth Amendments to the U.S. Constitution.

CHAPTER 11: THE CROWN JEWELS

143   **"provide crucial legal services"**: *Nomination of Kenneth L. Wainstein to be Assistant Attorney General for National Security,* Hearing Before the Senate Select Committee on Intelligence, 109th Cong., 2nd sess., May 16, 2006, http://www.gpo.gov/fdsys/pkg/CHRG-109shrg31315/html/CHRG -109shrg31315.htm.

143   **"play a central role"**: Ibid.

144   **"prevent another terrorist attack"**: "Fact Sheet: USA Patriot Act Improvement and Authorization Act of 2005," US Department of Justice, March 2, 2006, http://www.justice.gov/archive/opa/pr/2006/March/06 _opa_113.html.

144   **"barbarians at the gate"**: Interview with Department of Justice attorney, July 20, 2013.

144   **increasing the FBI's intelligence capabilities**: *Intelligence Reform Implementation at the Federal Bureau of Investigation: Issues and Options for Congress,* CRS Report for Congress, August 16, 2005, https://www.fas.org/ sgp/crs/intel/RL33033.pdf.

145   **"to protect our civil liberties,"**: *Nomination of Wainstein.*

145   **"cards we were dealt"**: Ken Wainstein, interview by author, August 14, 2014.

145   **"not sustainable"**: Ken Wainstein, interview by author, August 11, 2015.

146   **traveled via fiber optic cables**: Eric Rosenbach and Aki J. Peritz, "Electronic Surveillance and FISA," in *Confrontation or Collaboration? Congress and the Intelligence Community,* Belfer Center, July 2009, http://belfer-center.ksg.harvard.edu/publication/19156/electronic_surveillance_and _fisa.html.

146   **two-page list of phone numbers**: Ellen Nakashima, "Records Reveal Why Court Shut Down Bush-Era Spy Program," *Washington Post,* December 13, 2014.

146   **"the President has determined not to reauthorize,"**: Attorney General Alberto Gonzales to Senators Patrick Leahy and Arlen Specter, January 17, 2007, http://news.findlaw.com/cnn/docs/doj/agn1707fisaltr.html.

147   **Vinson refused to sign the order**: Patrick C. Toomey, "In 2007, One Judge Said No to the NSA," Just Security, December 18, 2014, https:// www.justsecurity.org/18541/2007-judge-no-nsa/.

147   **"disappointment"**: *A Review of the Department of Justice's Involvement with the President's Surveillance Program,* Office of the Inspector General, US Department of Justice, July 2009, 255, https://oig.justice.gov/reports/ 2015/PSP-09-18-15-vol-III.pdf.

148   **"nothing in the definition"**: OIG DOJ Report, 261.

149   **"turned FISA on its head"**: "ACLU Analysis of the Protect America Act,"

American Civil Liberties Union, https://www.aclu.org/aclu-analysis
-protect-america-act.

149 **"The new law simply makes clear"**: "Dispelling the Myths: Key Myths
About FIS Amendments in the Protect America Act," US Department
of Justice, n.d., http://www.justice.gov/archive/ll/paa-dispelling-myths
.html.

150 **never turned down a government surveillance request**: Foreign Intelligence Surveillance Act Court Orders 1979–2014, Epic.org, n.d., https://
epic.org/privacy/wiretap/stats/fisa_stats.html.

150 **"pretty elegant solution"**: Wainstein interview, August 11, 2015.

151 **"discussion . . . for another day"**: Peter Whoriskey, "Judge Rules Padilla
Is Competent to Stand Trial," *Washington Post,* March 1, 2007.

151 **Even some former prosecutors**: See, e.g., Andrew McCarthy, "National
Security Comes First," *USA Today,* March 3, 2005. After the trial other
prominent prosecutors, including attorney general nominee Michael Mukasey, concluded that the trial proved the inability of the federal system to
adequately try terrorism suspects. See Michael B. Mukasey, "Jose Padilla
Makes Bad Law," *Wall Street Journal,* August 22, 2007.

151 **relatively weak**: Adam Liptak, "Padilla Case Offers New Model of Terrorism Trial," *New York Times,* August 18, 2007.

151 **data sheet found in Afghanistan**: Abby Goodnough, "C.I.A. Officer
Testifies He Was Given Qaeda 'Pledge Form' Said to Be Padilla's," *New
York Times,* May 16, 2007.

151 **seven of the 230 intercepted calls**: Deborah Sontag, "In Padilla Wiretaps, Murky View of 'Jihad' Case," *New York Times,* January 4, 2007.

151 **"used by Arabs"**: Vanessa Blum, "CIA Agent Testifies in Padilla Trial,"
Sun Sentinel (Florida), May 16, 2007.

151 **could not find a witness**: Warren Richey, "At Padilla Terror Trial, a Witness's Surprise Effect," *Christian Science Monitor,* May 21, 2007.

151 **91 times . . . 100 in closing**: Laura Parker, "Padilla Prosecutors Focused
on Alleged Al-Qaeda Training," *USA Today,* May 14, 2007; Peter Whoriskey, "Prosecutors Insist on al-Qaeda Link as Padilla Case Goes to Jury,"
Washington Post, August 15, 2007.

152 **"put al-Qaeda on trial"**: Whoriskey, "Prosecutors Insist on Al-Qaeda
Link"; Carol J. Williams, "Al Qaeda Is Specter Shading Padilla's Trial,"
Los Angeles Times, May 15, 2007.

152 **"conditions were so harsh"**: Peter Whoriskey and Dan Eggen, "Judge
Sentences Padilla to 17 Years, Cites His Detention," *Washington Post,*
January 23, 2008.

152 **"I was then, and am now, dismayed"**: Jay Weaver, "Convicted Terror
Plotter from Broward County Resentenced to 21 Years in Prison," *Miami
Herald,* September 9, 2014.

152   **"a new prosecutorial model"**: Adam Liptak, "Padilla Case Offers New Model of Terrorism Trial," *New York Times*, August 18, 2007.

153   **"the best lawyering I've ever seen"**: Ken Wainstein, "Remarks on the First Anniversary of NSD," in author's possession.

155   **"[f]ew were trained"**: Abraham Affadavit, ii, http://www.scotusblog.com/movabletype/archives/AP%20Odah%20reply%206-22-07.pdf.

156   **"I was not assigned"**: Abraham Affadavit, vi.

156   **"Justice Kennedy had been moved"**: Jonathan Hafetz, *Habeas Corpus After 9/11: Confronting America's New Global Detention System* (New York: NYU Press, 2011), 157.

157   **"virtually identical"**: Transcript of Oral Argument at 33, *Boumediene v. Bush*, 553 U.S. 723 (2008) (No. 06-1195), http://www.supremecourt.gov/oral_arguments/argument_transcripts/06-1195.pdf.

157   **"limited to whether the CSRTs"**: Michel Paradis to author, October 8, 2015.

157   **"procedures are wonderful"**: Transcript of Oral Argument at 38–39, *Boumediene v. Bush*.

158   **"Protection for the habeas privilege"**: Opinion, *Boumediene v. Bush*, https://supreme.justia.com/cases/federal/us/553/723/.

158   **"so thin a reed"**: *Boumediene v. Bush*, 579 F.Supp.2d 191, 197 (D.D.C. 2008) (emphasis in original), *rev'd Bensayah v. Obama*, 610 F.3d 718 (D.C. Cir. 2010), https://ecf.dcd.uscourts.gov/cgi-bin/show_public_doc?2004cv1166-276.

158   **"this is a unique case"**: Lara Jakes Jordan, "Judge Orders Release of 5 Terror Suspects at Gitmo," *Washington Post*, November 20, 2008.

CHAPTER 12: THAT DOG WILL NOT HUNT

162   **$250,000 a day in fines:** Craig Timberg, "U.S. Threatened Massive Fine to Force Yahoo to Release Data," *Washington Post*, September 11, 2014.

162   **"to participate in surveillance"**: Transcript of Oral Argument, June 19, 2008, *In re Directives Pursuant to 105B of Foreign Intelligence Surveillance Act*, 551 F.3d 1004 (FISA Ct. Rev. 2008) (No. 08-01), at 8, http://www.dni.gov/files/documents/1118/19%20June%202008%20FISCR%20PAA%20Hearing%20Transcript%20-%20Declassified%20FINAL.pdf.

163   **president had the "inherent authority"**: Memorandum Opinion, *In re Directives to Yahoo! Inc. Pursuant to Section 105B of the Foreign Intelligence Surveillance Act*, No. 105B(g): 07-01, at 58 (FISC Ct. April 25, 2008), https://cdt.org/files/2014/09/29-yahoo702-redacted-memo-opinion-and-order.pdf.

163   **"not easily achieved"**: Ibid., at p. 97.

163   **"magnitude of the surveillance"**: Oral Argument, *In re Directives*, at 11.

163   surveillance was "rampant": Ibid., at 11.

163   "What's the damage to your consumer?": Ibid., at 8.

164   "the remotest interest": Ibid., at 14.

164   "privacy is intruded upon": Ibid., at 14.

164   "an effective and reasonable substitute": Ibid., at 30.

164   "a database on millions": Ibid., at 16.

165   "that dog will not hunt": *In re Directives*, Memorandum Opinion, un-redacted version, August 22, 2008, 551 F.3d 1004, 1011 (FISC Ct. Rev. 2008), https://fas.org/irp/agency/doj/fisa/fiscr082208.pdf.

165   "parade of horribles": Ibid., at 21.

166   "little more than a lament": Ibid., at 24.

167   "the rights and freedoms that define our nation": "Senators Block Con-sideration of Wiretap Bill," CNN, June 26, 1008; Paul Kane, "House Passes Spy Bill; Senate Expected to Follow," *Washington Post*, June 21, 2008.

167   no firm had challenged: Evan Hill, "Telecom Firm Fails in First Known FISA Court Surveillance Challenge," Al Jazeera America, April 25, 2014; Natasha Lennard, "Telecoms Firms Never Challenged NSA," *Salon*, Sep-tember 19, 2013.

168   other nongovernmental organizations: Other plaintiffs included Global Fund for Women, Global Rights, Human Rights Watch, International Criminal Defence Attorneys Association, *The Nation* Magazine, PEN American Center, Service Employees International Union, and the Washington Office on Latin America.

169   "narrowing dramatically": Jameel Jaffer, interview by author, Sep-tember 3, 2015. Later that summer the FISA Court noted that the FAA contemplates a very circumscribed role for this court. See *In re Proceed-ings Required by § 702(i) of FISA Amendments Act of 2008*, Misc. No. 08-01, 2008 WL 9487946, at 1 (FISA Ct. August 27, 2008), http://www.fas.org/irp/agency/doj/fisa/fisco82708.pdf.

169   "given the legitimate threats we face": "Obama: I'll Fight to Strip Tele-com Immunity from FISA," CBSNews.com, June 21, 2008.

CHAPTER 13: A NEW BEGINNING

173   "Congress may no more regulate": Steven G. Bradbury, Memorandum for the Files, "Re: Status of Certain OLC Opinions Issued in the Aftermath of the Terrorist Attacks of September 11, 2001," Office of Legal Counsel, US Department of Justice, January 15, 2009, http://www.justice.gov/sites/default/files/olc/legacy/2009/08/24/memostatusolcopinions01152009.pdf.

175   "we have . . . lost our way": Eric Holder, speech to American Constitu-tion Society, June 13, 2008.

176 **"rancid politicization"**: "Senate Confirmation Hearings: Eric Holder, Day One," *New York Times,* January 16, 2009.

176 **"blind loyalist"**: Ibid.

176 **"Waterboarding is torture"**: Ibid.

176 **"immunize acts of torture"**: Ibid.

176 **"a distance between me and the president"**: Ibid.

178 **"the potential synergies"**: David Kris, Confirmation Hearing, Committee of the Judiciary, http://www.gpo.gov/fdsys/pkg/CHRG-111shrg61992/html/CHRG-111shrg61992.htm.

180 **"a hefty litigation looking backward"**: Carrie Johnson, "Holder Hires Prosecutor to Look into Alleged CIA Interrogation Abuses," *Washington Post,* August 25, 2009.

180 **"who acted reasonably and relied"**: Siobhan Gorman and Evan Perez, "CIA Memos Released; Immunity for Harsh Tactics," *Wall Street Journal,* April 17, 2009.

181 **"to mount an effective legal defense"**: "Remarks by the President to CIA Employees," White House, April 20, 2009, http://www.whitehouse.gov/the-press-office/remarks-president-cia-employees-cia-headquarters.

181 **"Secretary of Defense determines that disclosure"**: H.R. 2712, 111th Cong., 1st sess., June 4, 2009, https://www.congress.gov/111/bills/hr2712/BILLS-111hr2712ih.pdf.

181 **the new law required a reconsideration**: Adam Liptak, "Supreme Court Overturns Decision on Detainee Photos," *New York Times,* November 30, 2009. The litigation is still pending as of November 2015.

181 **a civil suit against Jeppesen Dataplan**: The plaintiffs were suing using the Alien Tort Statute, which allowed foreign citizens to sue in federal court for human rights violations committed abroad in very limited circumstances. *Mohamed v. Jeppesen Dataplan, Inc.,* 539 F.Supp.2d 1128 (N.D. Cal. 2008), *aff'd* 614 F.3d 1070 (9th Cir. 2010) (en banc).

182 **"effectively cordon[ed] off"**: *Mohamed v. Jeppesen Dataplan, Inc.,* 579 F.3d 943, 955 (9th Cir. 2009) *overruled by* 614 F.3d 1070 (9th Cir. 2010) (en banc).

182 **"an unacceptable risk of disclosure"**: *Mohamed v. Jeppesen Datatplan, Inc.,* 614 F.3d 1070, 1089 (9th Cir. 2010) (en banc).

182 **The Supreme Court declined to review**: "Mohamed et al. v. Jeppesen Dataplan, Inc.," American Civil Liberties Union, November 15, 2011, https://www.aclu.org/cases/mohamed-et-al-v-jeppesen-dataplan-inc.

183 **the reality was more complicated**: "Department of Justice Withdraws Enemy Combatant Definition for Guantanamo Detainees," Department of Justice, Office of Public Affairs, March 13, 2009, http://www.justice.gov/opa/pr/department-justice-withdraws-enemy-combatant-definition-guantanamo-detainees.

183 **"a comprehensive detention policy":** Respondents' Memorandum Regarding the Government's Detention Authority Relative to Detainees Held at Guantanamo Bay, *In re Guantanamo Bay Detainee Litigation*, Misc. No. 08-442(TFH) (D.D.C. Mar. 13, 2009), http://www.justice.gov/sites/default/files/opa/legacy/2009/03/13/memo-re-det-auth.pdf.

184 **Colonel Morris Davis, had resigned:** "Former Chief Guantanamo Prosecutor Says Military Commissions 'Not Justice,'" *Democracy Now,* July 16, 2008.

185 **resuscitating and reforming the military commissions system:** Carol Rosenberg, "Pentagon Names New Guantanamo War Crimes Prosecutor," *Miami Herald,* June 23, 2011.

186 **"a legitimate forum for prosecutions":** David Johnston, "New Guidance Issued on Military Trials of Detainees," *New York Times,* June 29, 2009.

186 **Congress approved the bill:** It was part of the National Defense Authorization Act for 2010. For a good overview of the MCA 2009, see Jennifer K. Elsea, *Military Commissions Act of 2009: Overview and Legal Issues,* Congressional Research Service, April 6, 2010.

CHAPTER 14: WINNING FOR LOSING

191 **local police stopped him:** Matt Apuzzo and Adam Goldman, *Enemies Within: Inside the NYPD's Secret Spying Unit and Bin Laden's Final Plot Against America* (New York: Simon & Schuster, 2013), 63–64, 118.

191 **found no contraband in the car:** Paul Cruickshank, "Inside the Plot to Devastate New York." *CNN Security Clearance,* May 2, 2012.

193 **"toughest decision I've had to make":** Carrie Johnson, "For Holder, Much Wrestling over Decision," *Washington Post,* November 14, 2009. Holder also referred another five high-value detainees to military commissions.

195 **flashbacks to his torture:** Benjamin Weiser, "Psychologist Says Strip-Searches Traumatized Embassy-Bombings Suspect," *New York Times,* May 5, 2010.

196 **right to a speedy trial:** Benjamin Weiser, "Judge Refuses to Dismiss Terror Suspect's Case," *New York Times,* July 13, 2010.

197 **"Here you are asking me":** Memorandum and Order, *United States v. Ghailani,* No. S1098 CRIM.1023 (LAK) (S.D.N.Y. October 5, 2010), http://www.propublica.org/documents/item/10619-ruling-of-district-judge-lewis-a-kaplan-in-the-case-of-ahmed-kha.

197 **"If the government is going":** Benjamin Weiser, "No Appeal in Exclusion of Witness in Terror Trial," *New York Times,* October 10, 2010.

199 **"Ahmed's world":** Benjamin Weiser, "Ex-Detainee's Defense Calls Him Qaeda Dupe in Its Closing," *New York Times,* November 9, 2010.

199 **both sides had rested:** Ibid.

199   **"My conclusion it not going to change":** Adam Klasfeld, "Ghailani Jurors Question Burder of Proof in Terrorism Trial," Courthouse News Service, November 17, 2010, http://www.courthousenews.com/2010/11/17/31913.htm.

200   **bordering on 91 percent:** Center on National Security at Fordham Law, *By the Numbers: U.S. Prosecutions of Jihadist Terror Crimes Since 9/11* (July 2015), http://www.centeronnationalsecurity.org/node/1589.

202   **"This case should put to rest":** Stephanie Condon, "Ghailani Verdict: Where to Go from Here?" CBS News, November 18, 2010.

CHAPTER 15: LOSING GROUND

205   **the Moynihan courthouse would not be the venue:** Kenneth Bazinet, Wil Cruz, and Samuel Goldsmith, "Trial for 9/11 Mastermind Khalid Sheikh Mohammed Won't Happen in New York City," New York *Daily News,* January 30, 2010.

206   **"transfer, release, or assist":** *National Defense Authorization Act for Fiscal Year 2011,* Report of the Committee on Armed Services, House of Representatives, on H.R 5163, 111th Cong., 2nd sess., May 21, 2010, pp. 366–67, http://www.gpo.gov/fdsys/pkg/CRPT-111hrpt491/pdf/CRPT-111hrpt491.pdf.

206   **"I have reluctantly made the determination":** "No Civilian Trials for 9/11 Suspects," CNN Newsroom, April 4, 2011, transcript.

207   **"direction of extending the current":** "Congress Approves Extension of USA Patriot Act Provisions," *Washington Post,* May 27, 2011.

207   **"Now more than ever":** "Bin Laden Death Sparks New Talk over Patriot Act," *USA Today,* May 7, 2011.

208   **In twenty cases:** Mark Denbeaux et. al, "No Hearing Habeas: D.C. Circuit Restricts Meaningful Review," Seton Hall Public Law Research Paper no. 2145554, May 1, 2012, http://papers.ssrn.com/sol3/papers.cfm?abstract_id=2145554. See also "Guantanamo Habeas Scorecard," Center for Constitutional Rights, http://ccrjustice.org/files/2012-05-30%20Updated%20Habeas%20SCORECARD.pdf.

209   **"no reliable evidence":** *Al-Adahi v. Obama,* No. 05-280 (GK), 2009 WL 2584685, at 16 (D.D.C. Aug. 21, 2009), *rev'd* 613 F.3d 1102 (D.C. Cir. 2010), http://www.scotusblog.com/wp-content/uploads/2009/08/Al-Adahi-opinion-8-21-09.pdf.

209   **"each piece of the government's":** *Al-Adahi v. Obama,* 613 F.3d 1102, 1105–1106 (D.C. Cir. 2010).

209   **"infected the court's entire analysis":** Ibid., at 1106.

209   **"incorrect—indeed, startling—conclusion":** Ibid.

209   **"more likely than not a part of al-Qaeda":** Ibid.

210   **"to make up a story and a lie"**: Ibid., at 1111.

210   **"judicial deference to the government"**: Denbeaux et al., "No Hearing Habeas," p. 11.

212   **"There is serious question"**: *Abdah v. Obama,* No. CIV.A 04-1254 HHK, 2010 WL 3270761, at 9 (D.D.C. Aug. 16, 2010), *Vacated and Remanded sub nom. Latif v. Obama,* 666 F.3d 746 (D.C. Cir. 2011) and *Vacated and Remanded sub nom. Latif v. Obama,* 677 F.3d 1175 (D.C. Cir. 2012).

212   **"suffers from the same omission"**: *Latif v. Obama,* 666 F.3d 746, 756 (D.C. Cir. 2011).

214   **"calling the jailer to account"**: Jonathan Hafetz, "Calling the Government to Account: Habeas Corpus After *Boumediene,*" December 14, 2011, 63, http://dx.doi.org/10.2139/ssrn.1972542.

CHAPTER 16: FURTHER CONSEQUENCES

215   **so slick and topical**: Max Fisher, "Five Reasons to Doubt Al Qaeda Magazine's Authenticity," *Atlantic,* July 1, 2010.

216   **planning to send a drone after him**: Greg Miller, "U.S. Citizen in CIA's Cross Hairs," *Los Angeles Times,* January 31, 2010.

217   **The memo, authored by David Barron**: Charlie Savage, "Court Releases Large Parts of Memo Approving Killing of American in Yemen," *New York Times,* June 23, 2014.

217   **"use all necessary and appropriate force"**: David J. Barron, Memorandum for the Attorney General, "Re: Applicability of Federal Criminal Laws and the Constitution to Contemplated Lethal Operations Against Shaykh Anwar al-Aulaqi," July 16, 2010, https://www.aclu.org/sites/default/files/assets/2014-06-23_barron-memorandum.pdf. The first eleven pages of the memo are redacted. That section "compiled the evidence to support the intelligence community's assertion that Mr. Awlaki was not merely a propagandist but an operational terrorist." Charlie Savage, "Court Releases Large Parts of Memo Approving Killing of American in Yemen," *New York Times,* June 23, 2014.

218   **"the probability of American casualties"**: Department of Justice White Paper, *Lawfulness of a Lethal Operation Directed Against a U.S. Citizen Who Is a Senior Operational Leader of Al-Qa'ida or an Associated Force,* November 8, 2011, 7–8, http://fas.org/irp/eprint/doj-lethal.pdf.

219   **The order to fire**: "Get the Data: Drone Wars: Yemen: Reported U.S. Covert Actions, 2001–2011," Bureau of Investigative Journalism, December 24, 2009, https://www.thebureauinvestigates.com/2012/03/29/yemen-reported-us-covert-actions-since-2001/#YEM004.

220   **"filling the bucket with numbers?"**: Jo Becker and Scott Shane, "Secret

'Kill List' Proves a Test of Obama's Principles and Will," *New York Times*, May 29, 2012.

220 **more than two hundred drone strikes:** "Drone Wars Pakistan: Analysis," New America Foundation, n.d., http://securitydata.newamerica .net/drones/pakistan/analysis.html; and "Drone Wars Yemen: Analysis," New America Foundation, n.d., http://securitydata.newamerica.net/ drones/yemen/analysis.html.

220 **only one suspected terrorist abroad:** Ken Dilanian, "Terrorism Suspect Held Secretly for Two Months," *Los Angeles Times*, July 6, 2011.

220 **"Their policy is to take out high-value targets":** Becker and Shane, "Secret 'Kill List.'"

221 **"there are circumstances in which":** *Al-Aulaqi v. Obama*, 727 F.Supp.2d 1, 46 (D.D.C. 2010).

222 **"This isn't justice":** Hina Shamsi, "Relative of Americans Killed by Drone Strikes: No Justice in U.S. Courts," American Civil Liberties Union, June 4, 2014, https://www.aclu.org/blog/relative-americans -killed-drone-strikes-no-justice-us-courts.

222 **"he's responsible for the position of the United States":** Becker and Shane, "Secret 'Kill List.'"

224 **"Do you disagree with that judgment?":** *Nomination of Lisa O. Monaco to Be Assistant Attorney General for National Security, Depertment of Justice*, Hearing Before the Select Committee on Intelligence of the US Senate, 112th Cong., May 17, 2011, http://www.gpo.gov/fdsys/pkg/CHRG -112shrg72746/html/CHRG-112shrg72746.htm.

224 **"intelligence-led and threat-driven":** Bar Association of the District of Columbia (BADC), National Security Law Policy & Practice Committee, *Real-Time Legal Advice During National Security Ops, June 14, 2012*, notes in author's possession.

224 **"traffic light":** Ibid.

224 **fell by more than 50 percent:** Monaco, like Wainstein, would move up to be homeland security adviser to the White House. Her successor, her protégé and longtime colleague John Carlin, a prosecutor and former FBI official, would continue this pattern of relatively few terrorism indictments until the ISIS cases of 2014–15.

225 **"make us look terrible":** Amy Davidson, "Q & A: Ali Soufan," *New Yorker*, May 16, 2012.

227 **"a cascade of speculation":** Transcript of Oral Argument at 7, *Clapper v. Amnesty Intern. USA*, 133 S.Ct. 1138 (2013) (No. 11-025), http://www.su-premecourt.gov/oral_arguments/argument_transcripts/11-1025.pdf.

228 **"objectively reasonable likelihood":** Ibid., at 1148–49.

228 **Verrilli learned about the lack of notifications:** Eric Schmitt, David E.

Sanger, and Charlie Savage, "Administration Says Mining of Data Is Crucial to Fight Terror," *New York Times*, June 7, 2013.

CHAPTER 17: THE SNOWDEN EFFECT

231   **over an encrypted chat:** Ben Wizner, interview by author, October 7, 2014.

232   **"banging our head against this wall for nine years":** Kashmir Hill, "How ACLU Attorney Ben Wizner Became Snowden's Lawyer," *Forbes*, March 10, 2014.

232   **seeking advice about encrypted emails:** Wizner interview.

232   **"will subject [any American's] phone":** Congresswoman Jackie Speier, remarks, House of Representatives hearing on FISA, June 20, 2008, https://www.congress.gov/crec/2008/06/20/CREC-2008-06-20.pdf.

233   **projects with fanciful names:** For a good overview of the multiplicity of programs, see *The Washington Post*, e-book, *NSA Secrets: Government Spying in the Internet Age* (Diversion Books, 2013).

233   **"E-mail, Chat-video, voice":** Barton Gellman and Laura Poitras, "U.S., British Intelligence Mining Data from Nine U.S. Internet Companies in Broad Secret Program," *Washington Post*, June 7, 2013.

233   **nor was it sufficiently minimizing:** "How the NSA's Surveillance Procedures Threaten Americans' Privacy," American Civil Liberties Union, website, accessed November 24, 2015, https://www.aclu.org/sites/default/files/field_document/explainer_v4.pdf.

233   **"akin to snatching every American's address book":** ACLU Complaint for Declaratory and Injunctive Relief, *ACLU v. Clapper*, No. 13 Civ. 3994, at 1 (S.D.N.Y. June 11, 2013), https://www.aclu.org/sites/default/files/field_document/nsa_phone_spying_complaint.pdf.

234   **"not step right into the conflict zone":** Wizner interview.

234   **a three-year investigation:** Peter Finn, "Lawyers Showed Photos of Covert CIA Officers to Guantanamo Bay Detainees," *Washington Post*, August 21, 2009

234   **"for our activism on behalf":** Nick Baumann and Asawin Suebsaeng, "John Kiriakou and the Real Story Behind Obama's Latest Leak Crackdown," *Mother Jones*, January 23, 2012.

235   **a hero or a villain:** Frank Newport, "Americans Disapprove of Government Surveillance Programs," Gallup Poll, June 10–11, 2013.

235   **a whistleblower rather than a traitor:** "U.S. Voters Say Snowden Is Whistle-Blower, Not Traitor," Quinnipiac Poll, July 10, 2013, http://www.quinnipiac.edu/news-and-events/quinnipiac-university-poll/national/release-detail?ReleaseID=1919.

235   **"Mr. Snowden will not be tortured":** Attorney General Eric Holder to

Russian Minister of Justice, July 23, 2013, http://apps.washingtonpost
.com/g/page/world/full-letter-from-eric-holder-to-russian-justice
-minister/339/.

235 **"Repeated leaks of classified information"**: President Barack Obama,
"Remarks by the President in a Press Conference," White House, Office
of the Press Secretary, August 9, 2013, https://www.whitehouse.gov/the
-press-office/2013/08/09/remarks-president-press-conference.

237 **that didn't stop Kris**: David Kris, "On the Bulk Collection of Tangible
Things," Lawfare Research Paper Series 1, no. 4 (September 29, 2013),
https://lawfare.s3-us-west-2.amazonaws.com/staging/s3fs-public/
uploads/2013/09/Lawfare-Research-Paper-Series-No.-4-2.pdf.

237 **"How will the United States recalibrate?"**: Ibid., 66.

238 **"terminated as soon as reasonably practicable"**: *Liberty and Security in
a Changing World: Report and Recommendations of the President's Review
Group on Intelligence and Communications Technologies*, December 12,
2013, 119.

238 **"served an important function"**: Ibid., 145.

238 **"unless it has foreign intelligence value"**: Ibid., 146.

239 **"Nothing in the text"**: Transcript of Oral Argument at 4, *ACLU v. Clapper*, 959 F. Supp. 2d 724 (S.D.N.Y. 2013) (No. 13 Civ. 3994) *Vacated and
Remanded*, 785 F.3d 787 (2d Cir. 2015), https://www.aclu.org/files/assets/
transcript_of_oral_argument_2013.11.22.pdf.

239 **"This kind of dragnet surveillance"**: Dominic Rushe, "NSA Bulk Data
Collection Violates Constitutional Rights, ACLU Argues," *Guardian*,
November 22, 2013.

240 **"no reasonable expectation of privacy"**: Transcript of Oral Argument at
61, *ACLU v. Clapper* (2d Cir. 2015).

240 **"all other similarly situated consumers, users"**: Complaint, *Klayman v.
Obama*, June 6, 2013, http://cryptome.org/2015/08/klayman-3-001.pdf.

241 **"Generalized surveillance of this kind"**: Plaintiffs' Memorandum, *Klayman v. Obama*, No. 13-CV-851, at 3 (D.D.C. October 28, 2013), https://
cases.justia.com/federal/district-courts/district-of-columbia/dcdce/
1:2013cv00851/160387/13/1.pdf?ts=1387826995.

241 **"substantial likelihood of success"**: *Klayman v. Obama*, 957 F. Supp.
2d 1, 9 (D.D.C. 2013) *Vacated and Remanded*, No. 14-5004, 2015 WL 5058403
(D.C. Cir. Aug. 28, 2015), https://cases.justia.com/federal/district-courts/
district-of-columbia/dcdce/1:2013cv00851/160387/48/0.pdf?ts=13886
81326.

241 **"It's one thing to say that people"**: Ibid.

241 **"almost-Orwellian technology"**: Ibid.

242 **"does not provide an adequate legal basis"**: Privacy and Civil Liberties

Oversight Board (PCLOB), *Report on the Telephone Records Program Conducted Under Section 215 of the USA PATRIOT Act and on the Operations of the Foreign Intelligence Surveillance Court*, January 23, 2014, 10.

242   "out of step with the case law": Ibid., 10.

242   "concerns under both the First and Fourth Amendments": Ibid., 11.

243   "a strong showing of efficacy": Ibid., 13.

243   Obama had reportedly known: Lily Hay Newman, "Important Watchdog Review Group Says NSA Phone Call Surveilance Is Illegal, Should Stop," *Slate*, January 23, 2014.

244   "healthy skepticism toward our surveillance programs": "Remarks by the President on Review of Signals Intelligence," January 17, 2014, https://www.whitehouse.gov/the-press-office/2014/01/17/remarks-president-review-signals-intelligence.

CHAPTER 18:
THE EVER-ELUSIVE PENDULUM SWING

247   "We have kept faith with our belief": Statement by the President and Attorney General Eric Holder, White House, September 25, 2014, https://www.whitehouse.gov/the-press-office/2014/09/25/statement-president-and-attorney-general-eric-holder.

248   "I was right": Ryan J. Reilly, "Eric Holder: 9/11 Defendants 'Would Be on Death Row' If Case Proceeded in Federal Court Instead of Gitmo," *Huffington Post*, November 4, 2013.

248   The FBI was caught: Carol Rosenberg, "Accusation of FBI Spying Stalls 9/11 Hearing," *Miami Herald*, April 14, 2014.

248   "was working at the black site": Carol Rosenberg: "Guantánamo Hearing Halted by Supposed CIA 'Black Site' Worker Serving as War Court Linguist," *Miami Herald*, February 9, 2015.

248   had installed its own switch: Carol Rosenberg, "Guantanamo Judge Furious After Surprise Censorship During 'Black Sites' Testimony," *Miami Herald*, January 29, 2013.

251   persuaded the president to capture and try him: Mark Mazzetti and Eric Schmitt, "Terrorism Case Renews Debate over Drone Hits," *New York Times*, April 12, 2015; see also Conor Freidersdorf, "The Extrajudicial Killing That Didn't Happen," *Atlantic*, April 17, 2015.

253   "not an effective means of acquiring intelligence": Senate Select Committee on Intelligence, *Committee Study of the Central Intelligence Agency's Detention and Interrogation Program*, December 3, 2014, 9, http://www.ny times.com/interactive/2014/12/09/world/cia-torture-report-document.html.

253   "incommunicado for the remainder of his life": Ibid., 35.

254 **"Sometimes, the CIA knew detainees were lying":** Senator Dianne Feinstein, Remarks on Senate Floor, December 9, 2014, http://www.cnn .com/TRANSCRIPTS/1412/09/ath.02.html.

254 **"You don't know if the same person":** Josh Gerstein, "What's Not in the Senate Torture Report," *Politico,* December 9, 2014.

255 **A thirty-eight-page version of the report:** In response to a Freedom of Information Act lawsuit by *The New York Times,* the government declassified a 2009 report by five agencies' inspectors general about Stellar Wind, the group of NSA warrantless wiretapping and bulk phone and email records collection activities initiated by President George W. Bush after the terrorist attacks of September 11, 2001. In 2009 the government released a thirty-eight-page unclassified version that omitted discussion of many key facts that then remained secret. The agencies were Defense, the CIA, Justice, the Office of the Director of National Intelligence, and the NSA.

255 **"little feedback from field offices":** OIG DOJ Report, 300.

256 **The judge approved the application anyway:** Ibid., 75–76

257 **"that has changed the landscape":** *Hasbajrami v. United States,* No. 11-CR-623, 2014 WL 4954596, at 1 (E.D.N.Y. Oct. 2, 2014).

258 **"looking for any door or window":** Ben Wizner, interview by author, May 26, 2015.

258 **"Instead of using a sniper's rifle":** Transcript, Hasbajrami suppression hearing, January 23, 2015, 22.

260 **"ratified a program of which [they] were not aware":** *ACLU v. Clapper,* 785 F.3d 787, 820 (2d Cir. 2015).

261 **"unable to identify any major case developments":** Office of the Inspector General, Department of Justice, *A Review of the FBI's Use of Section 215 Orders: Assessment of Progress in Implementing Recommendations and Examination of Use in 2007 through 2009,* May 2015, vi, https://oig .justice.gov/reports/2015/01505.pdf.

INDEX

ABOUT THE AUTHOR

KAREN J. GREENBERG is the director of the Center on National Security at Fordham Law. A noted expert on national security, terrorism, and civil liberties, she is the author of *The Least Worst Place: Guantanamo's First 100 Days*, which was selected as one of the best books of 2009 by *The Washington Post* and *Slate*. She is the editor of *The Torture Debate in America* and *The Terrorist Trial Report Card, 2001–2011*. She coedited, with Joshua L. Dratel, *The Torture Papers: The Road to Abu Ghraib* and *The Enemy Combatant Papers: American Justice, the Courts, and the War on Terror*. Greenberg's work appears in many collections of essays on law and policy in the war on terror and has been featured in *The New York Times*, *The Washington Post*, the *Los Angeles Times*, the *San Francisco Chronicle*, *The Nation*, *The National Interest*, *The Wall Street Journal*, *Mother Jones*, *The Guardian*, TomDispatch.com, and on major news channels. She has a BA from Cornell, where she was a College Scholar, and a PhD in history from Yale. Greenberg is a permanent member of the Council on Foreign Relations.